UA 23 P

The New American Way of War

This book explores the cultural history and future prospects of the so-called new American way of war. In recent decades, American military culture has become increasingly dominated by a vision of 'immaculate destruction', which reached its apogee with the fall of Baghdad in 2003. Operation Iraqi Freedom was hailed as the triumphant validation of this new American way of war. For its most enthusiastic supporters, it also encapsulated a broader political vision. By achieving complete technical mastery of the battlefield, the US would render warfare surgical, humane, and predictable, and become a precisely calibrated instrument of national policy.

American strategy has often been characterized as lacking in concern for the non-military consequences of actions. However, the chaotic aftermath of the Iraq War revealed the timeless truth that military success and political victory are not the same. In reality, the American way of war has frequently emerged as the contradictory expression of competing visions of war struggling for dominance since the early Cold War period. By tracing the origins and evolution of these competing views on the political utility of force, this book will set the currently popular image of a new American way of war in its broader historical, cultural, and political context, and provide an assessment of its future prospects.

This book will be of great interest to students of strategic studies, military theory, US foreign policy, and international politics. It will be highly relevant for military practitioners interested in the fundamental concepts which continue to drive American strategic thinking in the contemporary battlegrounds of the War on Terror.

Benjamin Buley has a PhD in International Relations from the London School of Economics, and now works for the Foreign Office in London.

LSE International Studies
Series Editors: John Kent, Christopher Coker, Fred Halliday, Dominic Lieven, and Karen Smith

The International Studies series is based on the LSE's oldest research centre and like the LSE itself was established to promote inter-disciplinary studies. The CIS facilitates research into many different aspects of the international community and produces interdisciplinary research into the international system as it experiences the forces of globalization. As the capacity of domestic change to produce global consequences increases, so does the need to explore areas which cannot be confined within a single discipline or area of study. The series hopes to focus on the impact of cultural changes on foreign relations, the role of strategy and foreign policy and the impact of international law and human rights on global politics. It is intended to cover all aspects of foreign policy including, the historical and contemporary forces of empire and imperialism, the importance of domestic links to the international roles of states and non-state actors, particularly in Europe, and the relationship between development studies, international political economy and regional actors on a comparative basis, but is happy to include any aspect of the international with an inter-disciplinary aspect.

American Policy Toward Israel
The power and limits of beliefs
Michael Thomas

The Warrior Ethos
Military culture and the war on terror
Christopher Coker

The New American Way of War
Military culture and the political utility of force
Benjamin Buley

The New American Way of War
Military culture and the political utility of force

Benjamin Buley

LONDON AND NEW YORK

First published 2008
by Routledge
2 Park Square, Milton Park, Abingdon, Oxon OX14 4RN

Simultaneously published in the USA and Canada
by Routledge
270 Madison Ave, New York, NY 10016

*Routledge is an imprint of the Taylor & Francis Group,
an informa business*

© 2008 Benjamin Buley

Typeset in Times New Roman by
Newgen Imaging Systems (P) Ltd, Chennai, India
Printed and bound in Great Britain by
Biddles Ltd, King's Lynn

All rights reserved. No part of this book may be reprinted or
reproduced or utilised in any form or by any electronic,
mechanical, or other means, now known or hereafter
invented, including photocopying and recording, or in any
information storage or retrieval system, without permission in
writing from the publishers.

British Library Cataloguing in Publication Data
A catalogue record for this book is available
from the British Library

Library of Congress Cataloging in Publication Data
Buley, Benjamin, 1978–
    The new American way of war : military culture and the
political utility of force / Benjamin Buley.
       p. cm. – (LSE international studies)
    Includes bibliographical references and index.
    1. United States – Military policy. 2. Sociology, Military –
United States. 3. Strategy. 4. War. 5. Political culture – United
States. I. Title.
UA23.B7856 2007
306.2'70973–dc22   2007014370

ISBN10: 0–415–42995–1 (hbk)
ISBN10: 0–203–93416–4 (ebk)

ISBN13: 978–0–415–42995–5 (hbk)
ISBN13: 978–0–203–93416–6 (ebk)

For Mum, Dad, and Tim

Monarchy can go to war from policy or ambition, and if they do not find it suits their views they can, with almost equal ease, withdraw from the contest. But it is far otherwise with Republics. In these, before you enter a war, you must convince the mass of the nation that the war is virtuous and just in its principles, and unavoidable without disgrace. When a free people have become, by reflection, convinced of this, they become reckless of consequences; you rouse a deeper spirit; you concentrate a mightier wrath than a despotic government can ever know
Congressional Representative Alfred
Cuthbert of Georgia, 1824

By a combination of creative strategies and advanced technology, we are redefining war on our terms ... more than ever before, the precision of our technology is protecting the lives of our soldiers, and the lives of innocent civilians. ... In this new era of warfare, we can target a regime, not a nation. Our aim is to track and strike the guilty.
President George W. Bush, 2003

Contents

Acknowledgements xi
List of abbreviations xiii

Introduction: American ways of war, old and new 1

1 No substitute for victory: the separation of politics and strategy in the American military tradition 16

2 The science of strategy: war as a political instrument in the nuclear age 40

3 Overwhelming force: the American military and the memory of Vietnam 63

4 Immaculate Destruction: the impact of 9/11 on American military culture 84

5 The new American way of war: vision and reality in Afghanistan and Iraq 112

Conclusion: the rise and fall of the new American way of war 135

Notes 149
Bibliography 176
Index 191

Acknowledgements

This book is based on my doctoral thesis, which I would never have completed without the financial support of the International Relations Department of the London School of Economics. I am grateful not only for a generous scholarship and additional research grants, but also for the friendly environment of the IR department, which provided a wonderfully stimulating and enjoyable atmosphere in which to study. I would especially like to thank Professors Mick Cox and Chris Brown, LSE's Cold War Studies Centre, and the International Studies faculty of Columbia University for inviting me to test some of my ideas on an unsuspecting audience in New York. I am also grateful to Professor Brian Holden Reid and Dr Patrick Cronin for their constructive criticism in my PhD viva, which helped me considerably in honing my argument. The same goes for the insightful comments of my anonymous peer reviewers.

While studying I learnt a great deal from countless conversations with fellow graduate students, but I am particularly indebted to two friends who share my interest in the American way of war. I benefited throughout my research from the advice of Sebastian Kaempf, who also gave me the opportunity to present some of my early conclusions at a seminar of the Security Research Group at Aberystwyth University. I am also grateful to David Ucko for his feedback and suggestions on US strategy in general, and counter-insurgency in particular.

My greatest intellectual debt is to Christopher Coker, whose eclectic and uniquely rich approach to strategic studies was a constant inspiration from my arrival at the LSE as a Masters student in 2000. Consistently encouraging, thought-provoking, and ready to give up his time, Christopher was an exemplary supervisor.

Above all, I wish to thank my family for their love and support throughout my long years of studentdom, and in particular my mother for her patience in reading an entire early draft of the manuscript.

Abbreviations

ABM	Anti-Ballistic Missile
CENTCOM	US Central Command
CFLCC	Coalition Forces Land Component Command
CIA	Central Intelligence Agency
CPA	Coalition Provisional Authority
DARPA	Defence Advanced Projects Research Agency
IDF	Israeli Defence Forces
IED	Improvised Explosive Device
ISAF	International Security Assistance Force
JCS	Joint Chiefs of Staff
J-UCAS	Joint Unmanned Combat Air System
MAD	Mutual Assured Destruction
NATO	North Atlantic Treaty Organization
NSC	National Security Council
ORHA	Office of Reconstruction and Humanitarian Assistance
QDR	Quadrennial Defence Review
RMA	Revolution in Military Affairs
SAC	Strategic Air Command
SIOP	Single Integrated Operational Plan
SOCOM	US Special Operations Command
UAV	Unmanned Aerial Vehicle
VC	Viet Cong
WMD	Weapons of Mass Destruction

Introduction
American ways of war, old and new

The American way of war: from 'War is Hell' to 'Immaculate Destruction'

Amongst the many controversies associated with the 2003 Iraq War, perhaps the most widely discredited element was the military strategy adopted by the Pentagon under the guidance of Defence Secretary Donald Rumsfeld. 'Operation Iraqi Freedom' was portrayed by the Bush administration itself as a bold experiment in the pioneering of a 'new American way of war'. Of course, this phrase presupposed the existence of an older, more traditional American style of war which it was held to have rejected. For most of the twentieth century, the hallmark of the American approach to warfare was associated with its reliance on the mustering of an overwhelming margin of superiority through which opponents of the republic were utterly annihilated. In contrast, the hallmark of the new style was held to lie in the radical improvements in precision and efficiency afforded by the new military technologies of the information revolution. For a brief period – now unimaginably distant in the light of the chaos which now attends an Iraq on the verge or in the midst of a civil war (depending on one's point of view) – this new style of war appeared to permit the US to decapitate hostile regimes while leaving their surrounding societies almost untouched. The surgeon's scalpel appeared to have been substituted for the sledgehammer. Yet this simplistic contrast between an old and new American way of war only scratches at the surface of the more fundamental transition in the US military community's basic assumptions about war and the way in which it should ideally be fought.

The older concept of the American way of war was always associated with more than a simple penchant for strategies of annihilation. The more fundamental idea underlying this strategic preference concerned the characteristic American understanding of the relationship between war and *politics*. By extension, the continuities and discontinuities between the 'old' and 'new' American ways of war can only be properly understood if the new style of war is *also* placed in the broader context of its relationship to political utility. The most enduring theme associated with the older notion that there existed a distinctively American approach to war was its alleged rejection of the conception of war *as a political instrument*. The central argument of Russell F. Weigley's classic and still influential 1973 book *The American Way of War* was that the characteristic American view of strategy, unlike that of the famous Prussian philosopher of war, Carl von Clausewitz, tended to exclude from consideration the political purposes for which a battle or war was being fought. This apolitical concept of strategy, Weigley argued, meant that American military strategists had tended to give 'little regard to the non-military consequences of what they were doing.'[1] Yet while Weigley popularized the phrase 'the American way of war', the basic idea was much older. Writing in 1957, for example, Samuel P. Huntington asserted what would have been regarded as a truism at the time: 'American thought has not viewed war in the conservative-military sense as an instrument of national policy'.[2]

Reflecting the cultural heritage of American Exceptionalism, and the influence of a long formative period of 'free security' insulating the US military from the necessity of strategic thinking, Americans were held to have conceived of inter-state war not as a continuation of political intercourse, but as a symptom of its failure. This apolitical military culture was said to have fostered a penchant for total war, reinforced by the 'crusading' tendencies of American political culture. The American way was to distinguish sharply between the states of peace and war, and, once committed to the latter, to mobilize the republic's abundant resources behind an offensive of the highest possible intensity. The defining counter-image here was that of a more Machiavellian European tradition, which conceived of war as an instrument of imperial policing and great power rivalry. Conversely, the US military's characteristic resistance towards the intrusion of political considerations or limitations into their conduct of war was expressed in a preference for the annihilation of the armed forces of the enemy to achieve their unconditional surrender, rather than less direct or absolute means of employing military force for purposes of political bargaining. 'War', as General William Tecumseh Sherman famously stated, 'is Hell'. Or, as he put it elsewhere, 'War is cruelty, *and you cannot refine it*'.[3] By implication, once the resort to military force was undertaken, the political considerations that might have given rise to hostilities in the state of peace became increasingly irrelevant to the radically different state of war.

Over the last decade, however, increasing numbers of strategists, scholars, and commentators on US military affairs have begun to refer to a 'new' American way of war. This concept became particularly fashionable after the fall of Kabul in November 2001, as the Pentagon's initial euphoria was gradually replaced by more sober reflection on its implications.[4] Most of this commentary focused on the new technologies and tactics that had been employed to topple the Taliban regime, in a matter of weeks, in one of the most hostile military environments on earth. The new style of war was marked by the substitution of information, speed, and precision for mass, allowing small numbers of 'joint' ground, sea, air, and space forces sharing a common picture of the 'battlespace' to achieve radical economies of force. It was thus characterized by a more sophisticated operational style emphasizing manoeuvre over tactical attrition, a dependence on high technology rather than quantitative material superiority, and an emphasis on achieving the 'systemic paralysis' of the enemy's armed forces and infrastructure, rather than their annihilation.

Thus, in contrast to the older American way of war, the new approach was generally defined first and foremost as a *technological* phenomenon. Yet just because its broader implications were often left largely implicit, this did not mean that they were inconsequential. On the contrary, this concept of a technological and operational 'revolution' in the American style of warmaking also implied a concomitant revolution in the strategic and *political* dimensions of warfare. The new way of war would allow the United States to reconcile its own cultural misgivings with regard to the use of military power with its hegemonic (or, according to some commentators, imperial) aspirations to forcefully reshape the international environment in accordance with American interests. Military force could be utilized with unprecedented flexibility, precision, and with minimal bloodshed: warfare could even be rendered 'humane'. This vision of 'Immaculate Destruction', as the American foreign policy analyst Leslie H. Gelb dubbed it in the early 1990s, was far from original; indeed, as we will see, it had been first articulated in embryonic form in the late 1960s. Yet, with the Bush administration's decision to launch a preventive military campaign against Saddam Hussein's regime, it appeared to have come of age. President Bush told the journalist Bob Woodward in an interview in 2003 that to him 'the big news' was that the US had changed how war was fought and won.[5] Expanding on this theme in a speech in the immediate aftermath of the fall of Baghdad, Bush declared that,

> By a combination of creative strategies and advanced technology, we are redefining war on our terms ... more than ever before, the precision of our technology is protecting the lives of our soldiers, and the lives of innocent civilians. ... In this new era of warfare, we can target a regime, not a nation. Our aim is to track and strike the guilty.[6]

The central intellectual architect of the Iraq War within the administration, former Deputy Secretary of Defence Paul Wolfowitz, also spelt out the radical political implications of the new way of war. Musing on the intellectual trajectory of his late mentor, the nuclear strategist Albert Wohlstetter, he noted that Wohlstetter had been 'one of the first ... most influential people, to understand what a dramatic difference it would make to have accurate weapons'. Accuracy, in fact, translated into 'a whole transformation of strategy and politics'.[7] The new way of war promised to re-establish the link between the use of force and the rational pursuit of policy that had appeared severed by Mutual Assured Destruction (MAD) and the failure of conventional warfare in Vietnam.

This imagined transformation of the relationship between war and political *utility* was reflected above all in the decision to invade Iraq. Despite its protestations that the use of force against Iraq was a 'war of necessity' and a last resort – a claim that sought to frame the conflict in the tradition of America's past wars – in other statements the Bush administration made it clear that it conceived the war as a true political instrument. Wolfowitz, in particular, was remarkably candid about the war's underlying political rationale. As he explained after the war, the 9/11 attacks had demonstrated 'what 20 or 30 years of a failing *status quo* in the Middle East was bringing the world'; the administration consequently resolved to use American power to 'change the course of history there'.[8] Undersecretary of Defence for Policy Douglas J. Feith also stated that American strategy was guided by the idea 'that a successful, new Iraq could serve as a model to the Arab and Muslim worlds of modernization, moderation, democracy, and economic well-being. A free and prosperous Iraq could provide tens of millions of people with an alternative way to think about the future.'[9] The decision to bring about regime change, then, was conceived as the military dimension of a broader political strategy to reshape the politics of the Middle East.

This ambitious strategy of proactively reshaping the Middle East through 'preventive' military action – a strategic concept in severe tension with traditional American ideals of war – was unthinkable without the underlying belief that the US military had attained such complete technical control of the battlefield that the conduct of warfare had moved into the realm of the *predictable*. The Bush administration's strategy, in other words, reflected the underlying influence of a particular conception of war and the changing nature of military force in the twenty-first century. In this vision, technology would enable the US to wage war with ever more perfect precision and discrimination. Contrary to General Sherman, the cruelty of war might indeed be 'refined'. Warfare would *no longer* be 'Hell' – but potentially 'immaculate'. Consequently, it could be calibrated to the ends of national policy as never before. A central conceit of this discourse was the assumption that the Ba'athist regime could be removed with surgical finesse, leaving Iraq's infrastructure largely untouched and facilitating the rapid subsequent withdrawal of the majority of American troops. Thus, in its embrace of this strategic vision, the invasion of Iraq reflected the Bush administration's belief that it had perfected a form of warfare that would render the use of force the ultimate instrument of state policy. Underlying all the other calculations surrounding the decision to go to war were these basic, largely unquestioned assumptions about *control* in warfare: the assumption of predictability made a preventive military policy politically thinkable, rather than reckless, in the mind of the administration itself.

From the standpoint of early 2007, the Pentagon's fleeting vision of Immaculate Destruction seems hopelessly naïve, increasingly divorced from the messy reality of continuing violence in Iraq and Afghanistan. The chaos accompanying the post-war power vacuum in Baghdad was initially dismissed by Donald Rumsfeld as an inevitable reflection of the 'untidy' nature of freedom. Yet, as the realization dawned that the US military was facing a determined and increasingly vicious insurgency, the triumphalism surrounding the 'new American way of war' slowly ebbed away. The attention of the media and expert commentators turned to the military's apparent failure to anticipate any of the difficulties it would encounter after the termination of the conventional phase of combat. The central theme associated with the traditional American way of war – its separation of political and narrowly military considerations – suddenly appeared to acquire a new relevance. The Bush administration's strategists might have embraced the *principle* of the precept that political ends should govern the use of force, but in so far as its *execution* depended on the translation of military victory into political success – the essence of strategy – they appeared politically autistic, betraying an astonishing lack of foresight with regard to the likely political consequences of their cherished military strategy.

The US boasts the most powerful military machine, equipped with the most technologically advanced weaponry, and drawing on the intellectual capital of the most sophisticated community of professional military strategists that the world has ever seen. Yet, despite the unprecedented scale of this national project to render war a rational instrument of statecraft, the US was unable to convert its astonishingly rapid decapitation of the Iraqi regime into a stable political outcome. This paradox lies at the heart of my historical exploration of American military culture. Many of the specific decisions which contributed to this failure have already been discussed in great detail elsewhere – the lack of planning for post-conflict stability operations, the disbanding of the Iraqi army, the extent of the de-Ba'athification programme, to name but a few of the most significant. While each of these factors was undoubtedly important, my own interest is in the basic underlying assumptions about war itself that underpinned these fateful individual decisions. My thesis is that they were ultimately expressions of a broader failing – a military culture which refused to accept the full implications of Clausewitz's insight that war is a true continuation of politics.

From this perspective, of course, the continuities between the 'old' and the 'new' American ways of war begin to seem more apparent than the differences. Contemplating the American performance in Iraq, Lt.-Colonel Antulio J. Echevarria II of the US Army War College ruefully concluded as early as 2004 that, '... the American way of war tends to shy away from thinking about the complicated process of turning military triumphs – whether on the scale of major campaigns or small-unit actions – into strategic successes'.[10]

Yet the problem with simply reasserting the continuing relevance of the traditional account of the American way of war is that such an all-embracing characterization fails to differentiate sufficiently between *conflicting* visions of war and its relationship to politics that have successively struggled for dominance of American strategy. American military culture is far from a monolithic entity. As the battle to allocate culpability for the post-war chaos raged within the national security establishment, it became clear that influential voices within the military elite had been sceptical of Secretary Rumsfeld's strategy, and its rosy assumption that the chaos of war could be contained, from the beginning. At the root of this fracture were competing assumptions about war itself. Recently retired military elites were heard complaining furiously that the lessons acquired so painfully in Vietnam had been recklessly ignored by a new generation of civilian strategists.[11]

These invocations of Vietnam, and the US defence community's internal recriminations after Iraq, were indicative of an enduring cultural *fracture* with regard to the interpenetration of war and politics. My central argument is that, within American military culture, the proper relationship between war and political utility has been the subject not of consensus but of prolonged contention. There is no single American way of war or consensus over the proper relationship between war and national policy. While I argue that US military culture as a whole has failed to fully accept that the conduct of war is permeated by political considerations, American strategy since at least the early Cold War period has reflected the influence of a cultural dialectic between polarized conceptions of the political *utility* of military force. The traditional American conception of war as the *failure* of politics is only one of several 'cultural paradigms' – ideal templates for the use of military force and its proper relationship to political considerations – that have successively struggled for dominance of American military culture since the early Cold War period. This book explores the emergence and evolution of these competing conceptions of war, and the expression of this cultural dialectic in American strategy.

War as a political instrument and the American way of war

The assertion that war is a political instrument is associated most closely with the Prussian philosopher of war, Carl von Clausewitz (1780–1831). War, he famously contended, is 'a continuation of political intercourse, with the addition of other means'.[12] Conversely, the traditional view of the *American* approach to war was dominated by the theme that this Clausewitzian concept of war was incompatible with the American way. In the received wisdom about American military culture, its 'apolitical' character was held to reflect a dual political and military heritage: a political culture shaped by American Exceptionalism, which rejected the legitimacy of the European system of power politics, and a military culture shaped by long periods in which security was taken for granted, punctuated by brief, once-in-a-generation conflicts defined as punitive crusades against some evil transgressor of the principles of international society.

The most celebrated account of the American way of war was that of the late American military historian Russell F. Weigley, who coined the phrase 'American way of war' in his 1973 classic of the same title.[13] Indeed, as Brian M. Linn has noted, the book's central argument became so well known within the military history community that the very concept of the 'American way of war' became nearly synonymous with 'the Weigley thesis' (which is still required reading at service command and staff schools).[14] While he saw American ways of war as 'offshoots of European ways of war', and American strategic thought as 'a branch of European strategic thought',[15] Weigley nevertheless identified a number of distinctive features that justified discussion of a characteristically *American* style of warfare. His basic argument is still influential and well known: he identified the defining characteristic of the American style from the Civil War onwards as a penchant for strategies of 'annihilation', seeking the complete overthrow of the enemy's power, in preference to strategies of attrition, exhaustion, or erosion, usually employed by protagonists 'whose means are not great enough to permit pursuit of the direct overthrow of the enemy and who therefore resort to an indirect approach'.[16]

This American strategic preference derived from American attitudes towards the relationship between war and politics:

> Americans, especially American soldiers, often held to a still narrower definition of strategy than Clausewitz's, the time-worn conventional definition that calls strategy 'the art of bringing forces to the battlefield in a favourable position'. This latter view of strategy, unlike Clausewitz's, excluded from consideration the purposes for which a battle or war was being fought. ... The narrower definition of strategy meant that ... military strategists gave little regard to the non-military consequences of what they were doing. [17]

If the image of the old American way of war derived from the great crusades of the Civil War and the two World Wars, scholarly interest in a so-called new American way of war was sparked in the 1990s by the lone super-power's increasingly frequent exercises in coercive diplomacy. This interest quickened after the declaration of a 'War on Terror' that numerous commentators on both the left and the right of the political spectrum regarded as a proactive exercise in the policing of a *Pax Americana*. For some commentators, the new technologies show-cased in the first Gulf War – particularly those associated with precision guidance, satellites, stealth, and information technology – seemed to herald the dawn of a new era of warfare.[18] In combination with the US military's new emphasis on rapid manoeuvre (reflecting the all-volunteer force's post-Vietnam preoccupation with the operational dimension of war), the technologies of the emerging 'Revolution in Military Affairs' (RMA) offered the prospect of a vastly more efficient style of warfare that would reject the old reliance on tactical attrition.

It was not incidental that this concept of a 'new' American way of war originated in the new era of 'limited war' and coercive diplomacy ushered in by the end of the Cold War. Particularly when associated with President Clinton's reliance on air power and his refusal to contemplate the use of ground troops, the concept reflected the influence of contradictory impulses on American strategy: a political elite increasingly willing to contemplate the use of limited force to shape the international environment in accordance with American interests, constrained by a fickle and casualty-averse public opinion and a military establishment still traumatized by the memory of Vietnam. The American way of war, in other words, has always been defined largely in terms of its cultural orientation towards the political instrumentality of force, whether that orientation be its earlier rejection or more recent apparent embrace.

However, the notion of a simple historical transition from the 'old' way of war's rejection to the 'new' way of war's acceptance of the Clausewitzian concept of force is overly simplistic. The vision of 'Immaculate Destruction' that recently came to dominate US military culture had an important precursor in the notions of limited war developed by scientific civilian strategists in the 1950s and subsequently discredited in Vietnam, an experience which led to the temporary resurgence of the penchant for the doctrine of 'Overwhelming Force'. Thus, the recent ascendance of Immaculate Destruction as a guiding conceptual ideal (and, I will argue, its even more recent decline) can only be understood in the context of this protracted struggle. The evolution of American military culture has been marked not by a linear transition from one vision of war to another but by a struggle between competing conceptions of war. The notion that a 'new' American way of war has replaced the old is therefore useful in focusing attention on the *evolution* of US military culture. Yet the concept of a linear transition from one internally coherent military 'style' to another is one-dimensional. These popular images of the American way of war need to be replaced with a more complex and dynamic picture, which makes more allowance for the plurality of competing American conceptions of the political dimension of war, and for their evolution over time.

In reassessing American military culture's various interpretations of the relationship between war and political utility, this work is not intended as a study of the reception specifically of Clausewitz, or even of his most famous statement, within the United States.[19] Rather, I intend to explore the reception and interpretation within American military culture of the broad *conception* of war as an instrument of state policy, of which Clausewitz was the most famous advocate. The idea that war is governed by political instrumentality antedates Clausewitz by many centuries; it is certainly implicit in the 'realist' school of international relations which is generally dated at least as far back as Thucydides (and Clausewitz himself acknowledged an intellectual debt to Machiavelli[20]). Nevertheless, as Clausewitz is generally regarded as the most insightful student of the political dimension of war, and since this book is permeated by the vocabulary he bequeathed to conceptualize it, his discussion of the relationship between war and politics is a useful place to start.

Clausewitz's argument is perhaps stated most succinctly in a passage in Book VIII of his masterpiece, *On War*:

> It is, of course, well known that the only source of war is politics – the intercourse of governments and peoples; but it is apt to be assumed that war suspends that intercourse and replaces it by a wholly different condition, ruled by no law but its own.
>
> We maintain, on the contrary, that war is simply a continuation of political intercourse, with the addition of other means. ...
>
> How could it be otherwise? Do political relations between peoples and between their governments stop when diplomatic notes are no longer exchanged? Is war not just another expression of their thoughts, another form of speech or writing? Its grammar, indeed, may be its own, but not its logic.[21]

The implication, as he concluded in the first chapter of *On War* (the only one with which he was satisfied at the time of his death), was that, 'War should never be thought of as *something autonomous*, but always as an *instrument of policy*'. It was war's instrumental dimension as a servant of policy that gave it its 'logic', without which it would merely descend into meaningless bloodshed with no conceivable justification beyond its own sake. 'If we keep in mind that war springs from some political purpose, it is natural that the prime cause of its existence will remain the supreme consideration in conducting it.' This was not intended to imply that warfare was 'just' another instrument of policy, with no special characteristics which distinguished it from other forms of political or diplomatic intercourse. On the contrary, Clausewitz emphasized that he did not mean to 'imply that the political aim is a tyrant. It must adapt itself to its chosen means, a process which can radically change it.'[22] This is what he meant by his assertion that while war's 'logic' was that of politics, it had its own distinctive 'grammar': the grammar of human interaction and competition through organized violence.

In Colin Gray's words,

> What Clausewitz is saying is that the threat and use of force is not a self-validating exercise ... he insists upon a 'grammar', a distinctive character and dynamic of war that is inalienable, although it lacks any 'policy' logic of its own. ... We need to remember that it is the Janus-like

nature of war to be both a process of violence that will tend to escalate in the heat and the passion of the doing, and an instrument of policy.[23]

In particular, Clausewitz emphasized that, as a distinctive field of human activity, war's peculiar grammar was distinguished by its tendency to resist rational human control and direction. This derived from the necessarily imperfect informational environment (the 'fog of war') in which the warring sides directed their forces; the numerous unpredictable factors which tended to make the course of real war diverge from war as planned (or 'friction'); and above all, from war's inherently *interactive* and *competitive* nature as a contest of wills, that gave it its own innate tendency to escalate towards an ever more extreme form of violence, towards what he termed the 'absolute' form of war.[24] Nevertheless, despite his recognition of warfare's tendency to resist control, Clausewitz still insisted that, in so far as it *could* be subordinated to rational direction, it must be waged as the servant of policy. Thus, he insisted that the political aim must remain '... the first consideration. Policy, then, will permeate all military operations, and, in so far as their violent nature will admit, it will leave a continuous influence on them.'[25]

For Clausewitz himself, these various assertions about the political dimension of war no doubt all flowed logically from his central premise that war is a continuation of politics. While this may be the case, humans are incompletely logical beings; and, in so far as they accepted it at all, American strategists have interpreted the implications of that central premise with a high degree of selectivity. More specifically, a distinction may be introduced for the purposes of analysis between three concepts that for Clausewitz were no doubt intertwined: the *sovereignty* of politics in war, the political *utility* of force, and war as a *continuation* of politics.

To accept the sovereignty of the political dimension of war – in terms of Clausewitz's distinction between the 'grammar' and 'logic' of war – is to accept that war does not have its own logic, for its logic is that of policy. An important tradition in American military discourse has clung to the contrary view that war has a logic all of its own: the outbreak of war represents the failure of politics, which immediately gives rise (as Clausewitz put it in characterizing this view) to 'a wholly different condition' to that which preceded it. This is the tradition that was associated with the traditional paradigm of the American way of war; but from the Cold War onwards it has increasingly come under challenge within the American strategic community.

The political *utility* of warfare, in contrast, refers to the effectiveness of military force in achieving political objectives. An acceptance of the *sovereignty* of politics does not dictate any particular view of the utility of force; in fact, it is quite possible to accept the sovereignty of politics, and yet to retain a highly sceptical view of the political utility of force. This is apparent, for example, in the view expressed by George F. Kennan (the eminent diplomat generally recognized as the father of the 'containment' strategy adopted by the US during the Cold War) in 1961:

> The atom has simply served to make unavoidably clear what has been true all along since the day of the introduction of the machine gun and the internal combustion engine into the techniques of warfare ... that modern warfare in the grand manner, pursued by all available means and aimed at the total destruction of the enemy's capacity to resist, is ... of such general destructiveness that it ceases to be useful as an instrument for the achievement of any coherent political purpose.[26]

However, Clausewitz's most far-reaching claim was that war is a *'continuation'* of politics, in the sense that politics *permeates all military operations*. Numerous American military commanders (particularly in the post-Vietnam period) have accepted the sovereignty of political objectives in principle, yet have still sought to preserve a realm of purely military decision-making free from the intrusion of political considerations. Yet a true acceptance of Clausewitz's claim implies not only that the political dimension is ultimately sovereign over the military dimension, but that the two are inextricably intertwined. The military conduct of war is so penetrated by political factors that it is always unwise to consider either dimension in isolation. While American military culture has been fractured by diametrically opposed visions of the sovereignty of politics and the political utility of force, none of the most influential have accepted the full implications of this most far-reaching claim that war is a true *continuation* of politics. It is this common trait that constitutes the central continuity between the 'old' and the 'new' American ways of war, even though American military culture has been fractured by diametrically opposed views of the *sovereignty* of politics in war and the political *utility* of force.

War as a cultural phenomenon

Whether one agrees with Clausewitz's assertion that war is a continuation of politics or not, it is far from obvious that most societies, through most of human history, have thought of it as such; the very controversy with which his (in)famous statement is associated, in fact, suggests otherwise. Indeed, one eminent critic of Clausewitz, John Keegan, has suggested that,

> it is at the cultural level that Clausewitz's answer to his question, What is war?, is defective. ... War embraces much more than politics: ... it is always an expression of culture, often a determinant of cultural forms, in some societies the culture itself.[27]

This is somewhat unfair to Clausewitz, who himself remarked 'how every age had its own kind of war, its own limiting conditions, and its own peculiar preconceptions'.[28] Yet notwithstanding Keegan's interpretation of Clausewitz, his core premise – that war must be understood as a cultural phenomenon – is the basic theoretical assumption underlying this book: different societies' conceptions of war are inevitably conditioned by their unique cultural heritages. 'Being of the human condition', Paul Bathurst has written, 'people are necessarily enmeshed in a network of preconceptions'[29] – inherited cultural norms which necessarily condition a society's military and strategic behaviour as much as any other dimension of its communal life.

Many studies of national ways of war or strategic cultures attempt to classify them as if they were so many distinct specimens laid out in a collector's display, each distinguishable by their own unique characteristics. It is only fair to acknowledge that most such accounts also emphasize the frustratingly amorphous nature of 'culture' and the difficulty of making cultural generalizations. Indeed, there is an extensive academic debate on the relationship between 'strategic culture' and behaviour.[30] I tend to agree with Colin Gray's characterization of strategic culture as a dynamic context that shapes perceptions and strategic preferences without actually determining them, rather than the more positivist interpretation of culture as an 'independent variable' that determines behaviour through interaction with other factors. While I do not intend to engage in this debate here, it is necessary to clarify some of my core assumptions and definitions.

Throughout this book, I have used the term 'military culture' to refer to the basic assumptions about war of those groups within the wider society who are *professionally concerned with the use of military force*, whether they be uniformed military servicemen or civilian strategists. I have deliberately adopted this definition in order to narrow the scope of this study, in preference to broader concepts such as 'strategic culture' or 'ways of war' that encompass the wider society's understanding of war.

Secondly, my interpretation is indebted to John Lynn's theoretical distinction between what he terms the 'discourse' and the 'reality' of war. Lynn uses the term *discourse* to refer to cultural conceptions of war.[31] Lynn defines a discourse as a 'complex of assumptions, perceptions, expectations, and values on a particular subject.'[32] A compatible definition may be adapted from Isabel V. Hull's argument that military cultures are defined by sets of *basic assumptions* about war, which 'structure their perceptions of their own essence and purpose, of the problems they must solve, and of the way they should solve them'. Yet, while the basic assumptions of a particular discourse will tend to be internally consistent, few cultures are defined by a single conception of war or of any other subject, as Lynn notes.[33]

The existence of multiple discourses or cultural paradigms for the use of force within a single strategic community is a natural reflection of the resistance imposed by an independent military reality on cultural conception. Lynn calls this the 'feedback loop' between the discourse and the reality of war: 'Cultures try to change or control reality to fit conception, while reality modifies the cultural discourse to better match the objective facts of combat.'[34] This concept of military culture thus avoids the dangerous assumption that it must be both internally coherent and more or less static. Rather, military cultures may be fractured by rival conceptions of war that continually adapt to evolving strategic realities, a process that simply reflects a society's perpetual internal struggle to make sense of its military experience and shape its future strategy accordingly.

Lynn does not expand on the implications of the fragmentation of military culture, but for my analysis of American military culture it is essential: for, as we shall see, US military conceptions of the proper relationship between the use of force and national policy are more diverse and conflicting than is usually acknowledged. A simple way of conceptualizing the process through which rival military discourses coalesce is to focus on the *pressures* which are exerted on any military culture. Writing in 1957, Samuel P. Huntington suggested that,

> The military institutions of any society are shaped by two forces: a functional imperative stemming from the threats to the society's security and a societal imperative arising from the social forces, ideologies, and institutions dominant within the society. ... Military institutions which reflect only social values may be incapable of performing effectively their military function. On the other hand, it may be impossible to contain within society military institutions shaped purely by functional imperatives. The interaction of these two forces is the nub of the problem of civil–military relations. The degree to which they conflict depends upon the intensity of the security needs and the nature and strength of the value pattern of society.[35]

This insight points to a useful conceptual distinction between the internal and external pressures that will be exerted on any society's military culture. Any military culture which is perceived as diverging *too* radically from the values of the wider society is likely to be regarded as illegitimate, or even a threat to those values. Equally, any military culture which is perceived as being too 'dysfunctional' – that is, unresponsive to or incapable of addressing perceived strategic threats to national security – is likely to become equally discredited. In order to continue to command much influence within the military culture, therefore, any military discourse must appear to reconcile the tension between these perceived pressures. In combination, Lynn's distinction between the discourse and the reality of war and Huntington's distinction between societal and functional (strategic) imperatives have informed my conceptual model of the dynamics which have conditioned the evolution of US military conceptions of the political utility of war from the early Cold War period.

In conclusion, suffice it to say that perhaps an inevitable corollary of the search for cultural distinctiveness is a tendency to emphasize internal cultural cohesion over contradiction. In the search to differentiate *between* cultures, in other words, scholars have understandably tended to downplay apparent contradictions *within* cultures. This is certainly true of accounts of the American approach to war, of which numerous studies already exist. In this literature, arguably *the* defining feature of the American way of war was said to be its 'anti-Clausewitzian' concept of force. Rather than seeking to offer yet another account, therefore, of the various defining features of American military culture, my own approach is to focus on this particular *dimension* – the cultural interpretation of war as an instrument of national policy – in the hope that, by subjecting it to closer scrutiny, new light may be shed on the American way of war, its history since the beginning of the Cold War, and recent trends in its development.

The argument

From the beginning of the Cold War, there has been a striking polarization within the American strategic community between those who favoured the massive use of military power to overwhelm the enemy, and those who favoured more precisely calibrated doses of force to achieve more limited political objectives. At times this debate has been acrimonious and bitter, punctuated by recurring bouts of mutual recrimination (most recently in the aftermath of the Iraq War). Although this polarization has been expressed in military doctrine and behaviour, I call it *cultural* rather than doctrinal because it reflects very basic assumptions and attitudes about the nature of war. I am by no means the first to claim that such a polarization has existed or to explore its parameters, but I do seek to put it in a fresh perspective by arguing that, fundamentally, the cultural divide reflected diametrically opposed assumptions about the relationship between war and *politics*. The evolution of American military culture has been driven by a pronounced dialectic on the political *utility* of military force, which continues to be played out in the battlegrounds of the War on Terror.

In the early Cold War period, advocates of General Douglas MacArthur's famous statement that in war 'there is no substitute for victory' viewed war and politics fundamentally as things apart. One took over where the other left off (see Chapter 1). In later years, champions of General Colin Powell's doctrine of 'Overwhelming Force' did acknowledge that the conduct of strategy should be governed by the political objective, but they still sought both to restrict that objective to one that could be neatly achieved through the massive application of military power, and to maintain a realm of purely military decision-making that could remain unsullied by political considerations (see Chapter 3).

On the other side of the dialectic, the 'Limited War theorists' of the first half of the Cold War sought to restore the political utility of force in the zero-sum thermonuclear stand-off between the US and the USSR (see Chapter 2). Their optimism about the potential of science, game theory, and econometrics to render war controllable found pronounced echoes, in later decades, in the much-hyped Revolution in Military Affairs (RMA), which mutated more recently into former Defence Secretary Donald Rumsfeld's concept of Military Transformation (Chapters 4 and 5). Advocates of 'limited war' and 'flexible response' shared the same assumption of later RMA-enthusiasts that technology offered the potential to render warfare predictable, immaculate, and thus a usable instrument of national policy.

Yet, while they often regarded themselves as neo-Clausewitzians or, in later years, as having transcended Clausewitz, my argument is that they misread the true relationship between war and politics just as much as the proponents of 'no substitute for victory' and overwhelming force. In this respect I am unapologetically Clausewitzian, for I believe that more than any other strategic thinker Clausewitz perceived the inherent *unpredictability* of war, that meant its prosecution would always remain an art rather than an exact science. This unpredictability derived from war's very nature as an interactive contest between subjective beings. Thus, Clausewitz believed that in order to make any sense at all of war, we must accept that it should be governed by political objectives and that there is no such thing as a 'purely military' consideration. But he also saw that accepting the sovereignty of the political dimension of war gave no guarantee that war could be rendered 'surgical' or 'immaculate', for one could never factor out the enemy's quintessential human capacity to react in a creative and thus unpredictable way.

It is this basic refusal to contemplate that the enemy might react unpredictably – by refusing to fight on American terms – that has contributed to the most egregious strategic blunders of the War on Terror (and particularly the Iraq War). This refusal to fight according to the rules as the US military sees them is also the single most notable feature of the recent evolution of war itself, whether one labels it 'asymmetrical warfare', insurgency, 'new war', 'fourth generation warfare', or whatever. In my conclusion I turn to the implications of these recent trends for the American way of war, and its recent attempts to adapt its conception of the relationship between war and politics to these new strategic realities.

1 No substitute for victory

The separation of politics and strategy in the American military tradition

> Once war is forced upon us, there is no other alternative than to apply every available means to bring it to a swift end. War's very object is victory, not prolonged indecision. In war there is no substitute for victory.
>
> General Douglas MacArthur, 1952

The notion that the American military tradition rejected the concept of war as a continuation of politics has been central to the dominant image of the American way of war. As we shall see, this image became widely influential in the immediate aftermath of World War II. Yet, as an all-encompassing generalization about American military culture, this apolitical characterization was most valid for the period in which it emerged – that is, the period from the beginning of the Cold War up to the mid-1960s. Moreover, it depicted some elements of the US strategic community – above all the Strategic Air Command – more accurately than others – for example, the group of 'neo-Clausewitzian' civilian strategists discussed in the next chapter. Ironically, the latter group played no small part in tarring the traditional American way of war with the brush of apoliticism. Cold War realists and Limited War theorists interpreted earlier periods of US military history through the prism of the American strategy adopted in World War II, in an era when the logical culmination of that strategy appeared to have been realized in the terrifying prospect of 'Massive Retaliation'.

Russell Weigley once wrote that the strategy of unconditional surrender adopted by the Allies was a 'characteristically American war aim',[1] but he did not elaborate on what was characteristically American about it – perhaps because he regarded it as too self-evident to require explanation. Many of the central ideas that came to be associated with the American way of war were already well established before Weigley coined that phrase in 1973. In particular, a number of eminent 'realist' thinkers in the 1950s agreed that the legacy of American history had been manifested in a distinctive pattern of American military behaviour. Their conclusions reflected above all the recent memory of World War II, and were prompted by the new strategic imperatives of the atomic age and the Cold War.

The need for critical reflection on the American military experience was given added urgency by the coincidence of the Korean War with the loss of the US nuclear monopoly.

The father of containment, George F. Kennan, observed in 1950 that the American approach to international relations was distinctive in its excessive 'moralism and legalism'. Kennan argued that this moralistic–legalistic approach to world affairs, rooted in a desire to abolish war, paradoxically made warfare more enduring, more terrible, and more destructive to political stability than did more cynical motives of national interest: 'A war fought in the name of high moral principle finds no early end short of some form of total domination.'[2] The eminent political columnist Walter Lippmann agreed that what he called the 'Wilsonian system of ideas' that mobilized Americans to fight tended to demand nothing short of unconditional surrender. All wars, therefore, became wars *to end all wars*, all wars became crusades.[3] However, perhaps the most succinct statement of this realist critique came from the pen of Samuel P. Huntington, who argued in 1957 that the isolation of the United States from world politics in the nineteenth century had reinforced the dominance of liberalism. National security was 'a simple given fact – the starting point of political analysis – not the end result of conscious policy'. American awareness of the role of power in foreign politics was consequently dulled by the absence of external threats.[4] Thus, 'the United States by virtue of its non-involvement in the balance of power was able to pursue foreign policy objectives defined in terms of universal ideals rather than in terms of national interests'. Like Kennan and Lippmann, moreover, Huntington also saw liberal ferocity *in* war as the obverse of liberal pacifism *outside* of war:

> The American tends to be an extremist on the subject of war: he either embraces war wholeheartedly or rejects it completely. This extremism is required by the nature of the liberal ideology. Since liberalism deprecates the moral validity of the interests of the state in security, war must be either condemned as incompatible with liberal goals or justified as an ideological movement in support of those goals. American thought has not viewed war in the conservative-military sense as an instrument of national policy.[5]

This realist critique was not just of academic interest: it was also absorbed by some of the most eminent of the 'limited war' theorists writing in the late 1950s, during the era when Dulles' doctrine of 'massive retaliation' was official policy. Its influence was apparent in Henry Kissinger's contention in his *Nuclear Weapons and Foreign Policy* that Americans had confused 'the security conferred by two great oceans with the normal pattern of international relations'. Thus, he argued, Americans came to develop a purist and abstract doctrine of aggression: they either waged war all-out, with crusading moralistic fervour, or they did not wage war at all.[6] The influential limited war theorist Robert Osgood agreed that 'the deliberate limitation of war assumes a conception of the relation between power and policy that is, in many ways, antithetical to American ideas and predispositions in foreign relations'.[7] During the Kennedy and Johnson administrations, these ideas contributed directly to the formulation of military strategy in Vietnam. Thus, as the concept of 'limited war' gained influence within US military culture, it was often defined *against* the image of an older, characteristically American approach to war, as if limited war theory was itself beyond all cultural influence, rather than an alternative conception of war that was nevertheless equally 'American' in its preconceptions and basic assumptions.

Weigley's interpretation of the American way of war was pioneering in the sense that whereas the realists and limited war theorists had explained the American 'crusading' tendency in terms of the *political* culture of the US – the heritage of republicanism and liberal idealism – Weigley wrote a military history with particular sensitivity to the attitudes, unexamined basic assumptions, and educational bias of the military themselves. However, as we have seen, the core themes with which the American style of war is associated were already in common currency well before Weigley published *The American Way of War* in 1973. More specifically, the basic idea that Americans had historically rejected the Clausewitzian view of war as an instrument of state policy was something of a truism. Equally commonplace were its two associated concepts: that this rejection was nurtured during a long formative period of 'free security', and that the American 'crusading' tendency *in* warfare was the obverse of American passivity *outside* of war.

For the realists who coined this popular image in the 1950s, in the shadow of World War II and with the prospect of a long Cold War stretching ahead, the over-riding implication of American military history was that the American approach to war would have to change: as Lippmann put it, 'Voices are now beginning to be heard, asking whether we can break the deadly cycle, and by taking thought and by mastering ourselves, resist the destructive impulses of our democracy – which is to be too pacifist in time of peace and too bellicose in time of war.'[8]

The unrefinable cruelty of war: war as the failure of politics

For Weigley, the formative struggle which defined the American Way of War was the Civil War. Some scholars have seen General William Sherman's famous statement that 'War is Hell' as particularly illustrative. Indeed, if War is Hell, then it is not a continuation of politics by other means. General Sherman's famous adage is normally discussed in terms of its moral connotations, but it also suggests the difficulty of subordinating the chaos of war to any *political* objectives short of the unconditional surrender of the enemy. The assertion that 'War is Hell' could be taken, of course, merely as the idiosyncratic view of a lone general attempting to justify the harsh measures he had employed in the American Civil War. My argument, however, is that it represents something more than this: Sherman's military philosophy *can* be seen as a formative statement of a distinctive American understanding of the art of war, with profound implications for its relationship to politics, but one that became particularly influential amongst the uniformed military almost a century later. 'War is Hell' was merely the most succinct statement of a set of basic assumptions about the nature of warfare that came to dominate American military culture halfway through the twentieth century. This is not to say that the statement captures the complexity of Sherman's own attitude to war, which was more complex than is usually recognized.

General Sherman's comments on the nature of warfare must be understood in the context of his experience in the Civil War, and above all his infamous 'march to the sea', in which he not only made war against the enemy's resources more extensively and systematically than was considered acceptable by contemporary conventions, but also developed a deliberate strategy of terror directed at the minds of enemy civilians. In 1864, he ordered the evacuation of the entire civilian population of the city of Atlanta to rebel territory. When Mayor James M. Calhoun protested that this ruthless action would cause 'appalling and heart-rending' suffering, Sherman responded that he was aware of the consequences, but such was the nature of war: 'You cannot qualify war in harsher terms than I will. War is cruelty, and you cannot refine it.'[9]

Sherman's justification is usually discussed in the context of debates about the morality of warfare. Certainly, Sherman was expressing adherence to a distinctive military 'ethic', which resonated in later periods of American military history. It is important to note that Sherman's line of reasoning does *not* amount to a position of amorality or moral relativism. It does, however, pose a serious challenge to a central strand of the Western 'just war' tradition. The just war tradition rests on two concepts, the *jus ad bellum* – which specifies the conditions under which resort *to* warfare can be justified – and the *jus in bello* – which specifies the military means that can legitimately be adopted *in* warfare.[10] In ethical terms, the 'War is Hell' discourse rests on scepticism about the moral realism and thus the validity of core tenets of the latter concept, the *jus in bello*.

As John W. Brinsfield pointed out in his discussion of Sherman's ethics, 'Sherman, in his Civil War years, did not abandon his attachment to the law or to some of the ethical concepts he may have learned at West Point. Rather, he placed the laws of warfare on a continuum of expediency. The important thing was not the means but the end, and to this point Sherman was clearly a utilitarian thinker.'[11] In claiming that 'War is Hell', Sherman was implying that warfare represented the breakdown of all moral and political intercourse; consequently, it could only be morally justified by reference to an *external* standard of judgement, the *jus ad bellum* or cause for which it was waged. The second and less frequently quoted half of Sherman's statement that 'war is cruelty, and you cannot refine it', was 'and *those who brought war in our country* deserve all the curses and maledictions a people can pour on' (my emphasis). For in Sherman's view it was the Confederate states 'who in the midst of peace and prosperity plunged the nation into war', and therefore it was also they who bore the burden of moral responsibility for the 'unrefinable' cruelty that followed.[12]

There is a further moral implication of this philosophy of warfare. For if the cruelty of war cannot be 'refined', then once hostilities have begun, it follows that the most moral approach is to wage it at the highest possible intensity in order to finish it as soon as possible. For Sherman, this was how the burning of Atlanta was justified – for it brought the end of the war closer in sight. Had he been less ruthless, in his own eyes this would merely have prolonged the war and ultimately brought about more bloodshed. This position found particular support amongst proponents of strategic bombing in the twentieth century. Echoing Sherman's philosophy, General Curtis LeMay once remarked in an interview, 'I'll tell you what war is about. You've got to kill people, and when you've killed enough they stop fighting.'[13] In justifying the strategic bombing of Japan in World War II, he followed Sherman's line of reasoning precisely: 'Actually, I think it's more immoral to use *less* force than necessary, than it is to use *more*. If you use less force, you kill off more of humanity in the long run because you are protracting the struggle.'[14] Many American pilots in Vietnam found the castrating rules of engagement not just frustrating, but *immoral* – not the war itself, but the way it was fought, with so many constraints on the maximum use of force. A particularly extreme version of this philosophy was expressed by General Thomas S. Power (Strategic Air Force Commander) to a Pentagon audience in 1964: the task of the military in war was 'to kill human beings and destroy man-made objects', and to do it 'in the quickest way possible'. It had been 'the moralists who don't want to kill' that had given 'Hitler his start and got us into the mess in Cuba and Vietnam'.[15]

The 'War is Hell' philosophy was thus in severe tension with a central tenet of the *jus in bello* tradition – the principle of proportionality, which states that the means used to attack a particular target and the 'collateral damage' likely to result must be strictly in proportion with the military value of the target in question. For if attacks on civilians could shatter their will to resist and thus end war sooner, then in Sherman's view such attacks would be justified. As Michael Howard once suggested in a discussion of Western laws of war, 'it was laid down that the amount of force used should not be disproportionate to the object to be achieved – a moral imperative translated by military specialists into the principle of the economy of force. This principle ... is one that has never enjoyed a very high priority in the American Way of Warfare.'[16] The looser interpretation of the principle of proportionality adopted during the Civil War was reflected in the legal code of the US military: Francis Lieber, who authored the first comprehensive *jus in bello* code for the US Army in 1863, argued that, 'The more vigorously wars are pursued, the better for humanity. Sharp wars are brief.'[17]

The implications of the conviction that 'War is Hell' are not confined to the moral sphere, however – they also extend to the relationship between war and politics. In the 1800s, American military publications (like most contemporary Western publications) defined 'strategy' as 'the art of concerting a plan of campaign'. Yet the American concept of strategy remained narrowly military throughout the period of European great power politics and imperialism. In 1897, the senior instructor at the US Army staff college still stated that strategy was 'the art of moving an Army in the theatre of operations ... to increase the probability of victory'. According to *The Principles of Strategy* (1921 and 1936), 'Politics and strategy are radically and fundamentally things apart. ... All that soldiers ask is that once the policy is settled, strategy and command shall be regarded as being in a sphere apart from politics.'[18] Even when Americans read Clausewitz, the usual reception of his philosophy by the US Army as an institution 'left out the political aspect of war', and tended to interpret him as an unremitting proponent of 'total war'.[19]

In fact, Clausewitz believed that, 'At its highest level, the art of war is politics, but, no doubt, politics which fights battles instead of writing notes.'[20] This belief derived from Clausewitz's view that war had its own grammar, but not its own logic – for its logic was that of policy. In General Ulysses S. Grant's conception of the art of war, conversely, there is no sense that war's logic derives from anything outside the logic of force itself: 'The art of war is simple enough. Find out where your enemy is. Get at him as soon as you can. Strike at him hard as you can, and keep moving on.'[21] Due to its emphasis on the 'unrefinable' nature of military force, the 'War is Hell' discourse was profoundly hostile to attempts to impose political constraints on warfare. On the contrary, it demanded an anti-Clausewitzian view of the use of force as a response to the *failure* of politics or diplomacy rather than an instrument *of* politics or diplomacy. In suggesting that warfare takes over where politics leaves off, it rejected the sovereignty of the political dimension of war. The logic of policy *ceases to apply* once war begins. This hostility to political direction or constraints was based on an over-riding emphasis on the distinctive grammar of war: its innate tendency to gather its own momentum and resist attempts to subject it to political limits or rational constraints. President Lincoln had entered the Civil War, after all, with a determination to fight in as humane and conciliatory a manner as possible to facilitate a future rapprochement with the Confederate States;[22] yet by 1862 he had come to realize the extent of the bloodshed that would be required to end the war: 'No general yet found can face the arithmetic, but the end of the war will be at hand when he shall be discovered.'[23] In Sherman and Grant he found his generals. However, it was the experience of 'facing the arithmetic' in World War II that had the most lingering impact on US military culture, conditioning the outlook of a whole generation of military commanders facing the novel and different challenges posed by the onset of the Cold War.

Their emphasis on war's inherent tendency to defy attempts to limit or control its course was perhaps best stated by Rear-Admiral J. C. Wylie in 1967. Contradicting the Clausewitzian dictum, he questioned the utility of any active use of military force as a servant of policy except as a final resort. In contrast to the preoccupation of his contemporary strategists like Thomas Schelling with the precise calibration of force, he argued instead that military violence inevitably tended to cripple the policies in whose name it was invoked as it developed a momentum of its own:

> War for a non-aggressor nation is actually a nearly complete collapse of policy. Once war comes, then nearly all pre-war policy is utterly invalid because the setting in which it was designed to function no longer corresponds with the facts of reality. When war comes, we at once move into a radically different world.[24]

Thus war's innate momentum or tendency to 'escalate' meant that it would always resist attempts to subject it to complete technical control in the interest of rendering it a precise instrument of policy, and in this respect its conduct would always remain an art. Indeed the very concept of military 'escalation', inspired by the image of an escalator moving relentlessly upward, was originally coined by writers *sceptical* of the idea that wars using limited nuclear weapons could be controlled.[25] This emphasis on war's tendency to take on a life of its own meant that any resort to military action should be undertaken with extreme caution. It informed a deep scepticism of the political *utility* of force.

Once the threshold had been crossed, however, war should be waged with extreme vigour and relentless determination to win: as Vice-Admiral A. C. Davis put it with regard to possible US military intervention in Indochina in 1954, 'One cannot go over Niagara Falls in a barrel only slightly'.[26] A posture of strategic 'absolutism' – an 'all-or-nothing approach' – was thus conceived as appropriate.[27] 'Overkill' was considered a strategic virtue if it brought a quick end to hostilities. As the official Army history of World War II concluded,

> The efficient commander does not seek to use just enough means, but an excess of means. A military force that is just strong enough to take a position will suffer heavy casualties in doing so; a force vastly superior to the enemy's will do the job without serious loss of men.[28]

To deliberately restrain the force applied by one's own side introduced, as General MacArthur put it, 'the concept of appeasement, the concept that when you use force you can limit that force. ... To me that would have a continued and indefinite extension of bloodshed, which would have ... a limitless end.'[29] The implication of the 'No Substitute for Victory' discourse was that politics and diplomacy were the realm of the politician, while war – defined in narrowly military terms – was the province of the military professional. In a psychological sense, therefore, this philosophy derived from a concern to *redeem* war from the inevitable ambiguity, compromise, and mess of politics, by separating the political and military dimensions into distinct spheres.

The cultural sources of strategic absolutism

The notion that the American understanding of the relationship between war and politics was nurtured during a formative period of 'free security' has been a central theme in the literature on the American way of war. There is an undeniable element of truth in this notion. The uniqueness of the American geopolitical context from 1815 to 1945 is indeed striking. Although the American experiment in republicanism was acutely vulnerable in the first years of its confederation, the unprecedented degree of security bestowed by North America's geopolitical isolation became increasingly apparent after the War of 1812. Having experienced two apparent extremes in only a few generations – total insecurity followed by total security – one scholar has even suggested that the two extremes became perceptually linked: Americans developed 'the belief that military security was an absolute value, like chastity or grace'.[30] Others have warned against the dangers of retrospectively exaggerating this sense of 'free security'.[31] Nineteenth century pessimists feared a third war with England, a second with France, or a conflict with Spain over many long-standing clashing interests. Yet it is still the case that, *comparatively* speaking, Americans not only felt considerably more secure from the threat of external attack than Europeans, but they quite self-consciously celebrated the fortunate geopolitical position apparently bequeathed them by a benign Providence. The War of 1812 demonstrated that Britain could not project power into North America any more effectively than during the Revolution. No technological innovations had simplified the task of maintaining armies across the Atlantic, the cost of waging war in North America was still enormous, and the British still had to worry about Europe.[32]

A wealth of evidence demonstrates that contemporary observers were aware of the uniqueness of the American experience of security. As Thomas Jefferson noted, the fact that the United States was 'separated by nature and a wide ocean from the exterminating havoc of one quarter of the globe' was a blessing to the cause of American security.[33] Lincoln also saw that only Americans could destroy the United States: 'Shall we expect some transatlantic military giant to step the Ocean, and crush us at a blow? Never! ... If destruction be our lot, we must ourselves be its author and finisher.'[34] Secretary of War Elihu Root agreed two decades later that this sense of 'free security' had stymied any previous attempts at reform: 'The possibility of war seemed at all times so vague and unreal that it had no formative power in shaping legislation regarding the Army'.[35]

This comparative freedom from external threat was recognized as the geopolitical precondition of republican liberty and uniqueness. As the Swedish Minister in London remarked to John Adams in 1784, 'Sir, I take it for granted that you will have sense enough to see us in Europe cut each other's throats with a philosophical tranquillity'.[36] This was the exact line of reasoning followed by Senator Harry Truman over a century and a half later when he argued (before Pearl Harbor) that it was in the American interest to let Germany and the Soviet Union hack each other to pieces.[37] America's 'detached and distant situation', as George Washington put it in his famous Farewell Address, afforded the United States the luxury of pursuing 'a different course' to that of Europe, avoiding implication in the morally compromising 'ordinary vicissitudes and combination' of European 'friendships and enmities'. America's fortunate geopolitical situation thus nurtured and safeguarded the profound sense permeating American political culture of its own uniqueness – the belief in 'American Exceptionalism'.

If war is a continuation of politics, then it may also be said that military culture is a continuation of political culture, with all its internal contradictions. American Exceptionalism was 'Janus-faced': despite Secretary of State John Quincy Adams' celebrated injunction of 1821 that America 'goes not abroad, in search of monsters to destroy', Exceptionalism in the guise of Manifest Destiny or crusading Wilsonianism would also be used to justify foreign intervention in the cause of transforming the world in America's image. However, what *was* constant in the discourse of Exceptionalism was the sense that American behaviour in the international realm reflected less cynical calculations of national interest than those of the European monarchies.

The 'basic fact' about American thinking on the causes of war, Anatol Rapoport has written, is that, 'America, in declaring its independence, broke away from the European state system', and thus freed itself 'from the necessity of constant manoeuvring in the international power game with or without resort to organized violence, the predominant preoccupation of European potentates and statesmen'.[38] In rejecting the European balance-of-power system, moreover, the United States also rejected its legitimating ideology. American Exceptionalism – the belief in the uniqueness of the American experiment and its importance as an example to the rest of mankind (John Winthrop's 'city upon a hill') – has been deeply embedded in American culture since the late sixteenth century.[39] The Revolution, however, gave a powerful boost to this American sense of exceptionalism as American national identity came to be defined *against* American perceptions of Europe and particularly against the countervailing image of the former mother country and new arch-enemy, England. England came to be portrayed 'as the counter-image of a virtuous commonwealth, as a country in moral decline, unable to defend the liberty of its own people and intent on enslaving others'. Conversely, the colonies were seen 'as defenders of republican virtues and ideals, as guardians of the "sacred flame of liberty" enshrined in the ancient English constitution'.[40]

The revolutionary republicans believed that the monarchical system of government was the dominant source of war in the international system; they thus dared to hope, as John Adams did, that because she had republican institutions, America would be able to avoid all save defensive wars. This belief in the inherent pacifism of republican forms of government and the benevolence of the American experiment grew in the minds of the Revolutionary generation to acquire the status of a national orthodoxy.[41] Exceptionalism portrayed the United States as a uniquely virtuous nation that rejected the cynical *realpolitik* of the European great powers. Even in the most controversial of America's conflicts, such as the Mexican War, atrocious behaviour by the enemy could plausibly be presented as a justification for an American military response. Yet Exceptionalism found greatest expression in those conflicts where the republic's resources were mobilized for total war, where the sense of being a nation uniquely set apart permitted Americans to believe with crusading fervour in their *jus ad bellum*, and consequently to place less emphasis on *jus in bello*. As President Franklin Roosevelt declared to the nation in World War II, 'we must face the fact that modern warfare as conducted in the Nazi manner is a dirty business. We don't like it – we didn't want to get in it – but we are in it and we're going to fight it with everything we've got.'[42]

In alleging Nazi responsibility for beginning air war on cities, FDR stated that 'the Nazis and the Fascists have asked for it – and they are going to get it'. Even some religious publications like the *Christian Century* followed the 'War is Hell' line on the morality of strategic bombing – there seemed no way 'to draw a line between discriminate and indiscriminate bombing'. Indeed, it seemed 'idle to try to put a check upon the way in which weapons are used. If we fight at all, we fight all out.'[43] Public opinion polls taken during the war indicate that the vast majority of Americans favoured the strategic bombing campaigns against Germany and Japan.[44] Truman's justification for the use of the nuclear bomb echoed Sherman's logic precisely in putting the blame for the outbreak of war squarely on Japan, thus absolving the US of responsibility for the carnage that followed, particularly those measures that could bring a quick end to the conflict:

> We have used [the bomb] against those who attacked us without warning at Pearl Harbor, against those who have starved and beaten and executed American prisoners of war, against those who have abandoned all pretence of obeying international laws of warfare. We have used it in order to shorten the agony of war.[45]

Yet while mid-twentieth century realists like Kennan and Lippmann saw the use of the atomic bomb as a logical culmination of the American military experience, this is perhaps unfair. Comparisons with General Sherman's comments in the Civil War aside, it is a mistake to see the indiscriminate bombing of the final years of World War II as a characteristic expression of military culture. Indeed, before World War II began, FDR had denounced the massive aerial bombardment of cities (which actually dated back to the Japanese bombing of Chinchow and Shanghai in 1931 and 1932) in the strongest terms.[46] And, as Weigley himself notes, the US was far more preoccupied with daylight 'precision bombing' during World War II than the RAF. While strains of strategic absolutism (and certainly a characteristic apoliticism) can be found in the pre-World War II American military tradition, it was the memory of total war itself, combined with the innate destructiveness of nuclear weaponry, that did most to form the dominant mindset in the early Cold War period.

Yet while the resort to indiscriminate means must be seen in the context of the struggle that preceded it, the military establishment's belief that there is no substitute for victory – meaning the total defeat of the enemy – was a profound reflection of its uneasy relationship with the basic values of American democracy. In Russell Weigley's words, 'The great structural question throughout most of the history of American military policy was that of the proper form of military organization in a democratic society.'[47] In the eighteenth century, American colonists already displayed a pervasive suspicion of military professionalism.[48] Drawing on British Whig thought, which permeated and inspired the political outlook of the revolutionary generation, many pamphleteers drew a strong connection between liberty and the militia, and conversely between tyranny and standing armies. In the aftermath of the war, debate over the Confederation's peacetime military requirements reflected deep concern over the viability of the new republic. No one questioned the effectiveness of professional soldiers, but a regular Army symbolized the moral and political corruption to which republics had historically been susceptible. Federalists responded, however, that the danger of a tyrannical Federal government dominating its citizens with a standing Army would be guarded against through the intricate checks and balances of the Constitution, which gave the legislature control over the armed forces.[49] Until the Cold War, the characteristic American compromise was to rely on modest standing forces in 'normal times', to be supplemented with a rapid and massive mobilization of citizen-soldiers in times of emergency.

The Constitution appointed the president as Commander-in-Chief and also empowered the executive to make treaties and various appointments with the advice and consent of the Senate. Congress, on the other hand, was given powers to declare war; to provide for the common defence; to raise and support armies and navies; to govern the militia; and to establish taxes and spend monies. The Framers thus separated the purse from the sword, with the deliberate intention of making it *difficult* for the US to engage in war; by establishing a deliberative check to hasty action, they attempted to ensure that the decision to wage war would be made by those most accountable to the people.⁵⁰ The constitutional scholar Edwin Corwin once remarked that the Constitution thus amounted to 'an invitation to struggle for the privilege of directing American foreign policy'.⁵¹ It institutionalized republican attitudes towards war and the military, thus ensuring that future generations of Americans would continue to confront them as an objective reality constraining their freedom of action.

Once hostilities had been initiated, however, the logic of republican discourse tended to demand nothing short of complete victory. Woodrow Wilson's personal rationalization for entering World War I, for example, was to gain American influence to prevent a 'victor's peace' being imposed and to re-establish a balance of power in Europe. Limited American participation in World War I was not compatible, however, with the deep popular emotions Wilson decided he must arouse to support a declaration of war. Having mobilized public opinion on behalf of his crusade, Wilson was trapped between his own rhetoric and the 'unconditional surrender' wing of the Republican Party. He realized too late that Henry Cabot Lodge was correct in declaring that, 'the American people mean to have a dictated and not a negotiated peace'.⁵² Similarly, when projected casualty figures for the invasion of Japan in World War II led a number of American officials to argue for modification of Roosevelt's unconditional surrender formula, Secretary of State James F. Byrnes told Truman that he would be 'crucified' if he retreated from it.⁵³

Thus, American republicanism was profoundly ambivalent in its attitudes towards the professional military establishment. It is hardly surprising that the military were equally ambivalent towards republicanism in return. The logic of American political culture tended to starve the military of resources in peacetime, only to demand complete victory, with minimal casualties, in wartime. In order to square this circle, mobilization of the republic's human and material resources had to be massive in order to muster the requisite level of overwhelming force. American war leaders rightly feared, however, that the public would not tolerate such a massive mobilization of citizen-soldiers indefinitely. Victory, therefore, had to be achieved quickly. The professional officer class tended to regard itself as the guardian of American democracy and republican values. Yet, isolated from the rest of society by years of frontier duty, they tended to be regarded as misfits by their civilian contemporaries.⁵⁴ Thus, influential military intellectuals like General Emory Upton (1839–1881) were naturally resentful of what they regarded as the ingratitude of democracies to their military saviours. In a dual defensive response to public unease over militarism's threat to republican liberty, the military developed a concept of military professionalism whose hallmark was apoliticism, while paradoxically remaining acutely sensitive towards public opinion.

The American tradition of civil–military relations has drawn an unusually 'bright line to separate the realm of the soldier from that of the politician'.⁵⁵

After the Civil War, the Army professionalized itself in a state of isolation: Congress was content to leave the Army to itself as long as it did not request an increased budget, while Presidents, free from pressing external threats and fearful of Congressional accusations of meddling, left the Army to develop its professional standards free from civilian interference.[56] Isolated from American society on the western frontier and free from Congressional and Presidential interference, Army reformers like William Sherman and Emory Upton looked abroad for inspiration. An admirer of the Prussian military establishment, Upton was the most influential exponent of the separation of the armed forces from 'mere politicians'. In his *Military Policy of the United States*, he argued that in their conduct of military operations, officers should be free of civilian interference, which contributed to the imprudence and weakness of US policy. In Weigley's words,

> Emery Upton did lasting harm in setting the main current of American military thought not to the task of shaping military institutions that would serve both military and national purposes, but to the futile task of demanding that the national institutions be adjusted to purely military expediency.[57]

Between the world wars, *The Principles of Strategy* cited above continued to express the Uptonian view that, 'Any attempt on the part of statesmen to interfere in the conduct of military operations is likely to lead to disastrous results'.[58]

In contrast to the European experience, the US military developed its concept of military professionalism while trying to function within a liberal society. Professionalism thus became equated with the non-political, and with a primary focus on the technical military skills and competence required in the conduct of grand battles.[59] In Britain, conversely, power over grand strategy was much more centralized in the Cabinet, and the constant pressures of imperial policing demanded constant civilian oversight and interference in imperial affairs. Under civilian guidance, the British Army thus developed a critical attitude towards the lessons of Prussian and continental experience, and developed a self-image in which imperial policing was regarded as an integral part of their role and doctrine. 'Because the British Army, unlike the US Army, became professionalized under conditions of easy civilian intervention, Army purists were not able to set the agenda as to what counted as war.'[60]

Until World War II the Army regarded its core mission, appropriately for a republic in an era of apparently 'free' security, as continental defence. The Commanding General of the Army (Sheridan) wrote in 1884, 'Excepting for our ocean commerce and our seaboard cities, I do not think we should be much alarmed about the probability of wars with foreign powers, since it would require more than a million and a half of men to make a campaign upon land against us.'[61] For most of the era of free security, in peacetime the United States required only garrisons for the harbour fortifications and a constabulary to pacify the frontier and deal with unforeseen emergencies – tasks performed by a regular Army of 6,000 to 15,000 prior to the Civil War, and about 26,000 after the end of Reconstruction. In wartime, the Regulars' role was to provide professional expertise and guidance for the mass volunteer Army of citizen-soldiers. Regular officers were obliged to acknowledge that, as General Winfield Scott Hancock put it in 1876, 'As a *physical force*, our little standing Army can never be of appreciable importance after a great contest has set in'.[62]

In an accurate summary of the influence of republican political culture on the military, Colonel Arthur L. Wagner noted that,

> It is clear that our military future will not be shaped by theories based on military principles alone. The military policy of the United States will be strongly affected by the popular predilection for economical expenditures in time of peace; by a jealousy of standing armies; by reliance upon volunteers in time of war; and by a more or less active influence of popular opinion in the direction of armies in the field.[63]

Sensitivity towards the wider political and societal culture was especially marked in the Army, which had borne the brunt of Congressional fears of militarism from 1776 onwards (the Navy's presence was less visible, less associated with threats to republican liberty, essential in support of trade, and thus regarded as less threatening). As a result, Army officers tended to be more sensitive to congressional and public moods than their naval counterparts. During the 1930s, for example, these views were overwhelmingly pacifistic, isolationist, and Anglophobic, and Army planners deliberately factored such views into their war planning and views of national policy. In pressing for withdrawal from China and the Philippines on the grounds that the public was unwilling to use force against Japan, one officer noted that national objectives were not 'the whole of national policy any more than the objectives of a war plan are all of that plan. National policy consists of the objectives the nation pursues, *plus the means which the nation desires to employ, or is willing to employ in the attainment of those objectives*' (my emphasis). Lt.-General Stanley Embick, deputy chief of staff and Army commander between 1936 and 1939, warned against any involvement with Britain in either the growing European crisis or the Pacific, and supported appeasement of the Axis powers.[64]

Military sensitivity towards American public opinion and political culture was expressed most forcefully in unease over the inconstancy or fickleness of American support for military action. Relying as the republic did on the massive mobilization of citizen-soldiers, and generally fighting far away on foreign soil, military elites feared that American society would not tolerate being put on a war footing indefinitely. After the Civil War, Ulysses S. Grant wrote that, 'Anything that could have prolonged the war a year beyond the time that it did finally close, would probably have exhausted the North to such an extent that they might then have abandoned the contest and agreed to a separation'.[65] Popular ambivalence over war was equally apparent in August 1941, when three-quarters of voters opposed US military intervention on behalf of Europe. General Marshall remarked during World War II that Americans did not possess 'that tremendous spirit that comes of defending your own home' to the same extent as Europeans, a sentiment that also explained Roosevelt's private comment on what 'a good thing' it would be 'if a few German bombs could be dropped over here'. Years before the American entry into the war, Army War College planners were convinced that public stamina would be America's greatest weakness. During the conflict, the Joint Chiefs of Staff (JCS) believed that 'the prolongation of the war' was simply not an option for America, and their war planners repeatedly lectured the British that the public would 'not countenance a long war of attrition'.[66]

George Marshall remarked after the war that one of the most important lessons he had learnt was that a democracy 'could not indulge in a Seven-Years' War'. The factors that had been constantly on his mind in the European war, he explained, had been 'casualties, duration, and the Pacific'.[67] Richard Nixon expressed a similar conclusion in Vietnam: 'When a president sends American troops off to war, a hidden timer starts to run. He has a finite period of time to win the war before the people grow weary of it.'[68] One reason Generals Westmoreland and DePuy were so committed to the strategy of 'search-and-destroy' over 'pacification' in Vietnam was reflected in the question they repeatedly asked visitors: 'How long have we got to win this war?' They were convinced that pacification could not be the ultimate answer because it would *take too long* – they feared that the American public simply lacked the patience for such an approach. DePuy believed that the 'home front' was the US 'weak spot'.[69]

Seeking to defend the Joint Chiefs of Staff (JCS) against the charge of 'naïve apoliticism' in his account of US strategy in World War II, one scholar has pointed out that, 'Total victory over the Axis and its accomplishment as quickly as possible and with a minimum of US casualties were *political* goals. They were also fundamental political goals one would expect of a democratic society at war.'[70] Nevertheless, the political considerations identified here derived primarily from unease over the inconstancy of the support of the American public, rather than concern with the optimal political configuration of the post-war world. There was in fact no contradiction between the studied apoliticism of American military elites and their unease over the fickleness of public opinion – they both derived from the same ambivalence towards a political culture that in turn remained suspicious of the military.

In its sharp distinction between the states of war and peace, the absolutist mindset harmonized with the discourse on American Exceptionalism that dominated American political culture. In emphasizing war's internal momentum, it expressed a deep sensitivity towards the limits of popular support. In its preference for the use of overwhelming force unlimited by political considerations and constraints, it sought to achieve victory in the shortest time possible so that the republic could return to the 'normal' state of peace. As a discourse of military professionals, the absolutist conception of war thus sought to warn the republic against casual involvement in foreign military quarrels while ensuring that, once committed, the US would fight in a way that optimized republican strengths and minimized republican weaknesses. It can thus be seen as a distinctively republican discourse on the 'art of war'.

Cultural conception and the reality of war

In Russell Weigley's classic account, the American way of war was said to be distinguished by an enduring preference for strategies of 'annihilation' over those of 'attrition'. While this dichotomy is somewhat simplistic and confusing,[71] Weigley's underlying argument that American military elites sought as far as possible to prevent the intrusion of political considerations into their conduct of military affairs is an accurate characterization, at least for the first half of the twentieth century. It was no accident that this contempt for political interference in warfare reached its zenith in the early Cold War period, just as a new community of 'neo-Clausewitzian' civilian strategists emerged in dialectical opposition: the latter self-consciously set out to reform the traditional American way of war and adapt it to the new constraints of the Cold War, in which war between the great powers meant thermonuclear war, and only 'limited wars' could be fought.

From the Civil War onwards, American military education had come to be dominated by the cult of the Napoleonic 'decisive battle'.[72] This preoccupation with decisive battle, to the neglect of the broader political objectives that military action was intended to achieve, did have an enduring influence. President Woodrow Wilson's personal rationalization for entering World War I, for example, was to gain American influence to prevent a 'victor's peace' being imposed.[73] Yet General Pershing (commander of the American Expeditionary Forces) opposed the idea of an armistice in the belief that the United States must achieve an unconditional surrender of the enemy as Grant had in the Civil War. He believed 'that complete victory can only be achieved by continuing the war until we force an unconditional surrender from Germany; but if the Allied Governments decide to grant an armistice, the terms should be so rigid that under no circumstances could Germany again take up arms'.[74]

Pershing was determined to break out of the war's attritional stalemate and wage a war of movement, in order to restore momentum to the front, annihilate the enemy, and bring a quick end to the war.[75] The fact that the American preference for unconditional surrender was not discredited by World War I's terrible attrition may have been contingent on the fact that

Pershing's demand for a return to open-field tactics could be realized only under the special conditions of 1918.[76] 'At the deepest psychological level', as Eliot Cohen has pointed out, 'the American high command appears to have escaped the emotional scars that the World War I slaughter inflicted on Britain.'[77] In pursuit of Roosevelt's objective of 'unconditional surrender' in World War II, American Army strategists persistently clung to their insistence that a cross-channel invasion of Europe must take place as soon as possible, in contrast to the British preference for a more indirect 'peripheral' strategy. Whereas the British preference for a peripheral strategy focusing on the Mediterranean's 'soft underbelly' reflected their fear of a return to the old battlefields of France, the American preference for a direct advance on Hitler across the plains of Northern Europe perhaps reflected its different experience of World War I as well as the military preoccupation with ensuring total victory as quickly as possible. Once again, the success of the Normandy landings in 1944 seemed to justify these assumptions.[78]

Some scholars have connected the separation of politics and strategy with the reluctance of American military and political leaders to confront Stalin until much of Eastern Europe was irrevocably in his grasp.[79] There is some evidence to suggest that US military elites did indeed rationalize their decisions in these terms: Eisenhower responded to Churchill's pressure to seize Berlin before the Russians got there, for example, with the objection that, 'personally and aside from all logistical, tactical or strategic implications I would be loath to hazard American lives for *purely political purposes*' (my emphasis). George Marshall also believed that the military should stay away from political issues, in order to maintain their 'sacred trust' with the American people.[80] During World War II, he tried (as he put it) to 'make decisions without considering the political consequences', repeatedly stating that 'that was for the politicians'. In any case, he believed at the time that 'the destruction of the German armed forces is more important than any political or psychological advantages'.[81] Only after the war and with the political perspective of a secretary of state did he begin to take a broader view, recalling of Roosevelt's decision to invade North Africa in 1942 that, 'We failed to see that the leader in a democracy has to keep the people entertained. That may sound like the wrong wording but it conveys the thought.'[82]

Indeed, during the war, two US Army planners lamented the American tendency to separate political from military considerations: the US had been 'outmanoeuvred' at Allied conferences, they argued, 'primarily' because British war aims,

> based on national aims, have been clear-cut and understood by all concerned. In presenting their strategy and plans they have had the benefit of a nicely integrated politico-economic-military planning organization developed by experience over a long period of time. On the other hand our own war aims have not been so clearly defined and

the integration in our strategy of economic, and especially political factors with the purely military factors has not been so thoroughly effected.[83]

It was above all the experience of World War II itself that ensured the dominance of the absolutist mindset, and its lingering influence in the Cold War period. The memory of total war informed the attitudes of a military elite which remained distrustful of 'coercive diplomacy', or the limited use of force in support of political objectives. In his 1977 survey of civilian and military approaches to Cold War crises, Richard K. Betts noted that in decisions over whether to commit American forces, JCS views were frequently divided, and no clear civilian–military divide emerged. Yet, once discussion moved to the issue of the *degree* of force that should be committed, a clear pattern emerged: Generals preferred 'using force quickly, massively, and decisively to destroy enemy capabilities rather than rationing it gradually to coax the enemy to change his intentions'.[84]

The most famous expression of this mindset was General Douglas MacArthur's comment in his 'Farewell Speech' to Congress on the Korean War: 'once war is forced upon us, there is no other alternative than to apply every available means to bring it to a swift end. War's very object is victory, not prolonged indecision. In war there is no substitute for victory.' In 1952, he argued that, '*When politics fails and the military takes over* you must trust the military. ... There should be no non-professional interference in the handling of troops.'[85] He profoundly resented President Truman's attempt to exercise civilian supremacy in an active theatre of war: it 'introduces into the military a political control such as I have never known in my life or studied'.[86] MacArthur's distaste for limiting American objectives in the war was widely shared in the upper echelons of the Army. At the time of the armistice in July 1953, the US commander General Mark Clark told newsmen, 'I cannot find it in me to exult in this hour'.[87] The Joint Chiefs of Staff disagreed with MacArthur's proposals to widen the war, not so much because they did not share his philosophy of the nature of war, but because they thought Korea and Asia were not the main theatre of conflict with the Communists but a diversionary theatre[88] ('the wrong war, at the wrong place, at the wrong time, and with the wrong enemy', to quote JCS Chairman General Bradley).

Both the domestic unpopularity of the Korean War and the political restrictions placed on the use of American power fostered a 'never again' mentality within the Armed Forces. Roger Hilsman, who was appointed Director of the State Department's Bureau of Intelligence in 1961, later wrote that 'by 1961 it was a shibboleth among the Joint Chiefs of Staff that the United States ought never again to fight a limited war on the ground in Asia'. With regard to possible intervention in Laos, for example, Army Chief of Staff General Decker opposed the idea of limited intervention categorically: 'if we go in, we should go in to win, and that means bombing

Hanoi, China, and maybe using nuclear weapons'.[89] The dominant conviction amongst the Pentagon's military planners in the Eisenhower and Kennedy years was that there should be no more limited, local wars fought by American forces without freedom to use any weapons in the American arsenal, including nuclear ones. The frustrations of Korea were reflected in the advice of the Joint Chiefs of Staff in 1964 to escalate to an all-out attack on North Vietnam if it would not halt its aggression in the South.[90]

This absolutist mentality was also reflected in American planning for war with the 'real' enemy, the Soviet Union. The head of the Strategic Air Command during the early Cold War, General Curtis LeMay, was in many ways the embodiment of the 'War is Hell' mindset. He thought that the strategic bombing in Europe in World War II had been hampered by too much fussing about 'precision bombing'. LeMay's proposed war plan of delivering America's entire stockpile of nuclear bombs in a single massive attack became official policy in the Eisenhower administration's strategy of 'Massive Retaliation'. The 'Single Integrated Operational Plan' (SIOP-62) called for an all-out pre-emptive first-strike against the USSR, Eastern Europe *and* China, in response to an actual or merely impending Soviet invasion of Western Europe that involved no nuclear weapons at all.[91] There was thus some validity in Henry Kissinger's charge that, 'we added the atomic bomb to our arsenal without integrating its implications into our thinking. Because we saw it merely as another tool in a concept of warfare which knew no goal save total victory, and no mode of war except all-out war.'[92]

Refusing to fight on American terms: the American experience of 'small wars'

Assessing the state of American military education in 1960, the military sociologist Morris Janowitz was struck by the fact that, 'the curriculum does not focus on specific political consequences – past, present, or future – of military action. ... In fact, none of the war colleges focuses on the management of political warfare – that is, the practices involved in the co-ordination of military action with political persuasion.'[93] This apolitical bias had dysfunctional implications for the conduct of those conflicts that did not fit the idealized cultural conception of war against a conventional opponent in which the US could apply overwhelming force without political restrictions. The basic assumptions of the 'No Substitute for Victory' philosophy had little application to such categories as limited war, imperial policing, low-intensity conflict, and counter-insurgency. Indeed, the essence of counter-insurgency has been defined by Richard Betts as 'a delicate interweaving of political and military functions – the kind of fusion that irritated so many of the military elite who preferred a clear line of demarcation between the two spheres'.[94]

Historically, the Marine Corps was the only service to regard counter-insurgency and other forms of 'small war' or low-intensity conflict as an integral part of its mission and identity. In the early part of the twentieth century the Marines became known as 'State Department troops', a term that clearly evokes their purpose of utilizing force in support of diplomacy. Based on these experiences and Britain's colonial experience, the Marines wrote their own *Small Wars Manual* in the 1930s. The manual's contents went against the grain of mainstream American strategic thought in a number of significant respects, emphasizing the co-ordination of military force and diplomatic pressure, limited objectives, the primacy of politics, and a preference for employing a minimum of troops and a demonstration of power rather than overwhelming force.[95]

Yet, while the Marine Corps had a respectable record in such conflicts, their approach was confined to a minority culture, and the mainstream American armed forces never absorbed their hard-learned lessons.[96] Despite its engagement in an unconventional frontier war against the Indians in the nineteenth century, the Army objected to the use of the armed forces as a 'constabulary' force, regarding policing duties as beneath the soldier's proper vocation.[97] The Army's dominant cultural conception led it to fail repeatedly to institutionalize its experiences of small war:

> Whenever after the Revolution the Army had to conduct a counter-guerrilla campaign – in the Second Seminole War of 1835–1841, the Philippine Insurrection of 1899–1903, and in Vietnam in 1965–73 – it found itself almost without an institutional memory of such experiences, had to relearn appropriate tactics at exorbitant costs, and yet tended after each episode to regard it as an aberration that need not be repeated.[98]

The Army's experience in the Philippines is a particularly notable example. Some contemporary officers did question the Army's preoccupation with conventional warfare. The aftermath of the Spanish-American War, as one Colonel argued, showed that 'if Army officers and the Army have had to know something of the art of war, they have had to know and use far more the art of pacification'. In the Philippines, 'the work was four-fifths peace and one-fifth war making ... by the study of war alone we shall be but little prepared for by far the greater burdens which are to fall upon us'. Yet, whereas the British modified their doctrine to reflect the experience of the Boer War, the US Army's doctrine 'all but ignored the Philippines', and never made any systematic attempt to integrate the fighting of small wars into its core identity.[99]

This wilful amnesia recurred not only with regard to counter-insurgency and pacification but also with experiences of 'limited war'. Thus, the Air Force, for example, ignored the Korean War in the writing of doctrine. In 1955, Thomas K. Finletter, a former Secretary of the Air Force, said, 'The Korean War was a special case, and airpower can learn little there about its future role in United States foreign policy in the East'. The 1959 version of basic doctrine stated that 'the best preparation for limited war is proper preparation for general war'.[100] President Kennedy's interest in limited war was partly inspired by General Maxwell Taylor's book *The Uncertain Trumpet*, which coined the term 'flexible response' in an attempt to outline a new role for the Army in the nuclear age. Kennedy developed a keen interest in low-intensity conflict, which he sought to make one of the Army's central priorities. However, Taylor's own concept of flexible response focused primarily on creating an Army with the ability to wage a mid-intensity conventional conflict in the nuclear age; indeed, most military men perceived 'limited' as meaning non-thermonuclear, or local as opposed to global, war, rather than unconventional conflict or war in which political considerations might restrict the rules of engagement.[101] Thus, while the Army paid lip-service to Kennedy's enthusiasm for reform, it remained adamantly opposed to challenges to its basic conception of war and its central focus on preparing for a conventional conflict in Europe.[102]

General William Westmoreland consequently proceeded to develop a strategy for Vietnam that was fully in accordance with the apolitical tradition. He emphasized large-scale 'search-and-destroy' operations designed to carry the war to the enemy in a war of attrition by locating their forces, fixing them in place and annihilating them with superior American firepower. Indeed, asked in a press conference what the answer to counter-insurgency was, Westmoreland replied with one word: 'firepower'.[103] 'We'll just go on bleeding them,' he argued in 1967, 'until Hanoi wakes up to the fact that they have bled the country dry to the point of national disaster for generations.'[104] This was not a 'strategy' in the Clausewitzian sense of the word: it neglected the political dimensions of the war in favour of a narrow military focus on the physical destruction of the enemy armed forces. Consequently, Westmoreland devoted far fewer resources to the approach favoured by most students of counter-insurgency, which was to deny the insurgents access to the wider population (or of the 'fish' to the 'sea', in Mao's famous phrase) by diffusing light infantry through the main population centres in order to hold and secure territory.

In conventional Army thinking, there was scant difference between conventional limited war and counter-insurgency. It was assumed that, 'Any good soldier can handle guerrillas', as General Earle Wheeler remarked. Westmoreland's strategy of attrition was partly an attempt to minimize US casualties by emphasizing American strengths in firepower and strategic mobility.[105] Yet an Office of Systems Analysis study in 1966 showed that, regardless of the level of allied activity, the enemy lost a significant number of men only when they decided to stand and fight;[106] clearly, the Americans were fighting on Vietnamese terms. As the North Vietnamese General Giap himself later explained, Vietnamese strategy successfully aimed 'to draw American units into remote areas and thereby facilitate control of the population of the lowlands'.[107] Like the Army, the Air Force fought the Vietnam War without questioning its basic assumptions. Thus, in their attempt to develop a template for successfully applying air power, air planners created a rigid formula for success that eliminated such variables as war aims and the nature of the enemy's military effort. Doctrine was geared toward a general war with the Soviet Union, despite the fact that Vietnam was a pre-industrial, agricultural nation.[108]

'Retrospectively', a report on Vietnam sponsored by the Advanced Research Projects Agency noted in 1968,

> We didn't appreciate what we were getting into. ... Our approach followed our own American values and, in the military, a set of precepts and organizational practices institutionalized in conventional conflict. We strove to pattern the Vietnamese military after our own, and, largely ignoring Communist stimulated and supported insurgency in rear areas, set the defence of the 17th parallel as the mission.[109]

The central question posed by this account of the American experience in limited or unconventional conflicts is *why* the dominant cultural conception never adapted to the reality of war when strategic experience repeatedly refused to conform to expectation. This question is, of course, given added poignancy by the current challenges the US military face in Afghanistan and Iraq. A comparison with the British experience suggests several factors. Most straightforwardly, the US experiences were simply too brief and too intermittent and were thus regarded as 'aberrations'. The British imperial predicament, in contrast, required the British military constantly to use force in support of limited political objectives. Secondly, the diffusion of powers over warmaking demanded by republican political culture also gave the American military a level of autonomy from civilian interference that the British armed forces, subject to the centralized authority of the Cabinet, never experienced. Such constant civilian interference was central in maintaining the British military's comparative flexibility.[110]

More fundamentally, the republican political culture which nurtured the 'No Substitute for Victory' philosophy was founded on the principle of anti-imperialism. The use of American troops to police the internal affairs of other nations, whether in the Philippines or Vietnam, was thus in tension with the republic's dominant ideals to a degree that did not apply to the British imperial experience. The American experiment in colonialism was brief and remarkably controversial.[111] America's 'limited wars' in the Philippines, Korea, and Vietnam were also its most unpopular twentieth century conflicts. This was reflected in US strategic priorities – unlike some imperial powers, for example, the US never formed two distinct establishments for its colonial and metropolitan garrisons. The Pacific Army never received the resources to fulfil its designated mission in the Philippines, because it was regarded as secondary to the Army's core role of continental defence.[112] Ultimately, the American military could always rationalize its stubborn adherence to its conception of war by reference to the over-riding priority of preparing for war in which the application of overwhelming force would be required – whether the mission be continental defence, preparation for conventional war against the Great Powers of Europe, or nuclear war with the Soviet Union. The over-riding strategic imperative of preparing for World War III was reinforced by perceived societal imperatives: the perception that the American public would not tolerate heavy American casualties in wars for limited political objectives.

Conclusion: the loss of 'free security' and the dialectical evolution of US military culture

'One of the more basic and obvious facts of our time,' wrote Samuel P. Huntington in 1957, 'is that changes in technology and international politics have combined to make security now the final goal of policy rather than its starting assumption.'[113] This new strategic outlook was reflected at the outset of the Cold War by the replacement of the traditional term 'national defence' with the more elastic term 'national security', conveying the broader range and purpose of American strategic activities.[114] One scholar has located the origins of this new 'construction of national security' even earlier, in the period preceding American entry into World War II. While German armies advanced across Europe in 1940, President Roosevelt decried how a 'false teaching of geography' had created a sense of 'some form of mystic [American] immunity that could never be violated'; yet this was an illusion, for modern science had 'annihilated time and space'. The United States would never again be completely free from attack, and American security now entailed a global calculus: 'If the United States is to have any defence, it must have total defence. We cannot defend ourselves a little here and a little there.'[115] This new strategic predicament, moreover, would require a new conception of warfare that was fundamentally at odds with the desire for unconditional surrender at any cost. This new calculus was clearly expressed in 1950 in the top-secret strategy document NSC-68:

> if war comes, what is the role of force? ... In the words of the *Federalist* (No. 28) 'The means to be employed must be proportioned to the extent of the mischief.' The mischief may be a global war or it may be a Soviet campaign for limited objectives. In either case we should take no avoidable initiative which would cause it to become a war of annihilation, and if we have the forces to defeat a Soviet drive for limited objectives it may well be to our interest not to let it become a global war. Our aim in applying force must be to compel the acceptance of terms consistent with our objectives, and our capabilities for the application of force should, therefore, within the limits of what we can sustain over the long pull, be congruent to the range of tasks which we may encounter.[116]

In short, the new strategic imperatives imposed by America's rise to superpower status and the onset of the Cold War seemed to many critics of the military to require the adoption of a more Clausewitzian conception of force. Yet whereas the French military in the 1950s came to see 'revolutionary war' in the less developed world as the central threat posed by Soviet communism, and revised its military doctrine to reflect this perception, the American military establishment interpreted the challenge, in accordance with its cultural predispositions, as fundamentally a conventional military threat posed by Soviet strategic nuclear forces to the US or by Soviet conventional forces to America's allies in Europe.[117] The dominant American military culture resisted any fundamental reconceptualization of its basic assumptions about the nature of warfare.

A tension thus became increasingly apparent between the military's dominant conception of war and the new strategic imperatives of the Cold War. During the Cuban Missile Crisis, for example, President Kennedy was appalled by the narrow focus of recommendations from the Joint Chiefs. Eventually, he felt compelled to issue a national security action memorandum charging them to include political and economic factors into their recommendations.[118] Kennedy's Secretary of Defence, Robert McNamara, was equally shocked when he became fully cognizant of the all-or-nothing character of American nuclear strategy.[119] The evolution of US military discourse on the political dimension of war thus came to be marked by a *dialectical* trajectory. The failure of the absolutist mindset to adapt to the strategic imperatives of the Cold War contributed to the emergence of its own cultural antithesis: the apoliticism of the military elite's conception of war created the conceptual space for the emergence of a new scientific discourse on strategy that sought to render the use of military force a finely calibrated instrument of national policy. To add insult to injury, it would be civilians, rather than the uniformed military, who would be the high priests of this new concept of war.

2 The science of strategy
War as a political instrument in the nuclear age

> We're a young and new field, trying to discover ourselves. The parallel I think of is economics. The economists feel they have come to understand the broad workings of the economy and are able to control depressions. In the same way, we are trying to grasp the inner workings of war in order to control it.
>
> Donald G. Brennan, 1965[1]

From the end of World War II, American strategic thought was increasingly influenced by an emerging science of strategy pioneered by civilians. In its assumptions about the relationship between war and politics, this new scientific discourse on war represented the cultural antithesis of the absolutist philosophy that continued to shape the strategic thinking of the military. Whereas the latter tended to regard war as the failure of politics and were sceptical of the political utility of military force, the scientific civilian strategists enthusiastically accepted the primacy of political objectives and sought to restore, through scientific and technological means, the link between force and the rational pursuit of policy that appeared severed in the nuclear age. The evolution of US military discourse thus took on a pronounced dialectical character: the emergence of diametrically opposed conceptions of the political utility of war corresponded closely to the divide between military and civilian professionals within American military culture. The civilian strategists' intrusion into a realm traditionally regarded as the province of military professionals was legitimized by their scientific credentials and their focus on calibrating the use or threat of force to the ends of national policy. The military, conversely, regarded the civilians' emphasis on *limiting* and controlling force with deep suspicion, and were far more concerned with avoiding involvement in unpopular limited wars for ambiguous political objectives that might lack popular support.

Frustrated with what they regarded as the narrow parochialism and political naivety of the uniformed military, policy-makers were increasingly influenced by the new science of strategy. Yet, despite its acceptance of the primacy of policy, the scientific strategists' preoccupation with precise quantification and abstract modelling led, paradoxically, to a neglect of those subjective political 'imponderables' that could not be analysed with such precision. This epistemological bias was expressed in an emphasis on measuring enemy capabilities over the interpretation of enemy intentions – a bias which compounded the failure of the US to develop the sophisticated understanding of political complexities required in successful counter-insurgency.

The 'fine, internal structure of war'

'One of the most remarkable changes in the intellectual landscape over the past dozen years,' observed Bernard Brodie in the early 1960s,

> is the appearance of specialists in military strategy who are (a) mostly civilians and (b) trained in and accustomed to using scientific method in dealing with the problems of their chosen field. ... Although their numbers are still small ... they have been collectively of enormous influence. Most of the distinctively modern concepts of military strategy that have been embraced by the military services themselves have evolved out of their ranks.[2]

Beyond their civilian status and scientific aspirations, these strategists were collectively distinguished by their faith in the potential of the scientific method and technical ingenuity to manipulate, constrain, and control the course of warfare. This new interest in deliberately limiting and calibrating the application of military force was anathema to most military professionals. Indeed, the physicist Spurgeon Keeny (the civilian head of the Air Force's Special Weapons section) ultimately concluded that General Curtis LeMay's objection to restraint in war was *philosophical* rather than practical. Restraint, LeMay once told Bernard Brodie, was simply 'contrary to the principles of war'.[3] The scientific civilian strategists, conversely, sought to manipulate what one RAND strategist termed 'the fine, internal structure of war'. Their basic assumption, as one contemporary noted, was that rationality could triumph over irrationality, and the escalation of war could be controlled.[4] This preoccupation with controlling the 'internal economy' of war had moral, strategic, and political implications.

If the 'fine, internal structure of war' can be controlled, then *contra* General Sherman, war's cruelty may be 'refined' after all. Those civilians who sought to reform US nuclear strategy so that any future war might be waged with more finesse and discrimination were often caricatured in the press as amoral monsters in the mould of Dr Strangelove. Indeed, in a review of *On Thermonuclear War* by Herman Kahn – often regarded as 'the real Dr Strangelove' – James Newman wrote that, 'This evil and tenebrous book, with its loose-lipped pieties and its hayfoot-strawfoot logic, is permeated with a bloodthirsty irrationality such as I have not seen in my years of reading.' For Anatol Rapoport, similarly, Kahn's work represented the 'psychopathic' tendencies of strategic thinking, devoid of 'conscience' or 'moral sense'. Such reviewers were ethically more at ease with the indiscriminate destruction of Massive Retaliation which, in the simple choice it appeared to offer between peace or holocaust, made nuclear war unthinkable and, thereby, it was hoped, less likely.

Herman Kahn's point, conversely, was that since a possibility existed that nuclear war might nevertheless occur, strategists had a 'compelling obligation, at once moral and political, to examine and implement the kinds of steps that might greatly reduce war-related deaths, destruction and human suffering'. He stressed the continuing relevance of proportionality and the distinction between military and civilian targets that adherents of the 'War is Hell' mentality such as LeMay regarded as irrelevant in the context of nuclear war.[5] A congressman outraged by Kahn's cold-blooded emphasis on 'surviving' nuclear war once confronted him with the rhetorical question, 'Ten million or one hundred million dead, what is the difference?' Kahn's deadpan response – 'Ninety million, Senator' – expressed his fundamental conviction that nuclear war's nightmarish absurdities did not absolve war planners of the responsibility of attempting to mitigate the suffering it would unleash.[6] Kahn's explicit purpose in writing *On Thermonuclear War* was 'to create a vocabulary' so that strategic issues could be 'comfortably and easily' discussed, a vocabulary that would avoid the emotions surrounding nuclear war through its invocation of the dispassionate realm of scientific thought.[7]

However, such studied objectivity did not amount to a position of amorality. The formative experience for many of the strategists who later sought to bring discrimination to nuclear strategy was the planning of the strategic bombing campaigns of World War II. For example, Charles Hitch, Henry Rowen, Carl Kaysen, and Walt Rostow – who, after the war, would go to RAND and then join the Kennedy administration – spent much of the war at a British hamlet codenamed 'Pine Tree' attempting to combine techniques of photo-analysis with econometrics to estimate the amount of damage that Allied bombing was doing to the German war effort. The enormous civilian casualties that this effort was causing, Hitch later recounted, began to 'grow on him' after the war – at RAND, consequently, he sought an alternative to such indiscriminate destruction in order to 'return war to the soldiers'. An equally formative experience for many of those who became preoccupied with the *moral* economy of force was their first induction into the realities of SAC's nuclear targeting. The 'limited war' theorist William Kaufmann found SAC's war plan 'horrendous'. One observer also remembered Robert McNamara's 'stunned' expression at the end of his first SAC briefing – the first time he 'looked the subject of nuclear war down the throat'. For Daniel Ellsberg, the SIOP 'represented the pathology of military bureaucratic thinking to a degree that was almost unimaginable'. He thought that the Joint Chiefs were 'the most dangerous, depraved, essentially monstrous people. They really had constructed a doomsday machine.'[8]

Unlike the mainstream military, the scientific civilian strategists accepted the Clausewitzian notion that the 'logic' of war was that of *policy*. Indeed, their faith in the potential of science to control war made them far more optimistic than Clausewitz himself about the degree to which the grammar of war could be subordinated to the logic of policy. For the most optimistic, the new strategic science promised to restore the links between the use of force and both moral legitimacy and political utility that had appeared permanently severed in the nuclear age. Revising his theory of 'Limited War' in later life, Robert Osgood noted that limited-war strategy had originally grown in the 1950s out of opposition to the prevailing Eisenhower–Dulles strategy of increased reliance on nuclear deterrence. At the time, Osgood advocated an explicitly Clausewitzian approach which, he believed, represented the antithesis of the traditional American 'crusading' approach to strategy. For Osgood, the primacy of politics meant 'that military operations should be conducted so as to achieve concrete, limited, and attainable security objectives, in order that war's destruction and violence may be rationally directed toward legitimate ends of national policy'. Only by carefully limiting the dimensions of warfare, he concluded, could 'nations minimize the risk of war becoming an intolerable disaster'.[9]

One of the most influential civilian strategists, Thomas Schelling, argued that military power had indeed been transformed by nuclear weapons, but not in the way most people believed. In a sense, he thought, nuclear weapons made force *more* usable as an instrument of national policy in the speed with which they could be employed, the centralization of decision-making which they demanded, and in the consequent divorce of war from the domestic political processes (and thus the societal imperatives) that had previously restrained its conduct. These developments enhanced 'the importance of war and threats of war and threats as techniques of influence, not of destruction; of coercion and deterrence, not of conquest and defence; of bargaining and intimidation'. Nuclear weapons, in short, had transformed war into a purer 'diplomacy of violence'.[10] This view of the political utility of nuclear weapons was also explicit in Paul Nitze's evocative metaphor of the Cold War as a chess game: 'The atomic queens may never be brought into play; they may never actually take one of the opponent's pieces. But the position of the atomic queens may still have a decisive bearing on which side can safely advance a limited-war bishop or even a cold-war pawn.'[11] Contrary to the military's absolutist emphasis on the use of massive force, those seeking to transform war into a science sought to attune the degree of force applied as economically as possible to the political objectives at stake.

The scientific strategists did not merely accept the sovereignty of political objectives but rather sought to restore the political *utility* of force through scientific means. The belief that war could be rendered a science demanded a conception of strategy as primarily a *technical* process amenable to technical solutions: the aspiration was to gain a technical control over the social processes of war to equal that achieved in mechanical and electronic systems over the material dimension. For the study of human behaviour to be put on a 'scientific' basis, however, a level of abstraction and mathematical formalization was required that drew its greatest inspiration from economics, the science that focused on competitive behaviour. Schelling's contribution to the science of strategy, reflecting his own background in economics, was particularly influential. He took Clausewitz's insight that in some respects war resembled commerce, with battle as the 'cash payment', and using game theory developed it much further.[12] As a way of computing uncertainty, game theory sought to clarify the competitors' options and identify the optimal course of action. This depended, however, on the working assumption that the competitors would behave 'rationally'; although Schelling realized that this might be unrealistic, this recognition was outweighed by the consideration that the assumption of rationality was conducive to theory. Since the best course of action for each competitor depended on their perception of what the other participants were likely to do, it followed that the key to manipulating the outcome was to influence the other player's perception of one's own likely course of action. Theory – and, by extension, war – thus became concerned with the *communication* of messages to the other player leaving them with 'a simple maximization problem whose solution for him is the optimum for one's self', while destroying their ability to retaliate in kind.[13]

Like commerce, in this conception war was a form of 'bargaining', in which the object was to get the best deal. Other strategists such as Herman Kahn absorbed this idea. Kahn defined bargaining as 'the attempt by one side in a controversy to convince the other that a given solution is in both their interests'.[14] Such a concept of war, of course, was profoundly attractive in a nuclear context in which all-out war might well lead to disaster for both sides and complete victory was difficult to conceive – both sides, therefore, had an interest in keeping any conflict limited. Kahn acknowledged that he owed a lot to the classical economists, and also mused that, 'I must have the outlook of a businessman because I see them [the opponent] as businessmen, a different kind of businessman from myself but a businessman all the same. I know I am wrong to an important degree, but at least I know my bias.'[15] Kahn noted a natural tendency in bargaining for each side to counter the other's pressure with a stronger pressure of its own. In contrast to the original concept of escalation, which referred to war's innate tendency to develop its own momentum and escape rational control, Kahn's concept of escalation assumed the ability of the protagonists to manipulate the process rationally in order to gain some advantage. To explain the possibilities inherent in the tactic of deliberate escalation and escalation dominance, Kahn developed the idea of the escalation ladder – 'an ascending order of intensity through which a given crisis may progress' – and identified up to forty-four possible 'crisis levels'.[16]

The central emphasis the 'No Substitute for Victory' paradigm laid on war's tendency to defy attempts to restrain, humanize or control it underpinned its 'absolutist' strategic posture: war should not be embarked upon lightly, but once declared it should be waged with maximum force. The central article of faith in the scientific discourse of war, conversely, was that rationality and the scientific method could tame and control the course of war. The central strategic virtue deriving from this faith thus became *efficiency* in achieving objectives with the greatest economy in material resources and human life. The man who did more than anyone else to institutionalize this value in the defence bureaucracy was President Kennedy's Defence Secretary, Robert S. McNamara. As a statistical analyst in World War II, McNamara had raised by 30 per cent the flying time logged by General LeMay's bomber command.[17] The very term 'cost-effective' was coined by McNamara's future Pentagon Comptroller, the economist Charles Hitch, while he was working on the effectiveness of strategic bombing in relation to its costs (measured in terms of lives and materials) during the war.[18]

After the war, McNamara and his 'whiz kids' introduced the same techniques into business management with great success, and McNamara rose to become the youngest-ever president of the Ford Motor Company. The scientific management of business and war were thus intimately related from the beginning. The language and standards of measurement employed by the Operations Researchers in World War II were often borrowed from the balance sheet mentality of capitalism: their effort to construct a profit-and-loss statement of the progress of the air war reflected an assumption that entrepreneurial models were appropriate to war.[19] The difference was that, whereas business was concerned with the economy of production, war was concerned with the economy of force; and the measurement of efficiency in war depended, above all, on precise quantification. As Robert McNamara once remarked, 'I am sure that no significant military problem will ever be wholly susceptible to quantitative analysis. But every piece of the total problem that can be quantitatively analysed removes one more piece of uncertainty from our process of making a choice.'[20]

The American search for a science of war: cultural origins

The new civilian strategists tended to portray themselves as replacing an insular national tradition – the apolitical American way of war – with a body of scientific principles that were of universal application. Yet, in its basic assumptions and preoccupations, the new science of strategy was an authentically *American* enterprise: as Colin Gray has put it,

> A noteworthy strain in American defence analysis during the Cold War expressed transcultural confidence that it had unlocked the universal

mysteries of, for example, strategic stability in the nuclear age. Needless to add, such arrogant positivism was itself profoundly cultural.[21]

The association of American culture with technological rationality has a long genealogy. The eminent historian Charles Beard observed in 1930 that no theme, not even religion, stimulated such public interest and discussion in the United States as the meaning of 'machine civilization'. Its association with American culture was already well-established abroad: for example, the German psychologist Richard Muller-Freienfels argued in 1929 that the American culture cherished quantification, rationalization, efficiency, and utility, while suppressing agreeableness, the emotions, and the irrational. Yet, in response, Charles Beard celebrated the very American values that foreigners condemned.[22] The American faith in the ability of technology and science to impart technical control of warfare was a military expression of this broader American emphasis on man's ability to gain technical mastery of his material and social environment.

The systematization of war

A tendency to approach military matters primarily as technical problems has rightly been regarded as a defining characteristic of the US military tradition. Indeed, American military education was almost entirely technical in content until after the Civil War. West Point, for example, was founded as an engineering academy.[23] From the earliest days of the republic, American mechanization was closely connected to the needs of the military. Before it spread to other industries, what became known as the 'American System' of manufactures was associated above all with small-arms production and the quest for interchangeability of parts.[24] Perhaps the most potent early symbol of what American ingenuity could achieve through the mechanization of war was the machine gun. The machine gun was a characteristically American invention, not just because the four names with which it is most associated – Gatling, Maxim, Browning, and Lewis – were all Americans, but also because it was in America that there first developed the cultural and social environment conducive to such an invention. As John Ellis argues in his *Social History of the Machine Gun*, it was a military offshoot of the American cult of mechanization. A Gatling gun publicity broadsheet of August 1865 explained that,

> The gun can be discharged at the rate of two hundred shots per minute, and it bears the same relation to other firearms that McCormack's Reaper does to the sickle, or the sewing machine to the common needle. It will no doubt be the means of producing a great revolution in the art of warfare from the fact that a few men with it can perform the work of a regiment.

Yet paradoxically, the American Ordnance Department did not capitalize on the most significant developments in machine gun technology (all American) until World War I.[25] This apparent contradiction between the technological ingenuity of American society and the (pre-World War II) technological backwardness of the American military derived from the anti-militarism entrenched in republican political culture and nurtured by the American geopolitical predicament of 'free security'. After the Civil War, shortages of Congressional military funding made it difficult for the military to experiment and develop new techniques and weapons of warfare.[26] The institutionalization of links between the scientific, industrial and military sectors would have been perceived as 'un-American', a threat to the liberty of the republic. Only after the twentieth century experience of two world wars, and the onset of the Cold War, did the rise of the 'military-industrial complex' come to be accepted as a necessary evil.

Yet already by the 1880s, a strain of what has been called 'technological utopianism' could be discerned in American culture: a belief that 'a growing number, even a majority, of Americans were ... coming to take for granted: the belief in the inevitability of progress and in progress *precisely as technological progress*'.[27] During the Progressive era, a period of great social unrest, 'science' seemed to hold the promise not only of efficiency but also of impartiality and inevitability: technology appeared to offer an effective and uncontroversial substitute for politics. Thus the notion of 'efficiency' attained cult status during this period.[28] The craze for efficiency was embodied above all in the person of the mechanical engineer Frederick Winslow Taylor, whose famous book *The Principles of Scientific Management* lamented 'the great loss which the whole country is suffering through inefficiency in almost all our daily acts'. The remedy, he believed, lay in the systematization of processes in the workplace through the principles of scientific management. 'Taylorism' entailed the rationalization of the workplace through the analysis of work processes (time-and-motion studies to eliminate 'wasteful' motions). The objective was to ensure that the worker would work with machine-like precision, and thus become perfectly integrated into the mechanized system.[29] More than anyone else, however, it was Henry Ford's pioneering of the techniques of mass production that made the greatest contribution to production efficiency and symbolized America's technological contribution to the world. Ford's innovations and assembly lines raised productivity from 50 to 1,000 per cent with a relatively small additional investment in machinery. The miracle of 'Fordism' spread rapidly around the world and was held up as a specifically American ideal of technological behaviour.[30]

Frederick Winslow Taylor ended his *Principles of Scientific Management* with the claim that 'the fundamental principles of scientific management are applicable to *all kinds of human activities*, from our simplest individual acts to the work of our great corporations'.[31] This statement would prove a valid characterization of the American approach to warfare. American strategic thought was distinguished by a pronounced penchant for *systematization*, drawing its greatest inspiration not from Clausewitz but from Antoine Henri, Baron de Jomini, whose schematization of Frederickian and Napoleonic warfare became the foundation of the teaching of strategy at West Point. Azar Gat has pointed out that,

> All the translations of Jomini's major works into English were done in America. Indeed, and this has not been fully recognized, in no other country was Jomini translated so extensively. ... The Civil War was conducted by West Pointers, and it has been justly said that generals on both sides went into the war with a sword in one hand and Jomini's *Summary of the Art of War* in the other.[32]

Jomini's fondness for logic and order led him to define 'principles of war' that would form a neat system.[33] 'It is the Science of War in the broadest sense, not simply the Art of War, that we are to study,' Major-General John M. Schofield advised an audience of American officers in 1877. War's status as a 'science' was bound up with the process of military professionalism: the professional was to be distinguished from the amateur by competence in the technical expertise required by industrialized war. As one officer put it in 1906, the art of war had not 'escaped the regulating force of modern industrial specialisation. Starting as an instinct and the natural business of the entire body of adult males, it has steadily shrunk in its scope until it has become, with the advance of civilisation, a distinct profession and a special science.'[34] In the interwar years military thinkers like Stephen B. Luce believed that a proper study of military history would yield strategic generalizations comparable to the conclusions of the physical sciences. The proper application of science to the study of war, it was thought, ought to reveal universally applicable principles of war (the War Department published its first list of such principles in 1921).[35]

Major Bradford Chynoweth argued in 1921 that 'for all its glamour, war must be reduced to economics for technical study. Morale is supreme, but morale must subsist on matter.'[36] This managerial approach to war was identified by Martin van Creveld as a distinctive American trait in his comparison of the 'fighting power' of the German and American armies in World War II: whereas the German military culture was preoccupied with operational excellence and such human factors as morale and leadership in battle, in the US military culture 'scientific management and the optimum distribution and deployment of resources became the name of the game'.[37] A British officer who fought alongside the Americans in World War II was also struck by this 'corporate management' approach:

> The Americans were analytic. They approached warfare as they approached any other large enterprise; breaking it down to its essentials, cutting out what was superfluous, defining tasks and roles

and training each man as if he was about to take an individual part in some complicated industrial process. Indeed, the American system for basic training resembled a conveyor belt, with soldiers instead of motor-cars coming off the end.[38]

Perhaps the first sustained attempt to wage war according to entirely scientific principles, however, was the air campaign in World War II, with its emphasis on statistical and precisely quantifiable measures of 'success'. As the historian Michael Sherry has written, under Generals Curtis LeMay and Henry Arnold 'the greatest damage to the enemy for the minimum of effort' became a goal in itself, apart from such an abstract and unquantifiable concept as strategic success, largely because it was more easily measurable. Arnold's analysts focused on weight applied and damage done without pressing their connection to 'victory' in any *political* sense.[39] LeMay was a leader of the scientific management movement in the military, extending the emphasis on quantitative measurement throughout the Air Force when he became chief of staff in 1961.[40]

Casualty-aversion and the search for economies of force

As we saw in the previous chapter, American military and political elites have always been distinctly nervous about the fickleness of American public opinion in wartime. This was a natural concern considering the remoteness of war's harsh realities for many Americans. It is a remarkable record that from the War of 1812 until 11 September 2001, the mainland of the United States was never attacked by a foreign power. For the United States, wars were always 'over there' (in the words of a famous World War I song), and fought for second-order purposes – such as the restoration of the European balance of power, rather than the direct defence of the homeland. For example, in the early days of American entry into World War I, William Wiseman, intelligence chief at the British embassy, explained to the Foreign Office that, 'The American people do not consider themselves in any danger from the Central Powers. It is true that many of their statesmen foresee the danger of a German triumph, but the majority of the people are still very remote from the war.'[41] Similarly, in World War II, complaint about the war's unreality to Americans was a wartime commonplace – for example, *Life* magazine repeatedly regretted that Americans had only a 'Hollywood view of the war which the administration did little to deflate'.[42]

Concern over American resolve in wartime was thus an unusually pressing concern for American elites, and a characteristic response was to look for technological solutions. 'The war of the future, that is, if the United States engages in it,' remarked Thomas Edison in a *New York Times* interview in 1915, 'will be a war in which machines, not soldiers fight. ... Machines should be invented to save the waste in men.' Edison recognized that this would be a distinctively American contribution to warfare: 'America is the greatest machine country in the world, and its people are the greatest machinists. ... They can, moreover, invent machinery faster and have it more efficient than any other two countries. It is a machine nation; its battle preparation should be with machinery.'[43] Franklin Roosevelt adopted precisely this strategy in World War II. In one of his more famous 'Fireside Chats', on 29 December 1940, he explained that, 'We must have more ships, more guns, more planes – more of everything. ... We must be the great arsenal of democracy.' The nations already fighting Hitler, he insisted, 'do not ask us to do their fighting. They ask us for the implements of war ... Emphatically we must get these weapons to them in sufficient volume and quickly enough, so that we and our children will be saved the agony and suffering of war which others have had to endure.' After active American involvement became inevitable, Roosevelt and George Marshall adopted the same calculus: Roosevelt's call for a 'crushing superiority of equipment' reflected 'a shrewd calculation of America's comparative advantage in modern warfare and of the political dangers and economic opportunities that American belligerency posed on the home front'.[44] It would claim the smallest toll in American lives and run the lowest risk of alienating public commitment to the war effort. 'In winning this war,' he told Americans on the eve of the 1944 election, 'there is just one sure way to guarantee the minimum of casualties – by seeing to it that, in every action, we have overwhelming material superiority.'[45]

In 1944, the American economy produced four times as many munitions as the British with fewer than twice the workers.[46] The US consciously sacrificed some measure of quality (for example, in the Sherman tank and the Liberty Ship) in order to achieve higher production numbers and thus 'quantitative superiority'. Quantitative superiority permitted the US to mobilize a smaller segment of its population for service in its ground forces than any other power.[47] As General Henry Arnold's intelligence chief put it, 'American policy is to expend machines rather than men'.[48] Roosevelt and Marshall took the '90 Division Gamble', rejecting the 215 divisions that had initially been thought necessary to defeat Germany and Japan in favour of a smaller force that would rely not on masses of manpower but on maximum possible mechanization and mobility and the support of a gigantic air-arm.[49] As General Wedermeyer put it, 'We counted on our advanced weapons systems – technical prowess and stupendous production capabilities – to enable us to win the war'. Despite the Germans' pioneering of *blitzkrieg* and the superior quality of their tanks, the American Army was much more mechanized – ordinary German divisions remained dependent on horse transport and walking infantry.

As Eisenhower put it after the war, the American style in war was to 'overwhelm the enemy with an inundation of weapons'.[50] Echoing Edison remarkably closely, General Patton gave a similar summary of the American approach in his memoirs: 'The Americans, as a race, are the foremost mechanics in the world. America, as a nation, has the greatest ability for mass production of machines. It therefore behoves us to devise methods of war which exploit our inherent superiority.'[51] The ultimate technological force multiplier was the nuclear bomb. After the defeat of Germany, when some estimates of the cost of conducting an invasion of the Japanese home islands were as high as half a million American deaths, there was already a national 'end-the-war psychology', with 72 per cent of the public calling for partial demobilization. Yet 84 per cent of the public still wanted a total Japanese defeat.[52] Setting the pattern for American strategy in the Cold War, nuclear weapons provided the American solution to the contradictory public demand for grand strategic objectives with minimal levels of sacrifice.

David Kennedy thus sees the Manhattan Project 'as the single best illustration of the American way of war'.[53] Indeed, weeks after Hiroshima and Nagasaki, the radical critic Dwight MacDonald remarked that, 'Atomic bombs are the natural product of the kind of society we have created. They are as easy, normal, and unforced an expression of the American standard of living as electric ice boxes.'[54] In one sense, however, the Manhattan Project was a radical departure from republican principles – it confirmed the integration of civilian and military-industrial production in the US and the institutionalization of technological innovation within the armed forces that World War I had begun: 'The common defence provided what the general welfare had failed to produce – a consensus that technology should be shaped and mobilized by the government to accomplish a great public purpose, even at the risk of private profit and privilege.'[55] Military sponsorship of the new science of strategy, of which the RAND Corporation was the most famous beneficiary, was another reflection of this new public purpose.

In the aftermath of World War II the new global responsibilities of the US and its confrontation with the Soviet Union required it to maintain, for the first time in its history, a large standing Army in peacetime. Yet due to the unpopularity of mass conscription, the US seemed destined or doomed, as Bernard Brodie put it, to a permanent inferiority to the USSR in numbers of men on the ground in Western Europe. One way of compensating for this weakness, he suggested, was through technological force multipliers, and it was 'quite clear that weapons of this sort plus the conventional nuclear weapon introduce a fantastic augmentation of firepower'.[56] Paul Nitze's concern over the fickleness of republican resolve was reflected in the text of NSC-68:

> The democratic way is harder than the authoritarian way. ... A free society is vulnerable in that it is easy for people to lapse into excesses – the excesses of a permanently open mind wishfully waiting for evidence that evil design may become noble purpose, the excess of faith become prejudice, the excess of tolerance degenerating into indulgence of conspiracy.[57]

For Nitze, as for others, technology and particularly nuclear weapons could provide *a surrogate for national will*.[58] The unpopularity of the Korean War seemed to justify Nitze's concern. In 1952, Eisenhower made 'Koreanization' an explicit part of his election platform, and after his victory relied on the threat of nuclear escalation to end the war: 'Let it be Asians against Asians. ... Our boys do not belong on the front lines.'[59] Joseph Stalin was amongst those who perceived the tension between the republic's hegemonic aspirations and societal constraints, as a remark of his to Zhou Enlai in 1952 makes clear:

> They are pinning their hopes on the atom bomb and airpower. But one cannot win a war with that. One needs infantry, and they don't have much infantry, the infantry they do have is weak. They are fighting little Korea, and already people are weeping in the USA. What will happen if they start a large-scale war? Then, perhaps, everyone will weep. [60]

Many American military elites shared Stalin's judgement of the brittleness of popular support for limited war in the US. The 'War is Hell' discourse expressed a profound sensitivity towards the limits that American societal constraints imposed on the political utility of force. Yet many military scientists, civilian strategists, and policy-makers hoped that in the age of nuclear weapons and air power, high technology would offer a way of maintaining American hegemony while circumventing the constraints deriving from the casualty-aversion and fickleness of American democracy. The science of nuclear strategy would yield ways of coercing enemy behaviour without actually employing nuclear weapons, while, in conventional war, machines could be sacrificed in the place of men.

The ascendancy of the scientific strategists

In 1946, in the aftermath of Hiroshima and Nagasaki, Bernard Brodie made one of the most famous observations in the literature of strategic studies: 'Thus far the chief purpose of our military establishment has been to win wars. From now on its chief purpose must be to avert them. It can have almost no other useful purpose.'[61] The prospect of unrestricted nuclear war, he believed, had led to 'the end of strategy as we have known it'.[62] George Kennan agreed in 1961 that,

> The atom has simply served to make unavoidably clear what has been true all along since the day of the introduction of the machine gun and the internal combustion engine into the techniques of warfare ... that modern warfare in the grand manner, pursued by all available means and aimed at the total destruction of the enemy's capacity to resist, is ... of such general destructiveness that it ceases to be useful as an instrument for the achievement of any coherent political purpose.[63]

Many civilian strategists such as Albert Wohlstetter, however, were not content simply to leave it at that and accept the politically disabling logic of Massive Retaliation or Mutual Assured Destruction. They looked to the rational, scientific analysis of strategy to find a way to *restore* the political utility of force. As we have seen, many of the civilian strategists who would develop the new science of strategy experienced their first taste of war working for the strategic bombing campaign in World War II. However, in the aftermath of the war they parted company with absolutists like General LeMay in their emphasis on using science to render war a precise *political* instrument, constructing in the process, in Robert Kaplan's words,

> an intellectual edifice that military men of all stripes found utterly foreign, but that would have profound influence on the civilian community of defence officials for the next decade and beyond. It was a philosophy not only of using limited weapons, but of limiting, controlling, rationally calculating the very process of making war.[64]

The development of Operations Research, the Manhattan Project, and missile technology together marked the ascendancy of scientific influence over the formulation of strategy. This ascendancy coincided with increasing reliance on the computer (itself developed in the war to process the large quantity of statistical data used in operations research), whose application to the social sciences only reinforced the positivist pursuit of quantitatively guaranteed predictive capabilities with respect to human affairs.[65] Despite Clausewitz's prescient warning that theory could never provide all the answers to military problems, 'stamping out war plans as from a kind of truth machine',[66] from its beginning the development of the 'truth machine' – the computer – was intimately bound up with the desire to achieve technical control of war.[67] In many respects the computer was the perfect technological realization of the new science of strategy. Computers represent a particular way of understanding reality through formal techniques.[68] As George and Meredith Freedman have written, the computer is thus distinguished by its 'deeply embedded pragmatism': it 'does not deal with thought as the contemplation of the good or as the pursuit of beauty. Rather, it is a vast narrowing of the sphere of thought to what can be expressed in programming languages. But within that sphere, there is a dramatic deepening and magnification of reason's power.'[69]

At the RAND Corporation established after the war, a group of physicists and mathematicians were assembled to study war in the new conditions of the nuclear age. Although social scientists were also prominent among the new civilian strategists, the hard scientists and the mathematicians gave the new strategic studies, in Weigley's phrase, 'a distinctive quest for precision and sometimes also a distinctive dogmatism'. Quantitative analysis dominated the RAND approach. The new American strategic studies thus marked a shift in the roots of strategic thinking from history and political theory to economics, the 'hard sciences', and mathematics.⁷⁰ Wohlstetter and others were privately contemptuous of the more intuitive, historical approach of Bernard Brodie, which Wohlstetter denigrated as being in 'the essay tradition'. While Brodie was acknowledged by one RAND analyst to have written the 'primer on nuclear strategy', he thought that most at RAND 'had, in effect, gone on to graduate school and left Brodie behind'. RAND's most important contribution was not so much any specific study as a whole way of thinking – a 'systems philosophy of military strategy'. Herman Kahn and others argued that what they were doing was no longer Operations Research but 'Systems Analysis'. The difference was defined by one analyst as that 'systems analysis – while it does make use of much of the same mathematics – is associated with that class of problems where the difficulty lies in deciding *what ought to be done* – not simply how to do it'.⁷¹

For his part, Brodie was initially admiring of the 'scientific strategists', but experience, he remarked to a friend, had later shown him that 'the great majority of them (though with conspicuous exceptions) show an astonishing lack of political sense'.⁷² He believed that Systems Analysis was useful in solving problems of weapons procurement, but lacking in the political and historical judgement to direct strategy itself. 'We certainly need,' he once remarked, 'to stress the superior importance of the political side of strategy to the simple technical and technological side. Preserve and cherish the systems analysts, but avoid the genuflections.'⁷³ Nevertheless, the ascendancy of the technical bias in US military discourse was assured when Robert McNamara became Kennedy's Defence Secretary in 1961. McNamara institutionalized the principles of scientific management pioneered by Frederick Winslow Taylor in the Pentagon itself, observing that there was an 'absence of the essential management tools needed to make sound decisions on the really crucial issues of national security', and often compared the problems of managing the Defence department to the problems of managing a large corporation.⁷⁴ Under the guidance of McNamara and his civilian analysts (the so-called Whiz Kids), Systems Analysis became the *lingua franca* inside the Pentagon itself, the dominant discourse through which decisions were rationalized.⁷⁵

Thomas Schelling noted that in confronting many of the new strategic problems policy-makers had 'little or no help from an existing body of theory, but have had to create their own as they went along'. He recalled that when he was first introduced to military affairs, he found a 'great vacuum in military strategy'. A vacuum also constituted a *niche*, and it was the novelty of nuclear war, together with the civilian strategists' scientific credentials, that legitimized their intrusion into a strategic arena that had previously been the province of military professionals. The marginalization of Brodie's historical approach by the more technocratic methodology, therefore, was in a sense demanded by the 'expert' status to which the civilians aspired. 'RAND's subtleties,' one consultant noted, 'are likely to have a paralyzing effect on those who must deal with them' – principally the Generals who had either to learn to speak RAND's language of systems analysis or concede the superiority of its theoretical rigour.[76]

Alain Enthoven, first director of McNamara's new 'Office of Systems Analysis', explicitly rejected both experience and history as guides to military policy-making; instead, he wrote, 'modern day strategy and force planning has become largely an analytical process'. Similarly, former RAND economist and Pentagon comptroller Charles Hitch believed that in decisions regarding weapons development, 'no-one can ... answer by instinct, by feeling his pulse, by drawing on experience. ... This is the sort of thing an intellectual, by virtue of his training and his mental discipline, can do better than a military professional who is not an intellectual.' Herman Kahn agreed that, 'In some ways the unrealized and inexperienced, but historically plausible, problems of World Wars III and IV are more valuable than the experienced problems of World Wars I and II.' The revolution in strategic assumptions created by nuclear weapons created a 'level playing field' between professional soldiers and civilians. Kahn would ask officers who questioned his expertise, 'How many thermonuclear wars have *you* fought recently?'[77]

Unsurprisingly, the military professionals were frequently outraged at the interference of civilian academics and the alleged redundancy of their hard-earned experience. 'In common with many other military men, active and retired,' remarked General Thomas D. White, 'I am profoundly apprehensive of the pipe-smoking, tree-full-of-owls type of so-called defence intellectuals. ... I don't believe a lot of these often overconfident, sometimes arrogant young professors, mathematicians and other theorists have sufficient worldliness or motivation to stand up to the enemy we face.'[78] Such attitudes, however, did not simply reflect a military-civilian divide; they also reflected an underlying philosophical divide about the very nature of war. The tension between the absolutist mentality, with its assumption that the cruelty of war could not be 'refined', and the new preoccupation with manipulating the 'fine, internal structure of war', was illustrated most dramatically at a Strategic Air Command briefing on nuclear 'counterforce' strategy given by William Kaufman in 1960. Not two minutes into the lecture, General Thomas Power interrupted with a long tirade: 'Why do you want us to restrain ourselves? Restraint! Why are you so concerned with saving *their* lives? The whole idea is to *kill* the bastards! Look,' he concluded, 'At the end of the war, if there are two Americans and one Russian, we win!'[79]

General Douglas V. Johnson later criticized RAND in similar terms for introducing the concepts of limiting war that shaped strategy in Vietnam. Repeating a common misinterpretation of Clausewitz, he observed that for the civilian strategists:

> The object of the thing was to avoid provoking the enemy into nuclear attack by keeping these wars on a small scale. You kick me in the shins,

I'll kick you in the shins.... Well, it was a manner of making war which no military type has ever believed in. We had always thought from ... Clausewitz on, that the way to fight a war was to get in and win it, not this drawn out thing.[80]

War as a science: conception and reality

The scientific management of war: from Cold War to Vietnam

From the early Cold War period, the emphasis on scientific management was increasingly influential in the conduct of US strategy. The political approach of the 'Kremlinologist' George Kennan, who originally argued the need for a strategy of 'containment' of the USSR based on his interpretation of Soviet intentions, was supplanted by an emphasis on measuring Soviet *capabilities*. From a scientific perspective, it seemed wiser to base decisions on measurable quantities than on what Kennan himself admitted was 'the unfirm substance of the imponderables'. During the drafting of NSC-68 in the spring of 1950, Dean Acheson dismissed the attempts of Kennan and his fellow Soviet expert Charles Bohlen to rank the Kremlin's foreign policy priorities. The important thing, Acheson thought, was Moscow's *capacity* for aggression. There thus developed, as one eminent Cold War historian has argued, 'a tendency to equate the importance of information with the ease of measuring it – an approach better suited to physics than to international relations'.[81] Similarly, the authors of the influential report of the Gaither Committee in 1957 on *Deterrence and Survival in the Nuclear Age* constantly emphasized that, 'What's important is not what the Soviets *might* do; it's what they *could* do.'[82]

Yet the apparent objectivity of this approach concealed an uncritical ideological Manichaeism. NSC-68 in effect reduced the complexities of global politics to a giant equation, in which a Soviet advance anywhere would be considered a US retreat.[83] Unlike Kennan, whose subtle political analysis was careful to distinguish between areas of 'vital' and 'peripheral' interest to the US,[84] Paul Nitze and the authors of NSC-68 assumed the indivisibility of American interests ('a defeat of free institutions anywhere is a defeat everywhere') and thus conceived the strategy of 'flexible response' as 'symmetrical response'.[85] Rather like Newton's Third Law, every Soviet action would require an equal and opposite American reaction. Scientific strategists essentially took the Manichaean interpretation of the Cold War enshrined in NSC-68 and translated it into mathematical terms, in the process stripping it of any embarrassing ideological or political content that could not be stated 'scientifically'.

Despite its dispassionate approach, therefore, the result was to freeze the ideological interpretation of the struggle as a contest between two monolithic, symmetrical blocks. What was most influential about Albert Wohlstetter's famous *Foreign Affairs* article 'The Delicate Balance of

Terror', for example, was, in Kaplan's words, its 'almost mechanical concept of a very delicately balanced set of scales that once tipped even slightly off balance, threw the entire order of international relations out of kilter, wiped out the deterrent power of America's nuclear weapons and slid the world toward the precipice of a calamitously destructive war that the Soviet Union would almost certainly win'.[86] The Cold War was thus conceived as one gigantic 'closed system' or 'zero-sum game': all Soviet actions must be seen in terms of their effect on the grand competition.

The scientific strategists also sought to escape from the straitjacket of Massive Retaliation and restore the credibility of deterrence and the political utility of force through the doctrine of Flexible Response. In placing less reliance upon nuclear weapons and proposing to meet enemy aggression at the level of violence at which it was initiated, flexible response demanded a greater emphasis on non-nuclear forces. In the nuclear dimension, the 'counterforce' concept – based on the assumption that a nuclear war might be limited and controlled and civilian casualties minimized – promised what President Carter's National Security Advisor, Zbigniew Brzezinski, would later call 'strategic renewal'.[87] By offering nuclear options short of unlimited war in a crisis, counterforce appeared to offer an escape from the choice, in President Kennedy's words, of 'holocaust or humiliation'. Secretary McNamara began a complete revision of the SIOP to increase the President's options for responding to a Soviet attack, in accordance with the administration's declared policy of 'graduated deterrence'.[88]

James William Gibson has argued that,

> By adopting microeconomics, game theory, systems analysis, and other managerial techniques, the Kennedy administration advanced 'limited war' to greater specificity, making it seem much more controllable, manageable, and therefore *desirable* as foreign policy.[89]

'Desirable' may be the wrong word. Nevertheless, the civilian strategists' faith that scientific and technological rationality could render war controllable certainly made the resort to military action more *thinkable*. It shifted the emphasis from the avoidance of war at all costs, to the use of limited force to counter communist aggression. In 1965 Schelling praised President Johnson's 1964 decision to launch reprisals against North Vietnam following the Gulf of Tonkin incident as an admirable strategy of 'signalling'; Herman Kahn agreed that the US response was an 'exemplary' way to communicate a threat to the enemy.[90] 'The objective,' McNamara later recalled in terms that reflected the influence of their work, was 'to bend an opponent's will via the threat to continue on up the ladder of escalation.'[91] Vietnam became the testing ground of the new science of strategy; for McNamara and his key aides, the war was understood in terms of bargaining and communication, and the fine calibration of force to the limited political objectives at stake.

John McNaughton, an assistant secretary of defence, defined victory as follows: 'With respect to the word "win", this I think means that we succeed in *demonstrating to the VC that they cannot win.*' The bombing of North Vietnam, which could be tightly controlled by civilians, offered the greatest prospects to test the new strategic theories by communicating 'messages' to the enemy. Such models and assumptions underpinned the gradualistic Rolling Thunder air campaign which sought to gradually escalate the pressure on the North Vietnamese until it became 'rational' for them to capitulate. The rhetoric used to rationalize US strategy in Vietnam was replete with the vocabulary of commerce and bargaining. The bombing, concluded a study group led by National Security Advisor McGeorge Bundy, would 'set a *higher price* for the future upon all adventures of guerrilla warfare, and it should therefore somewhat increase our ability to deter such adventures'. Bombing would thus produce a global 'credit', even if Vietnam itself was a failure, or 'debit'.[92] Quantitative methodologies and assumptions based on the abstract, de-politicized models of game theory and economics permeated the Vietnam War. The most notorious contribution of Systems Analysis to the conduct of the war was the propensity to measure success and failure in quantitative, statistical terms. The 'body-counts' used to calculate American progress rested on the assumption that when the casualty rate reached a sufficient level the communists, as 'rational actors', would capitulate.[93]

Success in counter-insurgency thus tended to be defined as a function of the rate at which US forces killed VC, and was thus equally devoid of consideration of such subjective political factors as Vietnamese history and nationalist ideology. Even the inescapably political dimensions of 'nation-building' were stripped of their inherent subjectivity. If World War I was the chemists' war, and World War II the physicists' war, McNamara said, then the struggle for the Third World might well have to be considered 'the social scientists' war'. Yet this was a positivist social science inspired by the 'hard' natural sciences: McNamara put more than a hundred sociologists, ethnologists, and psychologists to work 'modelling' South Vietnamese society and seeking data sufficient 'to describe it quantitatively and simulate its behaviour on a computer'.[94] In 1966, for example, McNamara asked the CIA to create a technique to quantify trends in pacification, resulting in the 'Hamlet Evaluation Survey'. Advisers were tasked with evaluating the progress of pacification in individual districts on eighteen indicators; these reports were then processed by a computer into composite 'scores', which were then ranked according to a system in which numbers signified degrees of security.[95]

This 'Social Systems Engineering' approach to counter-insurgency conceived the insurgency as a 'system', a quasi-mechanical process subject to external manipulation. From this perspective, it was deemed far more effective, as one RAND report put it, to 'influence the behaviour and action of the populace rather than their loyalties and attitudes'. Behaviour, of course, could be monitored with more precision than such inherently ambiguous factors. Thus, in the shaping of strategy, the report concluded, 'the primary consideration should be whether the proposed measure is likely to increase the cost and difficulties of insurgent organizations rather than whether it wins popular loyalty and support'.[96] Yet it was ultimately these subjective, political dimensions of war that were crucial to achieving victory, defined in a proper strategic, rather than narrowly technical, sense.

Strategic abstraction and the reality of war

The central paradox of the new strategic science was thus that despite its acceptance of the sovereignty of political objectives in war, its obsession with scientific rigour led it to neglect those unquantifiable political factors that lie at its heart: for political complexities that could not be quantified or modelled in abstract or formalized terms tended to be excluded from consideration. Anatol Rapoport has noted the irony that although American strategic studies during the Cold War was deeply respectful of Clausewitz, many of its central thinkers,

> attempted to reduce nuclear war and deterrence to a matter of calculable rationality, susceptible to such mathematical technique as game theory. And ... it was precisely to this intellectualisation of war, this reduction of a bloody tragedy to a mathematical problem, this elimination of all moral and political content from the complex equation, that Clausewitz himself was objecting.[97]

As a distinctive mode of thinking about the world, the scientific discourse on war emphasized systems and models that relied on abstraction and formalism, to the neglect of experiential and situational knowledge. The *technical* interest in reifying the social dimension of war to facilitate its manipulation was given priority over the *hermeneutic* interest in interpreting the meanings the enemy assigned to their own actions. The result was a profound de-politicization of war. Writing of the strategic bombing campaign in World War II, Michael Sherry observed that, 'By the language they used, the methods they employed, and the concerns they focused on, the experts helped change the content of what decision-makers in the air war thought about, permitting them to see air war less as a strategic process aiming at victory and more as a technical process in which the assembly and refinement of means became paramount.'[98] This 'narrowing' of strategic thought was also apparent in the mentality of the RAND theorists, with their conscious decision to eschew the inherently ambiguous political dimensions of warfare for a focus on quantifiable data and abstract models.

The new science of war emerged out of the techniques of Operations Research that had been pioneered jointly by the Americans and the British in World War II. Systems Analysis, however, was a distinctively *American* development. Some of the former British Operations Researchers expressed concerns over the ahistorical and apolitical bias of the American researchers, warning that more was being sought in the 'scientific method' than could ever be provided. Sir Solly Zuckerman, for example, commented that, 'It is based upon assumptions about human behaviour which seem totally unreal. It neither constitutes scientific analysis nor scientific theorizing, but is a non-science of untestable speculations about Western and Soviet behaviour.'[99] A critic of the role of Systems Analysis in the Vietnam War even argued that it *'discourages* the study of one's opponents, his language, politics, culture, tactics, and leadership'.[100]

This neglect derived from the construction of an artificial 'strategic man', the belief that strategic theory would be most effective if based on the assumption that the enemy would behave rationally. In order to work, the conception of war as a process of bargaining and communication had to assume that the enemy would be undergoing a similar reasoning process and would interpret military 'signals' accordingly. In a top-secret 1959 study, for example, Andrew Marshall and Herbert Goldhamer argued that in 'trying to eliminate possible US courses of action, the Soviets would presumably attempt to construct their own version of the utility matrix' – in effect, Fred Kaplan has written, they simply assumed that the Soviets thought about the bomb in the same way as the RAND Corporation. The Whiz Kids' calculations of how much devastation would constitute 'Assured Destruction' of the USSR had little to do with any political analysis of what would deter the Soviets, but rather were based on the economists' concept of 'diminishing marginal returns'.[101] When McNamara perceived a 'tremendous philosophical gap' between Soviet and American thinking in nuclear strategy during talks over anti-ballistic missile (ABM) systems in 1967, it came as a revelation to him.[102] Kahn himself once acknowledged that he had 'committed the besetting sin of most US analysts and have attributed to the Soviets a kind of military behaviour that may in fact be appropriate only to US analysts – and not at all relevant to Soviet conditions and attitudes'.[103]

In Vietnam, this political and cultural parochialism contributed to the US defeat. McGeorge Bundy noted to President Johnson in 1964 that, 'In a curious way,' McNamara had, 'rather mechanized the problem [of Vietnam] so that he misses some of its real political flavour.'[104] When a White House aide once told McNamara that the war was doomed to failure, McNamara reportedly replied, 'Where is your data? Give me something I can put in a computer. Don't give me your poetry.'[105] Yet Bundy was guilty of precisely the same tendency: 'We should strike to hurt but not to destroy,' he argued in 1964, 'for the purpose of changing the North Vietnamese decision on intervention in the South.'[106] The Vietnamese failure to comply with American expectations led to the conclusion of a US Army 'lessons learned' report in 1967 that 'a more bizarre, eccentric foe than the one in Vietnam is not to be met', and that, 'the enemy in Vietnam deviates from what we consider normal'.[107] After the war, former Assistant Secretary of State Paul Warnke reflected that, 'The trouble with our policy in Vietnam has been that we guessed wrong with respect to what the North Vietnamese reaction would be. We anticipated that they would react *like reasonable people*.'[108]

It only belatedly occurred to those wedded to the assumption of enemy 'rationality' that the North Vietnamese might have a completely different casualty tolerance to the Americans; that, as one former policy-maker put it in later years, they might be 'more willing to die for it than we were willing to kill for it'.[109] The Vietnamese themselves perceived this much earlier. General Giap commented that, 'The United States has a strategy based on arithmetic. They question the computers, add and subtract, extract square roots, and then go into action. But arithmetical strategy doesn't work here. If it did, they'd have already exterminated us.'[110] Michael Sherry's observation about the air war in World War II was also true of Vietnam: 'The task, not the purpose, of winning governed.'[111] John Lewis Gaddis also noted 'the curiously myopic American fascination with process – a disproportionate fascination with means at the expense of ends'.[112]

Conclusion: Vietnam and the crisis of American military culture

'Vietnam,' declared Daniel Ellsberg, 'destroyed the centre.' For him, it revealed the limits of the 'attitudes and expectations associated with the American way of war', especially the American emphasis on measuring success in terms of numbers of enemy killed. The disillusionment fostered by Vietnam led some of the civilian strategists to question their own basic assumptions about the nature of war; the war, one political scientist observed, brought on 'a crisis not only of policy but of the theory behind the policy'. 'One realizes,' argued Philip Green (author of *Deadly Logic* and an early critic of the civilian strategists), 'with what misplaced abstractions the calculations of counterforce war and "limited nuclear war" have been conceived.' Pentagon Comptroller Charles Hitch, who left the Johnson administration in 1965, later responded to the suggestion that Systems Analysis should be elevated to a principle of government by remarking dryly that it had yet to solve the problem of rush-hour traffic in Cambridge.[113] Robert McNamara himself came to regret what he called the 'almost ineradicable tendency to think of our security problem as being exclusively a military problem. ... We are haunted by this concept of military hardware.'[114] From the Cuban Missile Crisis onwards, McNamara became increasingly disaffected with the ideas about 'nuclear war-fighting' that he had previously espoused so enthusiastically.

Vietnam represented a crisis in American military culture because, aside from any other considerations, it posed once again the central dilemma of the nuclear age: how to restore the political utility of force. By exposing the hubris of the faith in technical control at the heart of the new science of strategy, Vietnam extended this crisis beyond the nuclear realm to the conventional dimension of war. 'What was perhaps a surprise and a shock to some strategists,' as Robert Osgood later noted, 'was the limited utility of force.'[115] Indeed, Russell Weigley's classic account of the American Way of War, originally published at the end of the war, ended with the pessimistic conclusion that,

> It remains difficult ... to imagine tactical nuclear war that would not be either a very brief eruption giving way quickly to a different kind of bargaining if the world were very lucky, or the prelude to general war. Because the record of non-nuclear limited war in obtaining acceptable decisions at tolerable cost is also scarcely heartening, the history of usable combat may at last be reaching its end.[116]

Vietnam appeared to discredit both of the dominant American military discourses on the political dimension of war: in retrospect, the attempt to finely calibrate the degree of force applied to the limited political objectives at stake appeared just as flawed as the opposing philosophy of excluding political limitations from consideration. This double failure led to mutual recriminations: the 'scientific' approach of signalling American resolve to the enemy through the gradual escalation of American strategic bombing was regarded with deep contempt by military elites. As one SAC general put it, the 'computer types who were making defence policy don't know their ass from a hole in the ground'.[117] The military chafed against the political restrictions against an all-out assault on North Vietnam. Yet in the context of a guerrilla war, the 'War is Hell' philosophy was equally dysfunctional: the absolutist approach of waging counter-insurgency through the maximization of American firepower was arguably counter-productive in laying waste to the countryside and alienating much of the population. Neither approach emphasized the importance of Vietnamese history, politics, and culture. In the aftermath of the war, American military culture entered a period of introspection. However, the military were quicker than the civilian strategists to adapt their dominant discourse on the political dimension of war to incorporate an influential narrative of the 'lessons' of Vietnam.

3 Overwhelming force
The American military and the memory of Vietnam

> When this is over, we will have kicked, for once and for all, the so-called Vietnam Syndrome.
>
> President George H. W. Bush, during the first Gulf War[1]
>
> In US political discourse ... the horrors of the Vietnam War have been treated not in the obvious terms of tragedy – hubris, retribution, and expiation – but as a 'syndrome' that had to be 'got over.'
>
> Philip Windsor[2]

References to the 'Vietnam Syndrome' began appearing as early as 1976. The concept was taken to mean that after the trauma of defeat (itself an anomaly in a two-century military tradition that had known only victories, with the partial exception of the War of 1812), the American people would no longer support risky foreign interventions.[3] As Norman Podhoretz (the influential former editor of *Commentary* magazine) wrote in 1984, the lesson of Vietnam that had 'taken the deepest root in American culture' was that military force had become 'obsolete as an instrument of American political purposes'.[4] This heightened scepticism of the political utility of force also infected the military culture, fuelling the military's determination to circumscribe policy-makers' flexibility in using force as a political instrument. Despite President George H. W. Bush's claim that the spectre of Vietnam had been 'buried forever in the desert sands of the Arabian Peninsula', American strategy in the first Gulf War was actually the clearest expression of the lingering trauma of Vietnam. Far from having been 'kicked', memories of Vietnam continued to shape American strategy until the terrorist attacks of 9/11 replaced them as the defining reference point for US military culture.

The symptoms of the Vietnam Syndrome appeared clear – the American people had grown increasingly alienated from the military, and increasingly distrustful of the publicly stated objectives of national security policy. The military's attempts to 'kick' the syndrome thus concentrated on rebuilding their links with the American people; yet in the process the military's traditional sensitivity to the limits that a republican political culture imposed on military action transformed into hypersensitivity. The haemorrhaging of popular support following the 1968 Tet Offensive appeared to confirm the military's worst fears about the fickleness of Congressional and popular support. The central preoccupation of post-Vietnam military discourse was thus a re-orientation towards perceived societal imperatives. Amongst the military elite, the Syndrome took the form, in Brian Holden Reid's phrase, of 'a kind of pre-emptive cringe'.[5] The supposed lessons of Vietnam were enshrined in a new conception of the political dimension of war, which was articulated most explicitly in JCS Chairman Colin Powell's famous 'doctrine'. The Powell Doctrine codified the orthodox interpretation of Vietnam, and the military's perception of the limits of public support, for a generation of military leaders.

For the first two decades after the fall of Saigon, the new discourse of 'Overwhelming Force' dominated American military culture. However, for some policy-makers and strategists, its emphasis on societal constraints imposed an overly rigid template on the use of force that was increasingly in tension with perceived strategic imperatives on American strategy. The end of the Cold War soon made this new fracture over the political dimension of war readily apparent. By the mid-1990s, it had contributed to the emergence of competing conceptions that criticized the Overwhelming Force paradigm for its excessive risk-aversion and inflexibility.

War and policy: the 'bully's way of going to war'

In September 1989, then JCS Chairman Admiral William Crowe remarked that,

> every time I face the problem of having to deploy in third region [sic] – Third World contingencies, instabilities, what the American public wants is for the US military to dominate the situation, to do it quickly, to do it without loss of life, to do it without any peripheral damage, and then not to interrupt what's going on in the United States or affect the quality of our own lives.[6]

Crowe's remarks provide a concise insight into the military's post-Vietnam sense of resentment towards the unrealistic expectations of a political culture and a public increasingly divorced from the realities of war. Vietnam provided a powerful cautionary tale of the dangers of acquiescing docilely in these expectations. As a distillation of the supposed lessons of Vietnam, the discourse of Overwhelming Force thus evolved as a conscious attempt to re-orient the military culture towards the constraints imposed on the use of force by the nature of American society. This new emphasis on societal constraints shaped a new conception of the relationship between policy and the proper use of force. The traumatic memory of Vietnam informed a steelier determination to influence not only politicians' consideration of military options, but the formulation of policy itself. It was also reflected in the structure of the all-volunteer force that replaced the draft; in an unwillingness to contemplate operations with even minimal casualty levels; in a narrow conception of the kinds of missions that American forces should undertake; and in a new ideal of the proper application of military force.

In his study of pre-Vietnam Cold War crises, Richard K. Betts noted that, while the military tended to prefer the massive and decisive use of force over 'limited' applications, no clear divide was apparent between pre-Vietnam soldiers and civilian statesmen over *whether* to intervene in the first place – there were hawks and doves on both sides of the civil-military divide.[7] After Vietnam, conversely, a clear divide between soldiers and civilians emerged over the latter issue as well: the military became markedly more reluctant to recommend the use of force.[8] As the top military aide to Secretary of State Caspar Weinberger in the 1980s, Colin Powell was involved in the codification of these attitudes in the so-called Weinberger Doctrine, which laid out a set of principles governing the military's strategic outlook. Weinberger's purpose in outlining his 'doctrine' is suggested by the comment he made in his memoirs criticizing the National Security staff for 'spending most of their time thinking up ever more wild adventures for our troops'.[9]

As Chairman of the Joint Chiefs of Staff in the 1990s, Powell elaborated further on Weinberger's principles in the similar and more famous formulation that came to be known as the Powell Doctrine. By insisting that military intervention should only be undertaken in cases where there was the assurance of popular support, a close conformity between political ends and military means, a swift victory, and a neat exit strategy, the Weinberger and Powell Doctrines reflected the military's restrictive conception of the political utility of force. Military force *could* be used to achieve political objectives, but only if the military and political context conformed to a set of strict criteria. The Powell Doctrine can be summarized as follows:

1. The United States should only commit forces to combat overseas in circumstances where doing so is vital to the national interest.
2. If the US does commit troops, it should do so 'wholeheartedly', with the clear intention of winning.
3. The armed forces should have clearly defined political and military objectives.
4. The relationship between ends and means must be continually reassessed and adjusted as necessary.
5. There must be a reasonable assurance of the support of Congress and the American people.
6. The commitment of US forces should be a last resort.[10]

The Powell and Weinberger doctrines explicitly invoked Clausewitz in their own support, and Michael Handel has even concluded that 'the Weinberger doctrine reflects the adoption of Clausewitzian ideas and their adaptation to the post-Vietnam War era'.[11] Conversely, other scholars have concluded that, 'The Powell corollary was much less a new idea than it was an old idea whose time had come again'.[12] There is a partial truth in both of these statements: the post-Vietnam years did see a remarkable explosion of interest in Clausewitz within the US military, yet emphasis was laid on those aspects of Clausewitz's theory that appeared to reinforce the alleged lessons of Vietnam. Colonel Harry Summers' influential work *On Strategy* is a notable case in point. Summers used two Clausewitzian concepts to particular effect: the concept of war as a 'Remarkable Trinity' of the people, military, and government,[13] and the concept of 'friction'. The Remarkable Trinity was deployed to illustrate how politicians had erred in Vietnam by failing to rally the people behind the war effort, while Summers used 'friction' to illustrate his analysis of where US strategy had gone wrong. In all respects, the Powell Doctrine reiterated the thrust of his conclusions. The concept of friction, of course, also provided a powerful conceptual *caveat* against those who believed that war's 'internal momentum' could be harnessed and controlled in order to render force a precise instrument of policy.

The discourse of Overwhelming Force represented a kind of *synthesis* of the antithetical pre-Vietnam conceptions of war's proper relationship to national policy. In its emphasis on the importance of clearly defined political objectives and the constant assessment of the relationship between political ends and military means (conditions 3 and 4 of the Powell Doctrine), the discourse accepted the sovereignty of the political dimension of war. It accepted, in other words, Clausewitz's insight that war does not have its own 'logic', for its logic is that of policy. However, the distinctive *risk-aversion* of the new paradigm reflected the greater emphasis it laid on the unpredictable 'grammar' of war, and its tendency to overwhelm the logic of policy. In this respect, the lingering influence of the earlier distrust of limited applications of force could be detected. Indeed, in a sense the dominant post-Vietnam discourse resembled a self-conscious caricature of the military's earlier understanding of war, an idealization of the traditional 'American way of war' that had been betrayed in Vietnam.[14] For example, the first and sixth principles of the Powell Doctrine (demanding that force be used only in support of vital national interests and as a last resort) were faithful to the traditional American view that war 'takes over' where politics 'leaves off' – that is, the use of military force is not a 'continuation' of politics so much as a symptom of its failure. The second principle (demanding that there be 'a clear intention of winning') seems a platitude, until it is understood as an oblique expression of the military's aversion to the way force was deliberately limited in Vietnam for purposes of bargaining and communication.

Thus, despite the Overwhelming Force paradigm's acceptance of the principle that military means should be directed to the achievement of political ends, this did not extend to the deliberate limitation of force. Whenever possible, the mustering of an overwhelming margin of superiority effectively guaranteeing a decisive victory was to be preferred. In a 1995 interview, Powell characterized his favoured approach as 'the *bully's* way of going to war'.[15] The military's traditional sensitivity towards the tendency of war to defy rational control had only been reinforced by the debacle of Vietnam, and the hubris of the civilian limited-war strategists. The new discourse thus put an even greater emphasis on prudence over efficiency in the use of military means. Profligacy in the expenditure of military resources was a sign of proper caution. Thus, the discourse of Overwhelming Force sought to synthesize its more explicit acceptance of the primacy of political objectives with a *re-endorsement* of the traditional American ideal of war, reflecting the dominant military interpretation of what the United States did wrong in Vietnam.

Ironically, the dominant post-Vietnam conception of the relationship between war and policy tended to lead to a kind of *reversal* of Clausewitz: for, in practice, the Weinberger and Powell Doctrines' emphasis on clarity of objectives demanded that political objectives be formulated in terms that could be neatly achieved through military action. Military means thus tended to dominate the shaping of political ends, rather than the other way round. This is not to deny the genuine enthusiasm for Clausewitz that came to permeate American military education in the post-Vietnam years, but the US military, like so many others before them, took what they needed from Clausewitz to suit their needs – in this case to salvage what remained of the old American way of war for an age of limited war, quasi-imperial policing, and military professionalization. The military accepted the sovereignty of politics over war more readily than they had before Vietnam, but they still sought to redeem war from the inherent 'mess' of political ambiguity, by separating military concerns from wider political considerations as far as possible. Thus, by adopting a set of criteria that restricted the use of force to those cases where the military and political dimensions of war could be neatly separated, the discourse avoided confronting the full implications of the concept that war is a true *continuation* of politics, a concept which conflicted with the preference for the use of overwhelming force in every instance.

The cultural sources of the Overwhelming Force paradigm

The discourse of Overwhelming Force was inspired by two over-riding concerns: to restore the popularity and self-respect of a profoundly demoralized military establishment, and to ensure that hawkish politicians would never again involve the country in a war that would sever the links between the military and the American people. Demoralization within the Army in particular had reached chronic levels by the late 1960s: 'fragging' (the incidence of enlisted men trying to murder their own officers, most frequently with fragmentation grenades) more than doubled between 1969 and 1970, and continued to increase after 1971 despite 'Vietnamization'.[16] As the former JCS Chairman General Maxwell Taylor remarked, the Army had been sent to Vietnam to save that nation, but it had to be withdrawn in order to save the Army.[17] A 1973 Harris Poll revealed that the American public placed the military only above sanitation workers in relative order of respect.[18] In this respect the project of cultural regeneration would achieve its goals: in 1975 only 58 per cent of Americans expressed a great deal or a lot of confidence in the military; by 2002, this figure had risen to 79 per cent.[19]

The stab-in-the-back thesis and the post-Vietnam concept of civil–military relations

'One of the more simplistic explanations for our failure in Vietnam,' observed Colonel Harry Summers in 1982,

> is that it was all the fault of the American people – that it was caused by a collapse of national will. Happily for the health of the Republic, this evasion is rare among Army officers. A stab-in-the-back syndrome never developed after Vietnam.

There is some irony in this claim, for Summers' own work quickly became one of the most influential narratives of an American 'stab-in-the-back' thesis – albeit a more sophisticated version than the one Summers denied existed. In Summers' version, responsibility for the failure in Vietnam did not lie solely with one group and the American military themselves did not escape criticism, but he had no doubt that primary responsibility lay with the civilians in the White House and the Pentagon for imposing political constraints on the conduct of the war, and for breaking the sacred link between the military and the people. 'Having deliberately never been built,' he pointed out, 'it could hardly be said that the national will collapsed.'[20] There was some validity in Summers' argument. Breaking with the republican tradition of the American way of war, the Johnson administration refused to call up the reserves or mobilize a popular crusade and placed the entire burden for fighting the war on active-duty forces. In later years former Secretary of State Dean Rusk acknowledged ruefully that, 'we never made any effort to create a war psychology in the United States during the Vietnam affair. ... We tried to do in cold blood perhaps what can only be done in hot blood, when sacrifices of this order are involved.'[21]

Summers' analysis of the lessons of Vietnam became the mainstream interpretation: it was formally adopted by the Army, distributed to the entire general officer corps, incorporated within the syllabus of all the services' educational institutions. Copies were even sent to the White House and to all members of Congress.[22] Two orthodoxies became established in US military discourse in the years after Vietnam: firstly, that public support for the war had ebbed due to the politicians' deliberate decision not to rally public opinion; and secondly, that the military had been 'prevented from winning' due to the imposition from Washington of political constraints on the use of force. Writing from his retirement, General Westmoreland asserted that Vietnam had been a winnable war, and that MacArthur's dictum that 'there is no substitute for victory' should have been better heeded.[23] 'Bomb a little bit, stop it a while to give the enemy a chance to cry uncle, then bomb a bit more but never enough to really hurt,' Westmoreland characterized this approach in his memoirs: 'That was no way to win.'[24] Similarly, as former Air Force Chief of Staff General Dugan has remarked, 'Most Air Force officers believe to this day that if they had been allowed to bomb North Vietnam without limits the US would have won the war.'[25] In short, the defeat in Vietnam was attributed to a failure to follow the 'traditional' American way of war.

Having imposed political constraints on the conduct of the war that effectively rendered it unwinnable, it was believed, the politicians then allowed the American armed forces to bear the burden of blame for defeat. As one Army general put it, 'Those who ordered the meal were not there when the waiter brought the check'.[26] In 1980, 92 per cent of the Vietnam veterans polled by the Veterans Administration agreed with the statement, 'The trouble in Vietnam was that our troops were asked to fight a war which our political leaders in Washington would not let them win'.[27] 'I don't think there was a guy, from private to general,' reminisced one Marine General, 'who didn't have a stench in his mouth from the politics of the war.'[28] Moreover, many prominent politicians absorbed and thus reinforced this interpretation of the conflict. In 1980 Ronald Reagan reiterated the stab-in-the-back thesis: 'Let us tell those who fought in that war that we will never again ask young men to fight and possibly die in a war our government is afraid to let them win.' A decade later President Bush used the same rhetoric in a speech to the Reserve Officers Association: 'Never again will our armed forces be sent out to do their job with one hand tied behind their back.'[29]

The stab-in-the-back thesis led to a new interpretation of civil–military relations and the proper role of the military in providing advice to their civilian masters. In striking respects, the military's orthodox interpretation of Vietnam recalled the aftermath of the Korean War several decades earlier. Despite its 'never again' mentality after Korea, the military elite had allowed itself to be overridden once again by hawkish civilians when it came to Vietnam. Yet whereas stalemate in Korea could plausibly be presented as a strategic success in an age of limited war, defeat in Vietnam was unambiguous and fostered a steelier resolve. 'The big difference with the generation of military leaders from the Vietnam era,' former Secretary of the Navy James Webb has suggested, 'is that they are more comfortable stating publicly the downside of certain policy options.'[30] As General Colin

Powell wrote in his bestselling memoirs,

> Many of my generation, the career captains, majors and lieutenant colonels seasoned in that war, vowed that when our turn came to call the shots, we would not quietly acquiesce in half-hearted warfare for half-baked reasons that the American people could not understand or support.[31]

In explaining his willingness to actively question the American use of force in response to the Iraqi invasion of Kuwait, Powell's reference point was Vietnam: 'As a mid-level career officer, I had been appalled at the docility of the Joint Chiefs of Staff, fighting the war in Vietnam without ever pressing the political leaders to lay out clear objectives for them.'[32]

Thus the traditionally 'apolitical' American military elite became increasingly politicized, not in the sense that they acquired a more sophisticated understanding of the political dimensions of strategy, but in their more activist involvement in the *domestic* political process. Russell Weigley's summary of this shift is worth quoting at length:

> the Vietnam War had a poisonous effect on civil–military relations. The military found themselves waging war under policy constraints that they considered insuperable obstacles to military victory. ... In late August 1967, the Joint Chiefs of Staff seem to have reached the brink of a resignation en masse to protest civilian limitations on their conduct of the war. Although the old traditions retained enough vitality to draw back from the precipice, the event signalled a turning point. ... Henceforth, the Joint Chiefs campaigned consistently both to secure statutory authority for a military voice in deliberations on national policy and strategy, and through public pronouncements to influence policy-making in ways that will guard them against a repetition of waging war under the constraints against the application of overwhelming power that prevailed in Korea and Vietnam.[33]

Salvaging the citizen-soldier ideal: the Abrams 'Doctrine'

The all-volunteer force that replaced the draft was the politicians' way of avoiding the necessity of calling to serve those citizens who would not want to fight the next war.[34] Mass armies of citizen-soldiers are best suited, in Eliot Cohen's words, to 'desperate struggles and wars of mass mobilization'. Conversely, the citizen-soldier system was 'maladapted to the strategic challenges of risks run for ambiguous or second-order purposes' characteristic of an era of limited war such as the late twentieth century.[35] Yet the Pentagon's counter-initiative to the all-volunteer force – the 'Total Force' concept – was the military's way of ensuring that it would not be sent on costly imperial adventures in the future without popular backing. Under the guidance of Army Chief of Staff Creighton Abrams, the post-Vietnam force structure was consciously designed so that active-duty forces would depend on the reserves for critical support functions, such as engineers, civil affairs, and military police.

This arrangement, which came to be known inside the Pentagon as the 'Golden Handshake', thereby ensured that the military could not function without the reserves in a major crisis. Since mobilizing the reserves even temporarily required a presidential proclamation, this force structure guaranteed that any US military action would provoke intense political debate. The 'Abrams Doctrine' (as it came to be known) thus represented a compromise between the imperative for military professionalization on the one hand and the traditional republican ideal of the citizen-soldier on the other; and it also protected the military from being casually committed to future 'imperial' interventions without popular support. General John Vessey, who later became Chairman of the JCS, characterized Abrams' thinking as follows:

> Let's not build an Army off here in the corner someplace. The Armed Forces are an expression of the Nation. If you take them out of the national context, you are likely to screw them up. That was his lesson from Vietnam. He wasn't going to leave them in that position ever again.[36]

Abrams repeatedly told General Donn A. Starry and others, 'They're *never* going to take us to war again without calling up the reserves.'[37] In practice, the Total Force policy meant that combat roles stayed within the professional force and the Army 'shifted from being a Citizens' Army to one of professionals supported, in both senses of the word, by the public'.[38] Thus the Army fashioned a compromise which enabled it to focus on developing a new professional emphasis at the core of its identity, while simultaneously maintaining a link with the citizen-soldier tradition and guarding against reckless foreign interventions by institutionalizing its own dependence on the reserves. The Total Force structure thus institutionalized the military culture's new orientation towards societal imperatives: as Army Chief of Staff General Fred C. Weyand put it in 1976:

> The American Army really is a people's Army in the sense that it belongs to the American people who take a jealous and proprietary interest in its involvement. When the Army is committed the American people are committed. In the final analysis, the American Army is not so much an arm of the Executive branch as it is an arm of the American people. The Army therefore, cannot be committed lightly.[39]

Vietnam and the 'body-bags syndrome'

Much of the contemporary debate over whether the United States has become more casualty-averse since Vietnam ignores the wider issue of whether American society has *always* been casualty-averse relative to other cultures. Certainly, American military culture has always been distinctive in its anxiety over the fragility of popular support for military action. Relative to the experiences of other major belligerents, American casualty figures were low in both the World Wars. This experience of historically low casualty levels is most evident in comparison with the US's non-Western opponents. At Saipan and Iwo Jima, for example, Allied prisoners surrendered in a ratio of one prisoner to every three dead; on the Japanese side, there was one prisoner to every 120 dead.[40] General Marshall was well aware that American deaths on this scale would have been unacceptable to the American public: after Bataan he remarked that, 'If we took a third of the losses suffered by the Japanese, we would probably have been subjected to an investigation by Congress, certainly to considerable public clamour in the press'.[41] In the Vietnam War, the communist side suffered proportional military losses equivalent for the United States in the mid-1990s of 13 million Americans killed and 3.9 million missing in action. To put this in perspective, one scholar has calculated that the communist side sacrificed thirty-six times more of their own soldiers to unify Vietnam than did the Federal government to defeat the secessionist Confederate states in the American Civil War.[42] The American style of war has always been marked by a conscious attempt to sacrifice machines rather than men. This relative casualty-aversion can be largely accounted for by several factors: the strength of American individualism, a political system designed to maintain national security with the minimum possible coercion of states and individuals, and the remoteness of foreign wars, all of which made it much harder for American elites to justify massive US casualties. The sole exception to the rule of relatively low American casualty levels – the Confederate experience during the Civil War – was also the only American experience of prolonged fighting on *home territory* after the Revolution.

However, this 'traditional' intolerance of casualties appears to have been taken to extreme levels since the Vietnam War. Henry Kissinger, amongst others, has remarked that, 'We had 500 casualties a week when we [the Nixon administration] came into office. America now is not willing to take any casualties. Vietnam produced a whole new attitude.'[43] Numerous explanations have been proposed to account for this 'new' casualty-aversion. Edward Luttwak has suggested the controversial thesis that the rise of high-income/low birth-rate families has created a 'post-heroic' society, in which Americans and other citizens of the advanced Western democracies are increasingly unwilling to tolerate large numbers of deaths in battle.[44] Other analysts, citing some of the most sophisticated research yet conducted on public attitudes to casualties, argue persuasively that public attitudes to casualties are heavily influenced by the degree of consensus among political elites and media 'experts' over whether a particular intervention is justified or not.[45]

Regardless of the degree to which the wider American society has become more casualty-averse, however, there is little doubt that American *military* culture became radically more intolerant of casualties after

Vietnam. Indeed, evidence from opinion polls suggests that American military and political elites have become far *more* casualty-averse than the average American citizen. To some extent this is a simple function of the shift to the all-volunteer force: historically speaking, armies of highly trained professionals fighting for ambiguous goals have always been more casualty-conscious than crusading armies of citizen-soldiers fighting for existential causes, as in the world wars.

However, the shift towards greater casualty-aversion also reflects something historically contingent: the traumatizing effect of Vietnam and lingering memories of the collapse of Congressional and popular support for the war. A generation of post-Vietnam elites was notably reluctant to put troops in harm's way, convinced that public support for the projection of American force abroad, particularly in missions that were 'peripheral to vital national interests', would waver the moment the body-bags started to return home.[46] In 1990, Lt.-General Philip Davidson found one point of 'total unanimity' that the officer corps had absorbed from the experience of Vietnam: that 'the United States cannot sustain a prolonged, bloody, ambiguous, and limited war'.[47] General Marshall had doubted the resilience of the American people in 'a seven years' war'; the post-Vietnam generation of military elites' perception of the limits of public support was even less sanguine. Increased sensitivity to casualties was incorporated in training doctrine, with performance standards for the maximum number of allowable friendly casualties for particular missions set at levels that would have been regarded as unrealistically low by historical standards. Casualty-aversion also became enshrined in grand strategy – for example, in the first Bush administration's *Regional Defense Strategy*:

> In regional conflicts, America's stake may seem less apparent to the people. We should provide forces with capabilities that minimize the need to trade American lives with tyrants and aggressors. ... Thus, our response to regional crises must be decisive, requiring the high-quality personnel and technological edge to win quickly and with minimum casualties.[48]

'No more Vietnams': defining the national interest and the trauma of defeat

It is a popular cliché that military organizations have a tendency to attempt to 're-fight the last war'. With regard to the post-Vietnam period, however, this is misleading: the US military did not attempt so much to re-fight the war as to ensure that they would never have to fight such a war again. As we have seen, the US military already had a long history of failing to institutionalize the hard-earned lessons of fighting unconventional wars or counter-insurgency campaigns. In the case of Vietnam, this did not amount to an oversight but to a collective, willed amnesia. In F. G. Hoffman's summary,

> the military as an institution pushed the memories of the Central Highlands and the Mekong Delta out of its consciousness. Instead the Armed Forces focused therapeutically on the threat the Soviet Union posed in Europe. Over time, the 'lessons' of Vietnam passed implicitly into the military culture, into its doctrine, training and education, and thought process. The collective conclusion can be reduced to the simplistic cry of 'No More Vietnams'.[49]

Those who saw their careers most enhanced after the war had served in mainstream conventional positions as battalion commanders and main-force-unit staff officers, whose experience of counter-insurgency had been minimal. Instruction on 'foreign internal defence' at the Army's service schools virtually disappeared after the war; in effect, 'search-and-destroy' remained Army doctrine.[50] All the material on counter-insurgency housed at the JFK Special Warfare Centre and School at Fort Bragg was destroyed at the express direction of the senior Army leadership.[51] A 1989 survey that examined the 1,400 articles published by *Military Review* between 1975 and 1989 discovered only 43 articles dedicated to low-intensity conflicts.[52]

The coincidence of the American withdrawal from Vietnam with the 1973 Arab-Israeli conflict was important, as it enabled a military that was culturally predisposed to focus on conventional war to persuade itself that its future wars would resemble the latter more closely than the former. Reflecting this view that Vietnam had been an aberration, General William DePuy (one of the original architects of Search-and-Destroy tactics in Vietnam and the influential head of the Army's Training and Doctrine command immediately after the US withdrawal) argued that the Army should continue to capitalize on its strengths, rather than remedy its deficiencies in operations that blurred the boundaries between the military and political dimensions of war. DePuy believed that, 'Regular US Army troop units are peculiarly ill-suited for the purpose of "securing" operations where they must be in close contact with the people'. On the other hand, he thought they were 'perfectly suited for search-and-destroy'.[53]

Like the Army, the Air Force did not teach anything about Vietnam in its professional schools, and it was not mentioned in their doctrinal manuals. For the Air Force, the guerrilla struggle was an unacknowledged anomaly: bombing doctrine remained geared to a fast-paced conventional war, and the conviction that such doctrine was appropriate for any kind of conflict continued to permeate the service.[54] During Vietnam, General Curtis LeMay had put the case for overwhelming force in his characteristic idiom: 'We should stop swatting flies and go after the manure pile.'[55] Long after the war, this view resonated in US military discourse. As Lt.-General Mike Short reminisced after the Kosovo conflict (in which he was air component commander): 'For years in Vietnam we bombed a little bit, and then we backed off, and ... had pauses, and so on. Then finally we sent the B-52s north around January of 1973, and lo and behold, we brought them to the table.'[56]

Harry Summers' analysis of the Vietnam War provided one form of justification for this neglect of any sophisticated analysis of the political and cultural dimensions of the war. In Summers' view, failure to mobilize the reserves had prevented the military leadership from successfully pushing for 'strategic concepts aimed at halting North Vietnamese aggression' and led to 'campaigns against the *symptoms* of the aggression – the insurgency in the south – rather than against the aggressor itself'.[57] Effectively dismissing the guerrilla insurgency in the South as an almost irrelevant epiphenomenon of a conventional conflict, this argument conveniently rationalized a continued focus on conventional war in which overwhelming force could be applied without political restrictions. By focusing on political constraints and civilian meddling rather than conducting a searching critique of their own failures in the war, the military were able to rationalize their enduring conviction that the application of overwhelming force provided the key to victory.

Cultural conception and the reality of war: American military intervention from Vietnam to 9/11

In the decades after Vietnam, the Overwhelming Force paradigm was expressed both in military elites' attempts to influence policy-makers' decisions over whether to employ force, and in the strategies they sought to employ once committed to action. Between the Vietnam War and 9/11, very few American military interventions were judged to be in support of a 'vital national interest', at least as defined by the military. The military thus advised against potential involvement in the Horn of Africa in 1978, in the Persian Gulf in 1984, and in Libya in 1986.[58] In the Lebanon intervention (1982–1984), the Department of Defence and the Joint Chiefs also resisted sending any forces to stabilize Beirut, judging such a mission as peripheral to the national interest, and smacking too much of 'nation-building' and of low-intensity conflict to fit the Overwhelming Force paradigm.

The withdrawal of American forces after the tragic bombing of the Marine barracks in which 241 Marines died, in combination with the decision of the Clinton administration to pull American forces out of Somalia a decade later after the death of 18 troops in the 'Black Hawk Down' incident, appear to have confirmed the military's post-Vietnam conviction that policy-makers and the public lacked the stomach for military action in the absence of a 'vital national interest'. The Somalia episode led Ambassador Richard Holbrooke to coin the phrase 'Vietmalia Syndrome', combining Vietnam and Somalia.[59] Not even the ejection of Saddam Hussein from Kuwait fit the military's conception of a 'vital national interest': in 1990, the Joint Chiefs were far less hawkish than the Bush administration. Both JCS Chairman Colin Powell and CENTCOM commander Norman Schwarzkopf preferred drawing a line around Saudi Arabia that would deter the Iraqis from further advances, and waiting for sanctions to take effect, over military action. Ever concerned about the fragility of public support, Powell was convinced that, 'The American people do not want their young dying for $1.50 a gallon oil'.[60] It was also Powell who pressed for formal Congressional authorization to use force, in an attempt to ensure the rallying of public support behind the war effort.[61]

The military's dominant post-Vietnam concept of civil–military relations, reflecting the memory of the Joint Chiefs' 'docility' over Vietnam, was expressed in military elites' greater assertiveness in advising policy-makers. Military advice was frequently designed to steer policy-makers away from potential military action by emphasizing the potential risks involved. In response to the 1985 proposal by White House officials to overthrow Muammar Qaddafi with Egyptian assistance, for example, the military estimated it would need up to six American divisions, plus supporting air and naval forces.[62] During the lingering debate over potential intervention in Bosnia in the early 1990s, Colin Powell consistently advised that American military action against Serbia would require a massive number of troops – over two hundred thousand. Close associates of Powell told the writer David Halberstam that, fearing a 'Balkan Vietnam',

> One reason he had always put the number of troops needed to do the job so high ... was not necessarily that he felt it would take so many. It was a test for the civilians: How much do you really want this, how high a price are you willing to pay?[63]

The 'shattered bodies of Marines at the Beirut airport,' Powell later admitted, 'were never far from my mind in arguing for caution.'[64] In the recollection of Air Force chief of staff General Merrill McPeak, Powell's presentations to the White House on military options in Bosnia amounted to the following: 'Here's Option A, it is really stupid. Here's Option B, it is dumber than dirt.'[65] The American Commander in Europe, General Jack Galvin, shared Powell's caution: as he later put it, he believed that you could not just 'put your toe in'. A basic assumption of the dominant post-Vietnam discourse was that, if you 'put your toe in', the 'foot' and perhaps the whole body would inevitably have to follow.[66] Hawkish politicians learnt to deal with this risk-aversion by circumventing military advice altogether. The reason the JCS were blocked from planning for a ground-force campaign in Kosovo in February 1999, General Wesley Clark later told an interviewer, was because their intent in requesting the planning was

> to show all the costs and the risk. ... And once committed down this path, it would have gone something like this: 'Mr. President, you

realize if you go forward with this, you are talking about a 517,000 manned ground force, and our estimate of casualties is 117,000. ... Mr. President, the cost will be $62.7 billion, we will have to call up the reserves, ... and this is foolish. You don't want to drop the first bomb, Mr. President.'[67]

Until 9/11, the military elite also resisted involvement in counter-terrorism operations. According to Mike Sheehan, the State Department co-ordinator for counter-terrorism during the late 1990s, 'The Pentagon wanted to fight and win the nation's wars, as Colin Powell used to say. But those were wars against the armies of other nations – not against diffuse transnational terrorist threats.' Military culture was at the heart of this attitude: the Pentagon and particularly the Joint Staff did not *want* the authority to strike terrorists because such missions did not match their conception of the US military's proper role. Yet, if forced to contemplate such missions, they planned them in conformity with the preferred paradigm of Overwhelming Force. One former official interviewed after 9/11 recalled that when strikes against al Qaeda cells were proposed, 'the Joint Staff and the chairman would come back and say, "We highly recommend against doing it. But if ordered to do it, this is how we would do it." And usually it involved the 82nd and 101st Airborne Divisions. The footprint was ridiculous.'[68]

Once committed to military action, the orthodox ideal in the decades after Vietnam remained the employment of an overwhelming margin of superiority in order to minimize risk to American forces. The interventions in Grenada in October 1983 (Operation Urgent Fury) and Panama in December 1989 (Operation Just Cause) were fought in conformity with this paradigm. While these operations were perceived as successes (particularly the Panama operation), the military's continued focus on narrowly military concerns to the neglect of broader political considerations was apparent. Military contingency planning remained separated from the civilian national security agencies, and subject only to very restrictive review by civilian officials within the Department of Defence.[69] In both Grenada and Panama, this led to neglect of civil–military planning issues and the failure to anticipate the problem of breakdown of law and order, or plan for the reconstitution of the countries' security forces, political system and economy.

Paradigm triumphant? The first Gulf War

The clearest application of the cultural paradigm of Overwhelming Force was the Gulf War of 1991. 'The way the war was planned, fought, and brought to a close,' one history of the war concluded, 'had more to do with the culture of the military services, their entrenched concept of warfare, and Powell's abiding philosophy of decisive force than it did with the Iraqis or the tangled politics of the Middle East.' National Security Advisor

Brent Scowcroft thought that the force levels requested by Powell (the US ultimately deployed 500,000 troops) seemed excessive for the mission, but President Bush was determined not to interfere with the military's conduct of the war.[70] Military elites were thus free to formulate a strategy that reflected their dominant conception of the relationship between the political and military dimensions of war, a conception that was summarized in the remark by (Air Force Component Commander) Lt.-General Chuck Horner that: 'We will carry out any particular policy but as individuals we think that war is a very serious business and it should not be dragged out in an effort *to achieve some political objective*.'[71]

Thus, in 1991, Powell terminated combat operations *before* they fulfilled their objective of destroying the Republican Guard. The American media had obtained pictures of destruction at the infamous 'highway of death' out of Kuwait. 'We did not need another situation,' Powell later explained, 'where a large number of civilians were killed with Peter Arnett [from CNN, who made his reputation in Vietnam] all over the place.'[72] Thus, Powell's recommendation to end the war before completing the destruction of the Republican Guard was determined more by political than military considerations;[73] but those political considerations had little to do with the political configuration of the Middle East, and everything to do with domestic US politics and Powell's perception of the fragility of popular support. General Schwarzkopf was given an equally free hand in agreeing the terms of the military-to-military conditions that ended the war. His decision to allow the Iraqis freedom to fly their helicopters unimpeded after the war (a decision that was critical in allowing Saddam Hussein to repress Shiite uprisings and maintain his hold on power) reflected a 'surprising disinterest in the internal situation in Iraq'. The military's attitude, Paul Wolfowitz recalled later, 'was: we have won. Let's cut this cleanly and not let the civilians load us with a lot of missions.'[74]

In December 1990, National Security Advisor Brent Scowcroft had stated that the looming conflict posed an important question: 'Can the US use force – even go to war – for carefully defined national interests, or do we have to have a moral crusade or a galvanizing event like Pearl Harbor?'[75] Yet the President's concern not to micromanage the military in their conduct of the war allowed the latter to 'carefully define' (or rather restrict) the political objectives of the war to those that could be easily and neatly achieved through military action. This ruled out any objectives that might involve the US in messy stability operations in the aftermath of 'regime change'. Unfortunately, the unfinished business of the first Gulf War would eventually come back to haunt the US after 11 September 2001. At the time, the President's own ambivalence about the result was expressed in his surprisingly candid admission to a reporter two days after the ceasefire:

> You know, to be very honest with you, I haven't yet felt this wonderfully euphoric feeling that many of the American people feel. ... I think it's

that I want to see an end. You mentioned World War II – there was a definitive end to that conflict. And now we have Saddam Hussein still there – the man who wreaked this havoc upon his neighbours.[76]

The post-Cold War era and the changing realities of war

For two decades after Vietnam, American military culture was dominated by the paradigm of Overwhelming Force. Yet, by the early 1980s, prominent politicians were already beginning to chafe at the restrictions that it placed on the use of force as a political instrument. In his rejoinder to the Weinberger doctrine, Secretary of State George Schultz suggested that it was inappropriate for dealing with,

> those grey areas that lie somewhere between all-out war and blissful harmony. ... Americans have sometimes tended to think that power and diplomacy are distinct alternatives. This reflects a fundamental misunderstanding. The truth is that power and diplomacy must always go together or we will accomplish very little in this world.[77]

For those of Schultz's persuasion, who lamented the post-Vietnam loss of American resolve to forcefully 'shape the international environment', the potential of new military technology to provide 'low-risk' options for coercive diplomacy provided an increasingly attractive alternative to the paradigm of Overwhelming Force. If US strategy in the Gulf War represented the most perfect incarnation of the paradigm of Overwhelming Force, aspects of the air campaign nevertheless also presaged an alternative conception of war. Alvin and Heidi Toffler have characterized the air campaign as a 'dual war' – one a relentless war of attrition through the carpet-bombing of Iraqi forces (the old way of war), the other aiming at the 'systemic paralysis' of the Iraqi regime through precision bombing of those installations that permitted it to function (a glimpse of the future way of war). The latter effort was designed to persuade Saddam Hussein to pull out of Kuwait *without* the need for a ground war.[78] This reflected the initial concept for the air war conceived by Colonel John Warden, which he termed 'Instant Thunder' to present it as the antithesis of the gradualist 'Rolling Thunder' campaign in Vietnam. Defence Secretary Dick Cheney was particularly impressed by the possibilities of air power, once Warden's team explained the improvements in accuracy since World War II (they pointed out that new munitions were approximately 10,000 times more effective than the 'dumb bombs' of that era).[79]

Powell was at one stage concerned that the plan for the air campaign might prove *too* attractive to the civilians, tempting them to rely on air power alone. The deputy CENTCOM commander, Lt.-General Calvin Waller, also believed that the Air Force generals had a hidden agenda of 'victory through air power' throughout the war. In testimony to the Senate

Armed Services Committee in December 1990, Powell made his fears explicit:

> Many experts, amateurs and others in this town, believe that this can be accomplished by such things as surgical air strikes or perhaps a sustained air strike. And there are a variety of other nice, tidy, alleged low-cost, incremental, may-work options that are floated around. ... Such strategies are designed to hope to win, they are not designed to win.[80]

Powell had things his way during the Gulf War, and indeed for as long as he remained JCS Chairman. But as the 1990s progressed, his worst fears were increasingly realized. The relaxation of the restraints that the Cold War imposed on US military intervention ushered in a new era of American interventionism. Prominent civilian members of the Clinton administration did not share the risk-averse mindset of the military. When she was still Ambassador to the UN, Madeleine Albright famously asked Powell, 'What's the point of having this superb military that you're always talking about if we can't use it?'[81] As Clinton's Secretary of State she became an advocate of 'coercive diplomacy' through the use of limited force. The military itself became increasingly divided over this issue as the appeal of more discriminate weaponry exercised an ever-increasing influence within the military culture. For example, while the rest of the Joint Chiefs of Staff shared Powell's caution over American intervention against the Bosnian Serbs, the Air Force Chief of Staff, General Merrill McPeak, believed that the US could use air power to coerce the Serbs to hold peace talks. McPeak believed that air power had come into its own with the new technologies used in the Gulf War, and that confining the use of force only to those situations where America's vital interests were directly threatened was far too restrictive for the lone super-power. At this point the other services still tended to be intensely sceptical in response. As Powell said after one meeting in which a civilian extolled the potential of air power as an instrument for coercing Slobodan Milosevic into compliance, 'When I hear someone tell me what air power can do, I head for the bunker.'[82]

Yet, while the dominant discourse remained highly suspicious of Albright's enthusiasm for 'coercive diplomacy', some of the regional Commanders in Chief (CINCs) were more sympathetic.[83] General Wesley Clark, the Supreme Allied Commander for Europe (SACEUR) in the late Clinton years, became an enthusiastic advocate of an activist policy in the Balkans, and in particular of using NATO bombing to warn Milosevic against committing further abuses against the Kosovar Albanian population. The new military technology offered the appealing option of sacrificing machines rather than men. Operations Deliberate Force (against the Bosnian Serbs), Infinite Reach (against Osama bin Laden's infrastructure), Desert Fox (against Iraq), and Allied Force (against Serbia) all kept risks to American personnel to an absolute minimum through reliance on the US's stand-off precision strike capabilities – cruise missiles and smart weaponry delivered by air power. For General Clark, the Kosovo air campaign represented a 'low-cost, low-risk statement of intent';[84] for Clinton it was 'an exercise in coercion by manipulation of the enemy's risk'.[85] As one participant in the Kosovo air campaign reflected after the war,

> These remarkable weapons and the options they create undermine both the Weinberger Doctrine and the Powell Corollary regarding overwhelming force. The ease, speed, low risk, and high degree of detachment these weapons appear to allow permit policymakers to brush by such questions as 'Does some vital national interest require us to fight?'... With precision-guided munitions in the American arsenal, it was possible for Secretary of State Albright to prevail in her calls for two or three days of air-strikes to bring Milosevic back into line with the Dayton Accords, and it was those two or three days of strikes that grew unexpectedly into seventy-eight days of bombing and 38,000 sorties.[86]

The tension between the Overwhelming Force paradigm and the strategic imperatives of a new era of coercive diplomacy produced a peculiarly hesitant and indecisive form of warfare. In Bosnia and Kosovo, air power alone was insufficient to coerce the Serbs into compliance; yet the military's reluctance to commit ground troops to such a potential 'quagmire' forced a tacit dependence instead on 'imperial proxies' (the KLA in Kosovo and Croat ground forces, trained by the American private military company MPRI, in Bosnia). Just as European imperialists had frequently been embarrassed by the undisciplined behaviour of their locally recruited troops in the aftermath of battle, Washington was forced to turn a blind eye to the 'reverse ethnic cleansing' of Krajina Serbs and Kosovan Serbs by their victorious Croat and Kosovan allies.[87] The over-riding emphasis on 'Force Protection' severely restricted the ability of American troops to interact with civilians or engage in post-conflict reconstruction activities in the Balkans.[88]

In Kosovo, President Clinton publicly ruled out the use of ground troops at the start of the campaign, and pilots were forbidden to fly below 15,000 feet. This reliance on air power was inappropriate to the stated strategic objective of halting Serbian ethnic cleansing of Kosovar Albanians, which escalated after military action began.[89] General Clark's freedom of action was also circumscribed by the attitude of the Pentagon, where many of the senior officers had little sympathy for him: in one observer's summary, 'He had pushed to fight a war that was by Army tradition an alien use of American force and had violated every tenet of the Powell Doctrine, which most of them accepted.'[90] The Army successfully prevented Clark from using the Apache attack helicopters that he requested. In the *Washington Post*, Dana Priest concluded that the helicopters 'came to symbolize everything wrong with the Army as it enters into the twenty-first century: its inability to move quickly; its resistance to change; its obsession with casualties; its post-Cold War identity crisis.'[91]

Conclusion: the new dialectic in American military culture

In the post-Cold War period the grand strategic imperative on US grand strategy was quasi-imperial – the Clinton administration embraced the proactive management of international stability, or what the Pentagon euphemistically termed 'environment shaping'. However, the dominant military culture still remained highly sensitive towards perceived constraints on the American use of force deriving from the republican political culture of the United States, and the alleged casualty-aversion of American society. As Eliot Cohen wrote in *The National Interest* in 2000,

> The mentality of an imperial Army is, of necessity, utterly different from that of a mass Army. The former is composed of soldiers; the latter crusaders. The former accepts ambiguous objectives, interminable commitments and chronic skirmishes as a fact of life; the latter wants a definable mission, a plan for victory and decisive battles. In the imperial Army the trooper finds fulfilment in the soldier's life; in the mass Army in the belief that he exists 'to fight and win America's wars.' ... But to the extent that the American officer corps has developed a strategic lexicon rich in terms like 'end states', 'mission creep', 'clear objectives', and 'exit strategies', it clings to the strategic challenges of the last century.[92]

Colin Powell remarked in 1992 that the real threat remaining to American security was the threat of the *unknown*, the uncertain. The US no longer had the luxury of having a specific threat to plan for. When asked about the likelihood of US forces being used in future conflicts, he replied, 'Haven't the foggiest. ... That's the whole point. We don't know like we used to know.' What the US planned for now was 'that we're a super-power ... with responsibilities around the world ...'.[93] Yet, despite this insight, the Powell Doctrine imposed an essentially *reactive* posture on US strategy. Its emphasis on using force only as a last resort, with the assurance of public support, when vital national interests were at stake, and only when there was a clear exit strategy, appeared increasingly inflexible in an age of diffuse transnational threats. For those of a more proactive mindset, notions of 'risk management' moved centre-stage as a more forward-thinking means of coping with and structuring the new uncertainty.[94] A defining aim of 'risk management' is to act pre-emptively upon potentially problematic zones, to structure them in such a way as to reduce the likelihood of undesirable events or conduct occurring.[95] Clinton's Defence Secretary William Perry, for example, emphasized the importance of employing military-to-military relations for 'environment shaping' in peacetime, to seduce countries into the US sphere of geopolitical interests.[96]

Yet the use of force itself could also be justified in terms of proactively managing risk. Before the Kosovo conflict, NATO Secretary-General Javier Solana argued that 'the challenges of the next century suggest that our security policies must become increasingly proactive ... many problems and potential conflicts can be anticipated and many solutions devised, before it is too late.' President Clinton's remarks on commencing air strikes in Kosovo demonstrated that he was explicitly thinking of the action in terms of risk management: 'This action is not risk-free. ... However, I have concluded that the dangers of acting now are clearly outweighed by the risks of failing to act.' Clinton's December 2000 *National Security Strategy* noted that the United States had led the transformation of what used to be defensive entities into proactive instruments for meeting post-Cold War challenges.[97] This era of forceful 'risk management' appeared to require a less cautious and inflexible paradigm for projecting military power in support of political objectives. This tension between the dominant military paradigm and the strategic imperatives of the post-Cold War era led to the gradual ascendance of a military discourse that was far more optimistic about the potential to subordinate the grammar of war to the logic of policy. This emerging vision of 'Immaculate Destruction' was first conceived in the final years of the Vietnam War. However, its dominance within the military culture was not assured until the terrorist attacks of 11 September 2001.

4 Immaculate Destruction

The impact of 9/11 on American military culture

> To be sure, no way of war is a fixed thing. Under the right set of circumstances leaders and their society may accept very different styles of conflict. But barring some cataclysmic event – a twenty-first century Pearl Harbor – it seems likely that the American way of war will prevail for some time to come
>
> Eliot Cohen, 2001[1]

The 'twenty-first century Pearl Harbor' that Eliot Cohen imagined (with remarkable timing) might alter the American way of war did indeed occur on 11 September 2001. More precisely, the impact of 9/11 completed the marginalization of one cultural paradigm for the use of force as a political instrument, and assured the temporary ascendancy of its antithesis. Almost instantaneously, 9/11 joined Munich, Vietnam, and Pearl Harbor itself as defining reference points for the American national security establishment.[2] Considered through the prism of 9/11, many of the lessons of Vietnam enshrined in the Overwhelming Force paradigm appeared irrelevant to the strategic demands of the new age of shadowy threats and transnational terrorist networks. During the 1990s, Vietnam had symbolized the hubris in the civilian strategists' optimistic view of the political utility of military force. After 9/11, the pendulum swung back – those seeking to account for the failure of the Clinton administration to take decisive action against *al Qaeda* in the 1990s quickly identified the military elite's risk-aversion and restrictive conception of war as a contributory factor.[3]

The Bush administration regarded the post-9/11 period as one of revolutionary change in the basic assumptions governing national security policy, analogous to the early Cold War period when the concepts of containment and nuclear deterrence were first articulated.[4] It thus self-consciously set about revolutionizing the basic assumptions of US grand strategy. However, this revolution in strategic thinking required a corresponding shift in the nation's conception of war. The administration's concept of 'Military Transformation' thus acquired an important *cultural* dimension: it systematically attempted to transform not only the military's force structure, global defence posture, and weapons systems, but also, on a deeper level, the underlying set of cultural attitudes about warfare that crystallized in the decades after Vietnam. Defence Secretary Donald Rumsfeld consciously set out to purge the military culture of its risk-aversion, its rigid preference for the application of overwhelming force, and its restrictive concept of the political utility of force.

In their place, he sought to realize the full potential of a vision of a revolution in conventional warfare that had exercised an increasingly powerful hold over the Pentagon's collective imagination since the final years of the Vietnam War. This vision of 'Immaculate Destruction' (as the foreign policy analyst Leslie H. Gelb dubbed it in the early 1990s) promised to render military force an instrument of policy that could be wielded with hitherto unimagined discrimination and control. It thus provided an essential conceptual foundation of the decision to wage preventive war against Iraq in 2003.

The 'end of Clausewitz': mastering the grammar of war

In 1995, a senior American general remarked that the digitization of the battlefield meant 'the end of Clausewitz'.[5] He was referring to the fact that, for Clausewitz, two innate characteristics of warfare entailed that it could never be perfectly controlled – firstly, the 'fog of war' referred to the incompleteness of military information available to any commander deriving from battle's confusing nature. Secondly, 'friction' referred to warfare's unpredictability, deriving from a host of factors ranging from technical difficulties, to the weather, to the competitive and interactive nature of strategy. At the heart of the technological discourse that came to dominate the strategic assumptions of the G. W. Bush administration was precisely the opposite assumption: that warfare is fundamentally a *technical* process concerned with the achievement of complete technical mastery of the battlefield.

In the words of the authors of the influential strategic concept of 'Rapid Dominance' (more popularly known as 'Shock and Awe'), the aim is

> to ensure Control of the Environment or, to put it slightly differently, to impose the ultimate degree of shock and awe up to and including the realization by the adversary that resistance is futile. ... Properly applied, control will monitor and regulate what the adversary sees and understands and what is not seen or understood. ... The exercise of this type of control therefore must extend from shutting down and completely disrupting an adversary and its society to eliminating the ability of the lowest level military formation from carrying out its tasks and missions.[6]

The belief that total control *can* be achieved in warfare thus depends on two prior assumptions: that both the friction and the fog of war can be transcended through technical ingenuity. As early as 1978, the then Undersecretary of Defence William Perry claimed that the Department of Defence would soon have the ability to see everything of interest on the battlefield, hit everything that could be seen, and kill everything that could be hit.[7] Perry's revolutionary vision entailed overcoming the fog of war through complete situational awareness, while friction would be transcended through complete precision. The concepts of *information dominance* and *predictability* are thus central to the discourse of Immaculate Destruction.

A central conceit of the new military discourse is that the control of warfare centres around the control of information – the retention of a complete picture of the 'battlespace' combined with the simultaneous denial of such a picture to the enemy or even the precise manipulation of what the enemy 'sees'. In the apt metaphor of Lt.-General Liu Yazhou of the Chinese Air Force, the US military's new way of war depends on turning 'itself into a clairvoyant and clairaudient, able to see and hear from far away, while simultaneously rendering its adversary blind and deaf'.[8] Former Secretary of Defence William Cohen has argued that,

> We've had the age-old expression that knowledge is power, and absolute knowledge is absolute power. ... So, the actual domination of the information world will put us in a position to maintain superiority over any other force for the foreseeable future.[9]

Another enthusiast is Admiral William Owens, who as Vice-Chairman of the JCS from 1994–1996 was given the task of proselytizing this new vision of war within the military. In Owens' view, information technology promises to give military commanders, for the first time in history, an 'omniscient view of the battlefield in real time, by day and night, and in all weather conditions'. This revolution, he wrote, would challenge the 'hoary dictums about the fog and friction of war'.[10]

Once information dominance has been achieved, then the first of William Perry's requirements – seeing everything of interest on the battlefield – has been met. The second requirement – achieving the capacity to hit everything that can be seen – requires perfect precision in the guidance of munitions. If Perry's requirements can be met then, in the discourse of Immaculate Destruction, warfare moves into the realm of the *predictable*. Colonel John A. Warden, who originally conceived the 'Instant Thunder' air campaign during the first Gulf War, has argued that advances in precision technology make this prospect a reality:

> Precision weapons ... *change the nature of war from one of probability to one of certainty.* Wars for millennia have been probability events in which each side launched huge quantities of projectiles (and men) at one another in the hope that enough of the projectiles (and men) would

kill enough of the other side to induce retreat or surrender. Probability warfare ... was unpredictable, full of surprises, hard to quantify, and governed by accident. Precision weapons have changed all that. In the Gulf War, we knew with near certainty that a single weapon would destroy its target. *War moved into the predictable.* With precision weapons, even logistics become simple; ... we can forecast in advance how many precision weapons will be needed to defeat an enemy – *assuming of course that we are confident about getting the weapons to their targets.*[11]

With this last caveat – that the fundamental obstacle to 'predictability' is a *technical* one, dependent on the accuracy of weapons systems – this passage is perhaps the clearest expression of the underlying assumption that warfare is fundamentally a technical process, concerned with the efficient management of resources. The Air Force appears to have accepted the premise of predictability: it has now adopted the concept not only of 'Dominant Battlespace Awareness' but of '*Predictive* Battlespace Awareness', which provides decision-makers the ability to predict what actions the enemy is most likely to make. The former Commander of the Air Combat Command, General John Jumper, defined Predictive Battlespace Awareness in 2001 as 'a microscopic, all-encompassing understanding of the battlespace in all four dimensions, the ability to anticipate the right move rather than simply react to enemy moves. It's the art of prediction.'[12] Such is the military's faith in its capacity to achieve technical control of warfare that Secretary Rumsfeld's first Director of Force Transformation, Admiral Arthur Cebrowski, even claimed in 2004 that in planning for the future the American military can now discard the traditional 'inductive' approach (i.e. learning from experience and history) in favour of a 'deductive' method. In other words, as Williamson Murray has put it, 'the Department of Defense has supposedly reached a position where it can posit what the future is going to look like without reference to the past and thus determine what capabilities are transformational and which are not'.[13]

Humane warfare

One reflection of the degree to which Immaculate Destruction has become the prevailing discourse is the public's refusal to accept large-scale slaughter in war.[14] The traditional American way of war was associated with General Sherman's claim that, 'War is cruelty and you cannot refine it'. The 'War is Hell' discourse, suggesting the impossibility of subjecting the chaos of warfare to rational constraint, was employed in justification of American acts of indiscriminate violence from the burning of Atlanta to the firebombing of Tokyo. This line of argument also found echoes in the post-Vietnam era in the discourse of Overwhelming Force: during the first Gulf War, for example, General Norman Schwarzkopf kept near him a framed copy of

Sherman's adage: 'War is the remedy our enemies have chosen. And I say let us give them all they want.'[15] Colin Powell also described American strategy in that war in terms of similarly calculated brutality – the aim was to 'cut off' the Iraqi Army, and then to 'kill it'. This rhetoric partly reflected the casualties that the US itself expected to incur during the conflict: the Pentagon's best estimate was that about 18,000 American troops would be killed in action, a figure more than 100 times the actual losses it subsequently incurred.[16]

These extraordinarily low casualty levels shaped public expectations for the future. Before the Haiti intervention, President Clinton reportedly asked for the casualty figures for recent US military adventures in Panama, Grenada, and the Gulf, on the assumption that the public would support the average.[17] In the prevailing discourse that now conditions the American public's understanding of war, warfare is *no longer* Hell – but potentially immaculate. The implication is that the cruelty of war can not only be refined but precisely calibrated, placing a moral premium on efficiency in achieving victory with minimal loss of life for the US, enemy civilians, and armed forces alike. Information dominance, precision, and predictability should rule out the role of the accidental – both 'friendly fire' and 'collateral damage' are increasingly deemed unacceptable in the very terms of the discourse.

Admittedly, challenged at one point during Operation Enduring Freedom with the assertion that the US should have done more to reduce Afghan civilian casualties, Rumsfeld reverted to the 'War is Hell' argument: 'We did not start this war. So understand, responsibility for every single casualty in this war, whether they're innocent Afghans or innocent Americans, rests at the feet of the al Qaeda and the Taliban.' Much more frequently, however, US commanders emphasized the unprecedented precision of the campaign. 'I can't imagine there's been a conflict in history,' Rumsfeld claimed, 'where there has been less collateral damage, less unintended consequences.'[18] In Iraq, air commanders were required to obtain Rumsfeld's direct approval for any strike that might result in the deaths of more than 30 civilians.[19] Admiral Cebrowski, a devout Roman Catholic with a life-long special interest in just war theory and the ethics of warfare, stated that for him the Revolution in Military Affairs had 'great moral seductiveness', promising as it did 'to make it easier to protect the innocent'.[20]

The political desire for 'immaculate' warfare that can be conducted without casualties, collateral damage or risk to personnel also increasingly defines the R & D priorities of the defence industry. For example, Robert J. Stevens, the chief executive of Lockheed Martin (the US's largest military contractor and the strongest corporate force driving the Pentagon's vision of 'network-centric warfare'), has noted that Lockheed stands at 'the intersection of policy and technology', which requires 'thinking through the policy dimensions of national security as well as technological dimensions'. While Stevens acknowledges the existence of the 'Fog of War', he claims that it can be lifted, and envisions 'a world where you don't have any more fratricide'.[21] Given that the American public's concern over American casualties and high levels of 'collateral damage' (not to mention such atrocities as the My Lai massacre) were central to the decline of support in Vietnam, the notion that war can be waged humanely has been central to the post-Vietnam project of restoring the political utility of force.

The political utility of Immaculate Destruction

While the war in Afghanistan was presented by the administration as a vindication of its concept of Military Transformation, it was relatively uncontroversial as a projection of American military power in the service of national policy. The United States was reacting, after all, to a massive unprovoked attack on American soil by a terrorist organization harboured by a foreign regime. The invasion of Iraq, conversely, represented the ultimate 'proactive' use of force to reshape the international environment in conformity with American national interests. As the 2002 National Security Strategy made explicit, the use of force was conceived not as a symptom of the breakdown of diplomacy but as a preventive instrument to manage the risk of catastrophic threats arising in the future, in the Iraqi case either the regime's acquisition of nuclear weapons or a transfer of WMD to a terrorist group.[22] Beyond the debate over the existence of Iraqi WMD and links to terrorism, moreover, US intervention was conceived as a *political* instrument to reshape the Middle East, by sending a message of American power and resolve, reducing US dependence on Saudi Arabia, and by installing a more liberal regime that would encourage the democratic transformation of the region. As Deputy Secretary Wolfowitz explained after the war, 11 September had demonstrated 'what 20 or 30 years of a failing status quo in the Middle East was bringing the world'; the administration consequently resolved to use American power to 'change the course of history there'.[23]

The fact that the administration set about this ambitious project with such confidence, over-riding the caution of those in the military who warned of the risks of attacking Iraq, reflected its radical optimism with regard to the political utility of force. This optimism had been bolstered by a sense of vindication after the spectacularly rapid defeat of the Taliban, which quickly silenced early media speculation of an impending 'quagmire'. As President Bush declared in December 2001, soon after asking Rumsfeld and CENTCOM Commander General Tommy Franks to review the military's plans for war with Iraq,[24]

> Afghanistan has been a proving ground for this new approach. These past two months have shown that an innovative doctrine and high-tech weaponry can shape and then dominate an unconventional conflict. ... The conflict in Afghanistan has taught us more about

the future of our military than a decade of blue ribbon panels and think-tank symposiums.²⁵

Underlying the Bush administration's bold political strategy, therefore, was a distinctive set of assumptions about warfare. Most fundamental was the assumption that technology had rendered the battlefield transparent, predictable, and even humane; as such, force could be wielded with immaculate precision in the interests of American policy. When the fall of Baghdad followed the fall of Kabul, the Bush administration regarded its military vision as having been vindicated twice-over. 'To me the big news,' Bush told Bob Woodward, 'is America has changed how you fight and win war, and therefore makes [sic] it easier to keep the peace in the long run.'²⁶ Expanding on this theme in April 2003, he declared that,

> By a combination of creative strategies and advanced technology, we are redefining war on our terms ... more than ever before, the precision of our technology is protecting the lives of our soldiers, and the lives of innocent civilians.... In this new era of warfare, we can target a regime, not a nation. Our aim is to track and strike the guilty. Terrorists and tyrants have now been put on notice: they can no longer feel safe hiding behind innocent lives.²⁷

The vision of Immaculate Destruction: cultural sources

Like its antithetical paradigm of Overwhelming Force, the cultural well-springs of the vision of Immaculate Destruction derived from the American defeat in Vietnam. 'Of all the disasters of Vietnam,' the civilian strategist Albert Wohlstetter remarked in 1968, 'the worst may be the "lessons" that we'll draw from it.' For military officers of Colin Powell's persuasion, the way to 'kick' the Vietnam Syndrome was to acknowledge the limits that the republican political culture of the United States imposed on the exercise of American power abroad and to realign their conception of war within those restrictions. The emotional impulse behind this project derived from the need to restore the links between the military and the American people. For those of Wohlstetter's mindset, conversely, such a project was dangerously close to what he regarded as the 'new isolationism' advocated by the anti-war movement. He criticized the notion that 'our problem is not to use our power discriminately and for worthy ends but the fact of power itself, that we are better off reducing the choices available to us'.²⁸ In the later stages of the Vietnam War, the outlines of a future revolution in conventional warfare were already discernible. For some civilian strategists, military scientists and, increasingly, technological enthusiasts within the uniformed services themselves, the Vietnam Syndrome was to be overcome not by accepting limits on the political utility of force, but by embracing this technological revolution which offered the prospect of exercising military power with hitherto unheard of

Intimations of revolution: Vietnam and the electronic battlefield

The concept of the 'electronic battlefield' originated in Vietnam as a way of dealing with infiltration down the Ho Chi Minh Trail and across the Demilitarized Zone. In 1966, Roger Fisher, a Harvard Law School professor, suggested to Assistant Secretary of Defence John McNaughton that one solution might be the creation of a 'high-tech barrier'.[29] McNamara asked the Jason Division of the Institute for Defense Analysis, a group of about 45 scientists, to explore the concept further.[30] This scheme for the creation of the electronic 'McNamara Wall', as it came to be known, was soon abandoned, but it hugely increased the impetus behind the development of electronic sensors. In 1969, General Westmoreland compared the US performance in Vietnam to that of a 'giant without eyes'. The enemy's ability to find sanctuary in the dense jungles led to a great demand for mechanical sensors for the detection and surveillance of guerrilla forces. Leonard Sullivan, responsible for all Vietnam-oriented Defence Department research, argued in 1968 that the new sensor technologies offered a solution to the US dilemma in this 'porous war, where the friendly and the enemy are all mixed together'. Thus, as one analyst noted at the time, the urgency with which the Pentagon pursued the electronic battlefield concept was a direct result of the failure of conventional counter-guerrilla tactics in Vietnam.[31]

While the Marines and Army were initially sceptical in their attitude towards the new sensors, this mood changed after the siege of Khe Sanh in 1968, where the base commander estimated that without the sensors his casualties would have almost doubled. Westmoreland, formerly a lukewarm supporter, became amongst the most enthusiastic. Perhaps the most complete realization of the vision of the electronic battlefield in the Vietnam years was the Igloo White programme (c.1969–1972), whereby acoustic and seismic sensors were dropped along the Ho Chi Minh trail; truck or troop movements detected were then relayed to a fixed installation using computerized equipment, which then passed target information to strike aircraft. The system was the closest the US had yet come to the complete automation of military processes. In Paul N. Edwards' words, the overall conception was to achieve complete computerized control of the battlefield, in 'a kind of information panopticon where nothing and no one could move unobserved'.[32] By the end of the war it was already apparent that some of the new technological developments could have potentially revolutionary consequences. General Westmoreland was particularly taken with their potential. In a seminal October 1969 address to the Association of the United States Army, he outlined his vision of the 'Battlefield of the Future':

> Enemy forces will be located, tracked and targeted almost instantaneously through the use of data links, computer assisted evaluation, and

automated fire control. With the first round kill probabilities approaching certainty, and with surveillance devices, that can continually track the enemy, the need for large forces to fix the opposition physically will be less important. ... I see battlefields on which we can destroy anything we locate through instant communications and the almost instantaneous application of highly lethal firepower. In summary, I see an Army built around an integrated area control system that exploits the advanced technology of communications, sensors, fire direction, and the required automatic data processing.[33]

Westmoreland's vision of the future battlefield was, in short, a remarkably concise summary of what would come to be known by the 1990s as 'the Revolution in Military Affairs' (RMA). While the electronic battlefield concept originated as a technological solution to guerrilla infiltration, it quickly became apparent that it might have revolutionary consequences for conventional warfare (a shift in emphasis reinforced by the US neglect of counter-insurgency after Vietnam). Westmoreland declared that the US was on the 'threshold of an entirely new battlefield concept'.[34] In 1970, Senator Barry Goldwater went even further, stating that it constituted 'probably the greatest step forward in warfare since gunpowder'. Director of Defence Research and Engineering Malcolm R. Currie, testifying before Congress in 1974, agreed that, 'A remarkable series of technical developments has brought us to the threshold of what I believe will become a true revolution in conventional warfare'.[35]

The revolution in military affairs

Lawrence Freedman has noted that by the early 1970s the technologies that would make this 'revolution in contemporary warfare' feasible were already emerging: satellites were in use for reconnaissance purposes by 1961 and for communications in 1965; the first tactical computers were used in 1966; the internet can be traced back to a Pentagon-backed project to link together computers in the 1960s; and evidence of the devastating impact of 'smart' weaponry came with its use in the *Linebacker* campaigns in the closing stages of the Vietnam War. The essence of the revolution thus depended on the 'interaction between systems that collect, process, fuse and communicate information and those that apply military force'.[36] If the concept depended, in William Perry's formulation, on the ability 'to see everything of interest on battlefield' and 'to hit everything that could be seen', then the new sensor technologies provided the solution to the first problem, while precision guidance would achieve the second goal.

Albert Wohlstetter had been an early advocate for the development of the most accurate weapons possible, both nuclear and conventional.[37] He was instrumental during the 1970s and 1980s in promoting near-zero CEP (circular error probable) cruise missiles to provide the capability for discriminate long-range strikes with non-nuclear warheads.[38] 'Among the most revolutionary changes in precision that are in process,' he noted in 1985,

> some will permit one or a few non-nuclear warheads effectively to destroy a variety of important military targets which previously had been thought of as susceptible only to nuclear attack or to huge non-nuclear raids.

The new technologies would thus improve the US military's ability 'to keep destruction under control'.[39] Wohlstetter set up a group called the New Alternatives Workshop to examine the implications of the new technology. Many neo-conservatives later saw the influence of the forward-thinking of this group in the way that the first Gulf War was fought. 'It was a considerable matter of personal satisfaction,' Paul Wolfowitz later recalled, 'to watch those missiles turn right angles in the Gulf War in '91, doing what Albert envisioned 15 years before.'[40]

The second individual frequently credited with perceiving that the US was on the threshold of a 'Revolution in Military Affairs' (RMA) is Andrew Marshall, the Director of the Pentagon's Office of Net Assessment. According to another influential RMA enthusiast, Admiral William Owens, Marshall initially took his inspiration, ironically, from the debate within Soviet military journals from the mid-1970s onwards as to whether the US was undergoing a 'military-technical revolution' (a term that led American analysts to assume initially that the Soviets were discussing their own accomplishments). By 1993, Marshall and his colleagues within the Pentagon became convinced that the narrowly technical concept of a 'military-technical revolution' should be replaced with the broader concept of a revolution affecting the entire spectrum of military affairs.[41] Thus, by this point the vision of a revolution in conventional warfare that was embryonic in the electronic battlefield concept appeared on the cusp of realization.

Andrew Krepinevich has offered one much-quoted definition of an RMA:

> the application of new technologies into a significant number of military systems combines with innovative operational concepts and organizational adaptation in a way that fundamentally alters the character and conduct of a conflict.[42]

The second element of this definition – 'innovative operational concepts and organizational adaptation' – developed in the American case from the military's post-Vietnam rejection of tactical attrition in favour of a new focus on combined arms warfare, operational art, and rapid manoeuvre. This new operational style and focus on high-tech weaponry reflected several factors: the inspiration of the Israeli approach in the 1973 Yom Kippur war; an era of tight military budgets that demanded maximization of the potential of every weapon on the battlefield; and the increased professionalism of the all-volunteer force. Above all, it reflected the dilemma of how to confront a force vastly superior in manpower in the event of a Soviet invasion of Western Europe, a dilemma which contributed to the development of 'AirLand Battle' doctrine in the 1980s.[43] In combination with the technological dimension of the RMA, the new operational sophistication offered the prospect of a 'new American way of war' – a vastly more efficient style of warfare that could destroy the enemy with pinpoint accuracy from great distances while minimizing the exposure of US forces to enemy fire.[44]

The utility of force: political implications of the RMA

It should be noted that, as a 'cultural' phenomenon, the RMA had its origins in a revulsion against all those features of the Cold War strategic environment that had appeared to render force obsolete as a rational instrument of policy. This is true for both the individuals and the technologies involved. Albert Wohlstetter, of course, was one of the most influential pioneers of the new science of strategy in the early Cold War period, and his entire career can be seen in a sense as a search to restore strategic freedom of action to the US. Similarly, as a young RAND analyst in the 1950s, Andrew Marshall had been one of the earliest adherents of nuclear 'counterforce' doctrine that sought to increase US strategic options by making a limited nuclear war theoretically 'fightable'. Thus, in the post-Vietnam period, these scientific strategists continued their quest to restore the political utility of force through new technological means. Marshall remains an influential figure: in his 80s, he is still Director of the Office of Net Assessment and has been dubbed the 'Yoda' of Rumsfeld's Department of Defence.[45] Wohlstetter's continuing legacy is also felt through the influence he exerted on a whole generation of disciples, including two of the central architects of the 2003 Iraq War: former Chairman of the Defence Policy Board Richard Perle, and former Deputy Defence Secretary Paul Wolfowitz.[46]

The electronic battlefield concept originated in an effort to increase US effectiveness against the guerrillas whose asymmetrical tactics had nullified the political utility of *conventional* warfare. The technology of precision guidance that was so central to the embryonic RMA also had its cultural origins in this desire to subject the apparently uncontrollable and irrational course of *nuclear* war to 'rationality' (for 'controlled response' or 'counterforce' options required a high degree of accuracy in order to target specific enemy forces while avoiding cities and preventing escalation to all-out nuclear war). It was this interest in counterforce accuracy for ballistic missiles, concludes Donald Mackenzie in his study of nuclear missile guidance, which lay behind the American technological drive toward greater guidance accuracy;[47] or, as other scholars have pointed out, 'Precision-guided munitions were born from the womb of the nuclear culture. The search for nuclear-tipped missiles created the technology of precision that precision munitions drew on. The surveillance system created to guard against nuclear war was the foundation of their targeting systems.[48] This aversion to the inherent irrationality and uncontrollability of nuclear war – of Mutual Assured Destruction (MAD) – drove enthusiasm for the idealized vision of sanitized, perfectly controlled conflict that underpins the RMA.

The second broad cultural current fuelling enthusiasm for the RMA was the 'dot.com boom' of the 1990s. Just as the McNamara revolution was inspired by the cult of efficient management originating in the American corporate world, the faith in information technology that lies at the heart of the RMA concept was inspired by the corporate example of companies like Amazon.com, American Airlines, and Dell Computers:

> All of these companies attained dramatic 'competitive advantages' in their fields by creating vast and complex information networks. ... Information technology permitted enormous efficiencies by allowing corporations to make accurate predictions, minimize risk, and adapt rapidly to changing circumstances.[49]

Thus, as in McNamara's time, the corporate influence in American military culture continued to foster a distinctive set of assumptions about war: just as perfect knowledge of the marketplace could theoretically ensure perfect efficiency in the maximization of profits and the minimization of losses, so perfect knowledge of the battlefield should ensure an analogous efficiency in the management of destruction.

The narrowly technological terms in which the RMA tended to be discussed frequently disguised its radical implications for politics and strategy. Wohlstetter was amongst the first to recognize these implications. In his 1985 article criticizing reliance on the 'abhorrent doctrine' of Mutual Assured Destruction, he observed that,

> While ... precisely delivered non-nuclear weapons are not likely to supplant nuclear weapons completely as a means of responding to nuclear attack, they have a large political importance ... in reducing the pressures to resort to nuclear weapons. They would greatly increase the possibility of keeping a conflict under control.[50]

If such an observation could be made during the Cold War, the implications for a period in which the US was no longer restrained by its super-power rival would obviously be much more revolutionary.[51] After Wohlstetter's death, Paul Wolfowitz, his former student, credited him with being,

> one of the first ... most influential people, to understand what a dramatic difference it would make to have accurate weapons ... if you wanted to understand Albert Wohlstetter you've got to understand how somebody

can perceive that a seemingly cold technical fact like this fact about accuracy translates into a whole transformation of strategy and politics.[52]

Another of the earliest individuals to perceive these strategic implications was Les Aspin, President Clinton's first Secretary of Defence. In September 1992 Aspin, at the time the Chairman of the Armed Services Committee, delivered a speech criticizing the Weinberger–Powell Doctrine's restrictive criteria for using force. Aspin recognized that what he termed this 'all-or-nothing' approach was designed to allow 'the troops to go in, get the job done and get out quickly. And because it is done with overwhelming force you don't run into the problem of public support.' Yet, while he acknowledged that these criteria had served the US well, he argued that in the post-Cold War environment the formula was too rigid. It was ill-suited to such challenges as enforcing the no-fly zone over Iraq, or supporting humanitarian operations in Bosnia and Somalia. In contrast to the 'all-or-nothing' school, Aspin (who was a former economics professor and, briefly, a systems analyst in McNamara's Pentagon) proposed a 'limited objectives' school. Combined with the disintegration of the Soviet Union, he argued that technological advances (above all in air power) gave the US much greater freedom to exercise the use of 'compellent' military force in support of limited political objectives:

> What this means is that we have technology which has improved our ability to make air strikes with little, if any, loss of US lives and with a minimum of collateral damage and loss of civilian lives on the other side. This is a big, big change. But we've also become more sophisticated about targeting at a time when our adversaries have become more dependent on the kinds of things we can target. We can target ... the kinds of targets that national leadership and military commands hold dear.[53]

This new vision of Immaculate Destruction, in summary, appeared to offer the prospect of employing force with unprecedented precision, without the controversies associated with high-collateral damage, and, above all, without exposing American forces to hostile reprisals. This latter imperative had been at the heart of the new vision from its origins in the concept of the 'electronic battlefield'. General Westmoreland, for example, once argued that the US had a duty to take full advantage of those technological developments that could 'replace wherever possible the man with the machine'.[54] Indeed, Senator Barry Goldwater argued in July 1970 that one of the reasons that the US could move to a volunteer force was that the Army, 'the great user of men', was depending on the electronic battlefield.[55] Richard Cooper, a former Director of the Defence Advanced Projects Research Agency (DARPA), has spelt out the underlying cultural calculus most explicitly:

> It's my view that this society has decided that it will only use a certain fraction of its human effort in its own defence in peacetime. The imperative just isn't there ... so consequently we have no other alternative but to turn to high technology. That's it.[56]

The impact of 9/11: war within the Pentagon

The discourse of Immaculate Destruction grew increasingly influential in US military culture throughout the 1990s. However, it was 9/11 that facilitated its dominance over the antithetical paradigm of Overwhelming Force. The grand strategy the Bush administration articulated for the War on Terror required a concept of war compatible with the flexible and proactive use of precisely calibrated force to shape the international environment. In fundamental respects, such a concept was in tension with the 'lessons' of Vietnam that had been institutionalized in the military's force structure, doctrine and basic cultural assumptions. 'Rumsfeld might think we're at war with terrorism,' General Peter Schoomaker observed before Rumsfeld pulled him out of retirement to become Army chief of staff, 'but I'll bet he also thinks he is at war within the Pentagon. ... The real war's happening right there in his building. *It's a war of the culture.*'[57] To be more specific, Rumsfeld sought to marginalize one vision of the proper use of military force – the discourse of Overwhelming Force, most entrenched within the senior ranks of the Army – while championing the technocratic vision of Immaculate Destruction associated with the Pentagon's civilian strategists, military scientists enamoured with the 'Revolution in Military Affairs', and technological enthusiasts in the individual services.

Before 9/11, the American debate over Military Transformation tended to focus rather narrowly on weapons systems and how best to exploit technological innovation – whether, for example, the military should skip a generation of military technologies first conceived during the Cold War such as the F-22 Raptor and the Crusader artillery system to devote resources to more cutting-edge systems such as networked unmanned combat vehicles.[58] Rumsfeld's faith in new military technologies persuaded him that the US military could achieve decisive results with a far lighter structure; by the spring of 2001, Deputy Undersecretary of Defence for Policy Stephen Cambone was arguing that the Army could cut two divisions and the Navy two carrier battle groups, while the Air Force could sacrifice the new F-22 Stealth Fighter for more futuristic unmanned systems.[59] To Rumsfeld, the military's opposition to such reforms seemed excessively conservative and risk-averse. Yet, by the summer of 2001, Rumsfeld's inability to impose his vision on an increasingly disaffected military leadership had fostered a widespread view that he would be the first member of Bush's cabinet to resign. However, the strategic imperatives perceived in the aftermath of 9/11, the atmosphere of wartime emergency, and Rumsfeld's apparent vindication in the Afghan War gave him the stature to challenge the cultural inertia of the Pentagon head-on, and to purge America's military establishment of those entrenched forces that resisted his vision.

Preventive war: defining strategic imperatives through the prism of 9/11

Before Donald Rumsfeld became George W. Bush's defence secretary, he had an informal 'job interview' with the president-elect. Rumsfeld told Bush that, during the Clinton years, the country's natural pattern when challenged had been what Rumsfeld called 'reflexive pullback'. He said he believed that, in contrast, the new administration should adopt a 'forward-leaning' posture.[60] Rumsfeld's belief that the US could no longer afford a reactive posture derived from his preoccupation with *uncertainty*, which preceded 9/11. He routinely handed out Roberta Wohlstetter's *Pearl Harbor: Warning and Decision*, particularly recommending the cautionary foreword by Thomas Schelling: 'There is a tendency in our planning to confuse the unfamiliar with the improbable.' His interest in uncertainty was partly a product of his work as Chairman of the Ballistic Missile Commission during the late 1990s, which concluded that US intelligence had frequently learnt about significant weapons developments in other countries 5–13 years after they had occurred.[61]

The effect of 9/11 was to boost the executive's authority to force change on a stubborn military bureaucracy, while confirming and reinforcing this pre-existing preoccupation with managing uncertainty. Rumsfeld's famous concept of 'unknown unknowns' was much ridiculed in the press, although it was far from original (he appears to have borrowed it from the discourse of corporate risk management, perhaps reflecting his management experience in the private sector):

> There are things we know that we know. There are known unknowns. That is to say, there are things that we know we don't know. But there are also unknown unknowns. There are things we don't know we don't know.

Even before 9/11, Rumsfeld's strategic vision reflected a concern to minimize the risks associated with these 'unknown unknowns'. For example, the shift from a 'threat-based' to a 'capabilities-based' posture advocated in the 2001 Quadrennial Defense Review (QDR) explicitly reflected this concern with managing uncertainty.[62] The shift in focus enshrined in the QDR is consistent with the 2002 National Security Strategy. While a 'threat-based' force is reactive and defensive in nature, a 'capabilities-based' force is proactive and implicitly offensive in nature: rather than focusing on any specific threat, the US prepares for any and all contingencies by adopting an anticipatory, forward-leaning posture. The demands of proactively managing risks that might destabilize the *Pax Americana* put a premium on efficiency, flexibility, and rapidity in the projection of military power.

The most radical feature of the Bush administration's attempt to enunciate a new set of principles to guide US strategic thinking after 9/11 was the alleged redundancy, under certain conditions, of the structure of deterrence that governed the Cold War, and the assertion of a right to preventive military action that flows from this premise. At least during its first term, the Bush administration's rhetoric on anticipatory action since 9/11 was phrased in terms of 'pre-emption', but it in fact made a consistent case for preventive action.[63] The 2002 National Security Strategy obfuscated this distinction by arguing that, 'We must adapt the concept of imminent threat to the capabilities and objectives of today's adversaries'.[64] The administration's thinking on the redundancy of a reactive, deterrent posture was first systematically articulated in Bush's June 2002 speech at West Point: 'If we wait for threats to fully materialize, we will have waited too long. ... We must take the battle to the enemy, disrupt his plans, and confront the worst threats before they emerge.'[65]

The administration thus enshrined the 'precautionary principle' at the heart of its approach to national security. Somewhat ironically (considering the administration's sceptical stance on global warming), the precautionary principle originated in the environmental movement. The principle, now a recognized general principle of international law, first became current in the 1970s, when environmental impact assessments revealed gaps between significant risks of serious harm and accuracy of scientific forecasts. The 1992 'Rio Declaration' gave an oft-cited definition:

> a precautionary approach should be applied ... where there are threats of serious or irreversible damage, lack of full scientific certainty shall not be used as a reason for postponing cost-effective measures to prevent environmental degradation taking into account costs and benefits of actions or inactions.[66]

In essence, therefore, the principle lowers the standard of proof required before preventive measures can be taken to forestall catastrophic harm. This became a central pillar of the Bush administration's case for war in Iraq. The NSS declared that, 'The greater the threat, the greater is the risk of inaction – and the more compelling the case for taking anticipatory action to defend ourselves, *even if uncertainty remains as to the time and place of the enemy's attack*'.[67] During the search for evidence of Iraqi WMD programmes before the war, Condoleezza Rice famously stated that, 'We don't want the smoking gun to be a mushroom cloud', while Rumsfeld argued that absence of evidence did not amount to evidence of absence. Indeed, after the war he noted that, 'The coalition did not act in Iraq because we had discovered dramatic new evidence of Iraq's pursuit of weapons of mass murder. We acted because *we saw the existing evidence in a new light* through the prism of our experience on Sept. 11.'[68]

Purging the Powell Doctrine

One of the peculiarities of the Bush administration is that, in his position as Secretary of State, Colin Powell was perfectly placed as a senior administration insider to witness, yet apparently powerless to prevent, the systematic dismantling of the body of principles governing the conduct of warfare that he did so much to institutionalize during his time as Chairman of the Joint Chiefs of Staff. The Weinberger and Powell Doctrines were codifications of the military's determination to protect itself from 'future Vietnams'. Unsurprisingly, given Powell's prominence in Bush's cabinet, the administration's post-9/11 vision of war did not explicitly retract the Powell doctrine, but it implicitly contradicted every one of its stipulations. In an age of WMD-armed rogue states and apocalyptically minded terrorists, the Bush administration concluded that it was not sufficient to wait until a 'vital national interest' was threatened (condition 1) before contemplating military action.[69] In the search to apportion blame for the pre-9/11 failure to take firm action against *al Qaeda* in Afghanistan, the risk-aversion enshrined in the Powell Doctrine seemed an obvious culprit. As we have seen, far from stipulating that the use of force should be a last resort (condition 6), the Bush administration shifted the emphasis to anticipatory risk management, even on the basis of ambiguous intelligence. Equally, political and military objectives (condition 3), and the relationship between ends and means (condition 4) would of necessity be more ambiguous in the new context of preventive action against shadowy adversaries. Rumsfeld cautioned that Americans should 'forget about "exit strategies" ... we're looking at sustained engagement that carries no deadlines. We have no fixed rules about how to deploy our troops.'[70]

In this context the use of overwhelming force, in the traditional sense of committing forces in a ratio that would guarantee victory (condition 2), might simply not be possible; and, in the event, US forces were quickly spread thin as the Bush strategy called for stabilizing Afghanistan and occupying Iraq while simultaneously deterring North Korea and Iran and aggressively prosecuting the wider 'Global War on Terrorism' (GWOT). As Michael Ignatieff put it, the War on Terror appeared to require 'the exercise of American power everywhere at once'.[71] In contrast to the Powell Doctrine, the so-called Rumsfeld Doctrine claimed that decisive results could still be achieved with much smaller force levels through the exploitation of new technologies. Finally, the administration certainly hoped to sustain the support of Congress and the American people (condition 5), but this would have to be for the long-term and it could not be achieved through the 'zero-risk' strategies of the Clinton era; on the contrary, the attitude of the people would have to change. Rumsfeld (Bush confided to the journalist Bob Woodward) wanted nothing less than to 'change the psychology of how Americans viewed war'.[72]

The implementation of the Bush administration's grand strategy for the War on Terror, in short, seemed to require a wholesale purging of the post-Vietnam military culture that the Powell Doctrine had codified. In October 2001, Rumsfeld set up a new 'Office of Force Transformation' to spearhead his effort to reform the military and appointed Admiral Arthur A. Cebrowski, a leading enthusiast of the technocratic vision of Network-Centric Warfare, to be its first director. At the end of 2001, Rumsfeld also began doing something unprecedented for a defence secretary: interviewing officers for two- and three-star promotions (traditionally only four-stars received such scrutiny).[73] Rumsfeld's efforts to purge the military were facilitated not only by the new climate of deference to civilian executive authority created by wartime emergency, but also by the course of the Afghan war itself. The media's early fears of a quagmire were quickly replaced by jubilation and a widespread consensus following the fall of Kabul that the campaign had been a spectacular success.

Surveys of officer attitudes conducted between 2000 and 2002 revealed a corresponding shift of attitude towards the new high-tech technologies that had been show-cased in the conflict. In 2000, Army and Marine Corps officers were consistently more sceptical of the proposition that the US was experiencing a technological revolution in warfare than their Navy and Air Force counterparts, and were the most doubtful of the need for change. By late 2002, Army attitudes had shifted significantly towards those of the Air Force and Navy officers and away from those of the Marine Corps officers, and were much more supportive of the need for the Army to reduce its reliance on heavy forces.[74] The timing of this attitudinal shift suggests that the Afghan war, in which victory was achieved by networking small numbers of Special Forces with precision air power, was a critical factor. The difficulties of establishing a significant Army presence inside Afghanistan until the war was all but won underlined the need for Army reform.

After 9/11, Rumsfeld also made strenuous efforts to overcome the military's institutional hostility to Special Forces-led counter-terrorism efforts, developing a new vision of 'hunter-killer' teams that would pursue terrorist targets around the globe. To this end he boosted the budget of the Special Operations Command (SOCOM) – an 81 per cent increase in the baseline budget between 2001 and 2006, according to Pentagon figures[75] – and significantly increased its authority by changing it from a 'supporting command', which can only contribute to other combatant commands' missions, into a 'supported command', which can plan and operate its own independent operations.[76] Rumsfeld abandoned the Clinton administration's decree that the military must have an official 'finding' signed by the president before taking any action; instead, Special Forces were given more authority to take anti-terrorist action on their own initiative.[77] Rumsfeld's replacement of General Eric Shinseki as Army Chief of Staff in August 2003 by bringing out of retirement (itself an unusual move) a former commander-in-chief of SOCOM (the aforementioned General Schoomaker), was of great symbolic importance in reflecting a determination to transform the risk-averse regular Army culture.

In fact, General Shinseki became the public personification of the tension between the Army's cultural preference for overwhelming force, and Rumsfeld's faith in technological force multipliers. Shortly after 9/11, Rumsfeld reviewed all the military's extant war plans and pronounced that they were all improperly designed: 'Either it's world peace or it's World War III. Either the switch is off or on ... we're not going to do it that way.' Rumsfeld argued instead that, 'The only way these things can be done well is *if risk is elevated* ... instead of trying to mitigate it down below at a level where you don't have the benefit of trading off with and balancing risk'. During the planning process for the Iraq War, Shinseki expressed concerns to Rumsfeld and General Franks that the attacking ground force might be too small.[78] The Army's initial recommendation was for an invasion force of 400,000 troops; Rumsfeld's idea of the right size was reportedly about 75,000. Rumsfeld viewed Shinseki as a personification of the military culture he was attempting to purge. Accordingly, Rumsfeld announced who his successor would be in the spring of 2002, fourteen months before the scheduled end of Shinseki's term: an unusual move which converted the incumbent into a 'lame duck'. In a now notorious episode, Shinseki publicly indicated his concerns over the war plan in his February 2003 appearance before the Senate Armed Services Committee, in which he estimated that 'several hundred thousand soldiers' might be needed to stabilize post-war Iraq. Two days later, Deputy Secretary Wolfowitz went out of his way to tell the House Budget Committee that such notions were 'wildly off the mark'.[79] According to the journalist Rowan Scarborough, after Shinseki retired, about a dozen two- and three-star generals – protégés of Shinseki – were informed that they would retire too.[80]

Army Secretary Thomas White, who contradicted Wolfowitz by defending Shinseki's estimate in front of the same committee a week later, was soon also requested to retire by Rumsfeld. Interviewed after the Iraq War, he spoke of the powerful unease within the Army over the size of the attacking force and a sense that the lessons of Vietnam were being ignored:

> Everybody sitting around that table, all of us were Vietnam veterans, and this business of the Powell Doctrine – and I guess it came from Weinberger as well before that – was, 'We're not going to do Vietnam again'. And what we did in Vietnam is we kind of went in an uncommitted way. The strategy was flawed. We didn't have adequate forces to execute it ... and it ended up destroying the United States Army and

seriously damaging the country. ... And we were just not going to be a party to anything that looked like that again. It came up in the '80s; it came up in the Gulf War. We assembled an overwhelming force – we waited until we had two full corps on the ground rather than going with one – because we wanted to be able to conduct an overwhelming offensive operation, not just a parody type of thing.[81]

Bob Woodward relates that Powell himself was deeply concerned that the Army leadership would allow itself to be talked into using a smaller force than necessary, and in the summer of 2002, he tried to impress this caution on the President: *'You are going to be the proud owner of 25 million people. ... You will own all their hopes, aspirations and problems. You'll own it all.'*[82] General Hugh Shelton, JCS Chairman until October 2001, was also deeply alarmed when the subject of war with Iraq was brought up after 9/11.[83] Outside the administration, some of the staunchest critics were retired military officers. In an exaggeration that nevertheless contained an important element of truth, retired CENTCOM Commander Anthony Zinni even remarked that, 'It's pretty interesting that all the generals see it the same way and all the others who have never fired a shot and are hot to go to war see it another way'.[84]

However, these competing visions of war no longer corresponded quite as clearly to a neat civilian-military divide as Zinni's remark suggests. One Army maverick whose enthusiastic publications on Army reform had caught Rumsfeld's eye, Colonel Douglas MacGregor, was invited to brief the Pentagon civilian leadership before the run-up to the war. He presented his own vision of Immaculate Destruction that envisaged decapitating the Iraq regime with as few as 50,000 troops, in a lightning *blitzkrieg* to Baghdad that would deliberately avoid the destruction of the bulk of the Iraqi military forces.[85] In CENTCOM Commander Tommy Franks, Rumsfeld found another Army commander who would conform to his vision, creating a war plan that relied on troop numbers that were low by conventional Army standards (although still higher than Rumsfeld's initial preference). In his autobiography, Franks pours scorn on the service chiefs and also describes himself as a 'maverick', accustomed to thinking 'way outside the box of conventional doctrine', who had frequently found himself 'on the outside of the Army's conservative mainstream'.[86] While this may have been the case, his faith in the potential of the new technologies to substitute for manpower was, by the early twenty-first century, far from unconventional in other parts of the American military.

Abolishing the Abrams Doctrine

The traditional American way of war was a 'republican' way of war: the American dependence in wartime on the mass mobilization of citizen-soldiers derived from the republican fear of large standing armies. The Cold War eroded this arrangement in two steps: the first was the maintenance of the draft in an era of 'cold' peace. The second was the establishment of the all-volunteer force after the ending of the draft. However, as we have seen, the all-volunteer force was structured in such a way through the 'Total Force' policy that the fully professional component of the Army could not function in large-scale operations without the mobilization of the Reserves, thus maintaining a link with the republican citizen-soldier ideal. This compromise was designed to ensure that the US would not go to war without popular support. The disruption of the lives of mobilized citizens from the Reserves would also create pressure to bring hostilities to a quick end. The War on Terror, however, quickly revealed a tension between this ideal and the simultaneous deployment of troops to apparently interminable commitments in several different theatres. This tension prompted Secretary Rumsfeld to propose reforms which would enable the military to act with much greater independence of the Reserves, in effect abolishing the post-Vietnam settlement which defined the citizen's obligations of military service.

Since the end of the Cold War, the 'Total Force' arrangement had come under increasing strain.[87] Yet the strain imposed by the military interventions of the 1990s was insignificant in comparison to the demands that the War on Terror would make on the military. The armed forces were soon stretched thin: by July 2003, for example, only three of the Army's 33 active-duty combat brigades were free for a new mission.[88] Rumsfeld was forced to accept a temporary increase of 30,000 soldiers in the active-duty force. In other signs of strain, the Army lowered some standards for recruitment in 2004, instituted a 'stop-loss' policy to prevent thousands of deployed troops from leaving the service on schedule, and called up the Individual Ready Reserve (troops who have left the service but who are legally obliged to help out for several years after their discharge should the government decide it necessary). Pentagon officials also identified 300,000 jobs done by people in uniform that could be turned over to civilians in order to free up combat troops.[89]

In this context particular strain was exerted on the Reserves, to the extent that in January 2005 a leaked memo by Lt.-General James Helmly, the Chief of the Army Reserves, declared that they were 'rapidly degenerating into a broken force'.[90] The call-up of reservists since 9/11 represented the second largest reserve call-up since 1945 (only the Korean War mobilization was larger). Whereas President Lyndon Johnson could avoid calling up the Reserves during the Vietnam War through his reliance on the draft, the Bush administration was loath to reintroduce it. The 'Total Force' was structured in such a way, moreover, that certain non-combat components that were deemed to be essentially civilian functions, including military police, engineers, and civil affairs, were allocated almost entirely to the Reserves. The unexpected demands of counter-insurgency and post-conflict stabilization in Afghanistan and Iraq put such skills at a premium. In March 2004, Reserves accounted for 97 per cent of the military's civil affairs units, 70 per cent of its engineering units, and 66 per cent of its military police.[91]

In an apt imperial analogy, the historian of the great powers, Paul Kennedy, noted in 2003 that the US might have 'to move to a sort of Cardwell System'.[92] The Cardwell System was created by Edward (later Lord) Cardwell, British Secretary of State for War between 1868 and 1874, and was a solution to a strategic predicament with close parallels to that of the contemporary United States:

> Cardwell was faced with a number of problems. Britain's imperial interests were expanding in various parts of the world, and required military muscle.... Cardwell was also aware that there was no question of emulating the Prussians and the French by using conscription and compulsory reserve service.[93]

Cardwell's solution was the multi-battalion regiment, which provided both for regular rotation (thus maintaining morale) and imperial flexibility. Rumsfeld's proposed solution to America's 'imperial overstretch' was similar to Cardwell's: the Army is being reorganized to change its deployment unit of choice from the division to the smaller-sized brigade combat team (BCT). The theory is that this reorganization will in time give the Army greater strategic flexibility by increasing the number of active-duty combat brigades from 33 to 42. The Army will also retrain thousands of active-duty soldiers as military police officers, civil affairs experts, and intelligence analysts, thus reducing dependence on the Reserves for post-conflict stabilization.[94] Another solution is to rely on the private sector: by September 2004 there were reportedly 20,000 troops from Private Military Companies (PMCs) serving in Iraq alongside 138,000 American troops. Private contractors thus made up the second largest contingent of forces in Iraq after the US military itself – larger even than Britain's troop deployment.[95]

As one of the earliest members of Congress to propose the creation of the all-volunteer force in the late 1960s, Rumsfeld made it clear that he would not contemplate a return to the draft. His solution was, in effect, the opposite: rather than drawing on the resources of the American citizenry, he sought to introduce a further step towards a fully professionalized military. In December 2002 he remarked that

> If you think about it, a decision was made a number of years ago for the United States military to put in the Reserves and the Guard, as opposed to the active forces, a whole set of capabilities that are necessary if you are going to in fact be engaged in the use of force. That means that you cannot do the things you normally would do with active

forces ... in the event the president makes such a decision, without activating Reserve and Guard. ... It's a shame that we're organized that way, and we intend to see that we're no longer organized that way in the future.[96]

This project represented a further erosion of the ideal of the citizen-soldier that was historically central to American military culture, and at least in theory it will make it easier for a president to launch and sustain military operations without popular support. In his post-9/11 radio address to the American people, Bush invoked the language of a national crusade:

> We have ... much to ask of the American people. ... You will be asked for your patience; for the conflict will not be short. You will be asked for resolve; for the conflict will not be easy. You will be asked for your strength, because the course to victory may be long.[97]

However, in his address to Congress five days later, the sacrifices required for this crusade seemed rather more modest: the main demand on American citizens, beyond prayer, was their 'continued participation and confidence in the American economy'.[98] If the pre-eminent concern of the republican military ethic was to maintain the link between the military and the wider American society, then the hallmark of the grand strategy of the War on Terror has been the opposite: to insulate the average American citizen from the burdens and consequences of a new 'long, twilight struggle' without a foreseeable end.

Efficiency: the Rumsfeld 'Doctrine'

During the Iraq War, there was much discussion of a so-called Rumsfeld Doctrine replacing the Powell Doctrine.[99] The use of the term 'doctrine' was misleading in two senses: firstly, because Rumsfeld never set out a formal set of principles governing the proper use of force as Weinberger and Powell did, and secondly, because to some extent the analogy with the Powell Doctrine compared 'apples with pears': the Powell Doctrine was as much about *when* military force should be used as *how* it should be used. Yet in a broader sense the comparison was valid in that Rumsfeld and Powell did subscribe to fundamentally different concepts of warfare. For advocates of the Overwhelming Force paradigm, a central concern is the unpredictability of war. The central strategic values that flow from this premise are risk-aversion and prudence; a degree of 'overkill' is not necessarily a bad thing (recall Powell's remark that he believed in 'the bully's way of going to war').[100] A central premise of the vision of Immaculate Destruction, conversely, is that war *can* be rendered predictable. The central strategic value, therefore, becomes not prudence but *efficiency*. Risk-aversion is regarded as a form of inefficiency.

Like McNamara before him, Rumsfeld's preoccupation with efficiency reflected his corporate background. In the words of one commentator, Rumsfeld 'wanted the Pentagon commanded like a profit-conscious corporation, from the top down', and to that end he handpicked service secretaries with extensive corporate experience: Air Force Secretary James Roche had been an executive with Northrup Grumman; Navy Secretary Gordon England had been with General Dynamics; and Army Secretary Thomas White with Enron.[101] After his years as Defence Secretary for the Ford administration, Rumsfeld himself had made his name by his ability to turn big companies around. In a speech on Transformation in January 2002, Rumsfeld argued that, 'We must promote a more entrepreneurial approach to developing military capabilities, one that encourages people ... to be proactive and not reactive, to behave somewhat less like bureaucrats and more like venture capitalists'.[102]

With regard to military strategy, Rumsfeld rejected the central characteristic of Powell's own preferred way of war – the reliance on a margin of such overwhelming superiority that all risks were minimized – in favour of increased efficiency in the use of military resources. As Major-General Robert Scales put it, instead of overwhelming force, the Rumsfeld approach called for 'just enough force to strike at the enemy's brain.'[103] According to former Army Secretary Thomas White,

> Rumsfeld was always of the view that the military was excessive in its manpower demands and that they would always ask for three or four times more people than they really needed just to give them an enormous measure of assurance; ... his role in life, therefore, was to save them from themselves and to discipline the process by convincing them that they could do a lot more with a lot less.[104]

Precision provides one way of maximizing efficiency: in Rumsfeld's own words, 'Our use of precision weapons, with greater accuracy, can maintain lethality while reducing both the operational footprint and the logistics tail, thereby reducing force requirements'.[105] As we have seen, this ideal of achieving 'economies of force' was reflected in the planning for the Iraq War. However, it was exemplified even more clearly in the US strategy in the Afghan War. General Tommy Franks' initial planning for the attack on Afghanistan called for three Army divisions, perhaps in a devious attempt to *thwart* any deployment of a large US ground presence (for the resulting logistical requirements would have made any decisive action impractical for months). CENTCOM's improvised solution, from a narrowly military perspective, was admirably efficient: the innovative use of Special Forces permitted American air power to be effectively co-ordinated with the ground offensive of the Northern Alliance's 'fourth-world Army'. This dependence on Special Forces in the campaigns in Afghanistan and Iraq, in conjunction with an increasing reliance on unmanned aerial vehicles (UAVs), also point to two other dimensions of the Pentagon's preoccupation with efficiency: the super-empowerment of the individual, and the increasing automation of war.

The super-empowerment of the individual

According to Admiral Cebrowski, 'The ultimate attribute of the emerging American Way of War is the super-empowerment of the war fighter, whether on the ground, in the air, or at sea'.[106] DARPA Director Tony Tether elaborated one variant of this vision of super-empowered individuals in 2002:

> Think about our military commanders years from now. Envision them commanding warfighters who can then do things merely by thinking about them; who remain in action and effective for seven days and nights without sleep; who, if injured, can self-administer rapid-healing medications that enable them to stay in the fight, and who, if *seriously* injured, could be placed in temporary hibernation to prolong their lives until they can be evacuated to a hospital.[107]

Such futuristic visions aside, Network-Centric operations already seek to maximize not only the potential of each *weapon* through precision guidance, or even of each individual weapons platform, but also of each individual warrior through their integration into the network. 'Jointness' – the ability of the individual services to interact and thus support each other's capabilities – is a prerequisite, as only with the seamless integration of warriors and weapons into a 'system of systems' can the vision of Network-Centric Warfare be fully realized. As Dana Priest has noted, 'Just over three hundred men were pivotal in undoing the Taliban'.[108] In fact, the number of really critical individuals may have been even smaller: it was the Special Forces, and in particular the several dozen Combat Air Controllers, who called in the precision air strikes that devastated the Taliban, that provided the 'connection' Colin Powell celebrated between the 'fourth-world Army' of the Northern Alliance and the 'first-world air force' of the United States.

As US Army Chief of Staff Gordon Sullivan stated in 1994, the concept of Network-Centric Warfare envisages that battle command will be based on 'a near-perfect appreciation of the real situation', dependent on 'the electronic linking of every weapon system in the Battlespace'. There is thus an underlying vision of the entire military organization as 'one large synchronized machine, a massive large-scale technical system'.[109] Such an integrated system, of course, requires a high degree of machine-like precision in its guiding intelligence in order for it to sort through the chaos of the battlefield with the requisite speed and efficiency; and as Admiral Cebrowski has remarked, 'what we try to do is move the human mind to successively higher levels of thinking and of problem-solving, if you will, so as soon as you can relieve humanity of a lower-level decision-making process, you should do that'.[110] The super-empowerment of the individual is thus conceptually linked with the *automation* of military processes.

Imagining the future: the automation of war

For warfare to become truly immaculate, the element of human fallibility must be minimized or removed altogether. If warfare can be *automated* through the substitution of mechanical, electronic, or computerized processes for human judgement and labour, then those human frailties that lead to error and inefficiency, such as fear or fatigue, can be eliminated. As DARPA Director Tony Tether explained in his 2002 outline of DARPA's work, this does not necessarily entail removing the human element altogether: 'Ultimately, our vision is a more adept human warfighter who uses microelectronics to achieve machine-like precision.' DARPA's vision is focused not so much on developing autonomous machines, he claimed, as on *'blending the best traits of man and machine'*. In its plans for unmanned combat drones (now termed Joint Unmanned Combat Aerial Systems or J-UCAS), for example,

> There is always a person-in-the-loop to provide the timeless qualities of human judgement and insight to supervise the unmanned systems and manage the battle. Operators will be assisted by decision aids that allow them to focus on the operational art of war, leaving the implementation details to this synergistic blend of man and machine intelligence.[111]

During the second Bush–Kerry debate in the 2004 election campaign, President Bush argued that advances in American military technology meant that the US no longer required mass armies – 'some really interesting technologies', 'more effective weapons', and 'unmanned vehicles' could replace manpower.[112] This is already occurring. A particularly significant example occurred in November 2002, when an unmanned aerial drone destroyed a civilian vehicle containing six suspected *al Qaeda* members (including the alleged mastermind of the 2000 USS *Cole* bombing, Qaed Senyan al Harthi), as his convoy moved across the Yemeni desert. According to Lt.-General Michael DeLong (at the time Deputy Commander of CENTCOM), rather than requesting permission, CIA Director Tenet 'informed' Yemeni President Saleh of the impending operation.[113] The use of the Predator drone as a strike rather than reconnaissance tool was contemplated but never approved in the risk-averse 1990s.[114] Thus, the use of remotely piloted strike drones after 9/11 represented the antithesis of the 'massive footprint' demanded by the military for counter-terrorism operations in the 1990s.

Moreover, the Pentagon envisions that by 2010 the J-UCAS currently under development, the X-45, will be able to attack targets independently in designated 'kill boxes'. According to a statement by Colonel Michael Leahy, the programme's director in 2002, 'If the aircraft sees a target that matches its memory, it hits it and tells the humans about it later'.[115] Robotic vehicles not only offer the prospect of war without casualties; they also embody the very principle of *efficiency*. The Pentagon estimates that pilotless aircraft will cost less than half as much as piloted fighter jets like the F-15, largely because they lack humans. The human body requires food, sleep, training, and pay; pilots are prone to error and can only tolerate so much G-force; unmanned aircraft have the potential to be more dependable and, at least theoretically, to perform to higher standards in combat.[116] As Dr M. Franklin Rose, an electrical engineer working on unmanned ground vehicles for the Army, points out, robots can not only keep soldiers out of harm's way and do the most boring tasks, but they can 'keep going long after a soldier is exhausted. And they have no fear. ...'

The political appeal of such robotic warriors is clear. In the rationale of the president of SenTech, a company working on military robotics, 'We seem as a society, thank God, very averse to taking casualties. ... We'll continue putting as much effort as possible into keeping the humans in a safe location and do this dirty job remotely.'[117] In 2002, former Air Force Secretary James Roche also highlighted the possibility of eliminating risk to humans:

> The computer chip may very well be our most useful warfighting tool. Although it's never a good thing when we lose a Predator on the battlefield, I look forward to many more computer chips dying for their country.[118]

The X-45 will be used for the most dangerous tasks that currently put pilots at risk, such as the suppression of enemy air defences, a prerequisite for the establishment of US air superiority. Unmanned aerial vehicles like the Predator have already played an important role in the Afghan and Iraq campaigns (both for reconnaissance and, increasingly, air strikes), a fact reflected in massively increased funding: the Pentagon spent $3 billion on unmanned aerial vehicles between 1991 and 1999, but is expected to spend upward of $10 billion by 2010.[119] A Congressional mandate also calls for one-third of ground combat vehicles to operate unassisted by 2015. Given that the greatest constraints on the projection of American military force are the fear of casualties and the political risk associated with the large-scale deployment of troops, the implications for the political utility of force are clear.

Conclusion: the Pentagon's vision on the cusp of the Iraq War

The Bush administration did not invent the concept of a revolution in conventional warfare that would allow the United States to use force with unprecedented precision in support of American policy. Its vision of Immaculate Destruction had its roots in the final years of the Vietnam War, when advances in sensor technology and precision-guided weaponry first coalesced in the futuristic vision of the 'electronic battlefield', while enthusiasm for the so-called Revolution in Military Affairs had exercised an increasingly powerful hold over the American military imagination throughout the 1990s. Nevertheless, in the Clinton years the paradigm of Overwhelming Force acted as a countervailing influence, circumscribing the use of military force as an instrument of national policy. By marginalizing those military elites who subscribed to the latter philosophy of war in the aftermath of 9/11, the Bush administration sought to purge the military culture of the 'risk-averse' mentality that conflicted with its bold strategic vision.

In its emphasis on flexibility, efficiency, and unprecedented discrimination in the projection of military power, the vision of Immaculate Destruction seemed perfectly suited for the new strategic imperatives of the War on Terror. Moreover, the prospect of a new American way of war that could be fought without casualties or collateral damage, and without demanding any price from the average American citizen, promised to transcend the societal constraints that had traditionally circumscribed the American use of military force. Thus, underlying the decision to decapitate the regime of Saddam Hussein was a radical optimism about the political utility of force. However, the implementation of this vision soon encountered unforeseen obstacles. This lack of conformity between cultural conception and the reality of war in Afghanistan and Iraq is the subject of the next chapter.

5 The new American way of war
Vision and reality in Afghanistan and Iraq

> War is not an exercise of the will directed at inanimate matter, as is the case with the mechanical arts. ... In war, the will is directed at an animate object that reacts.
>
> Clausewitz[1]

> This Zionised American Administration ... came to Iraq. ... It thought that the matter would be somewhat easy. ... But it collided with a completely different reality. The operations of the brother Mujahidin began from the first moment.
>
> attributed to Abu Musab al Zarqawi, 2004[2]

In August 2002 the US military concluded 'Millennium Challenge 2002', a war game costing $250 million, designed to test the concepts of Transformation and Network-Centric Warfare championed by Donald Rumsfeld. The game attracted some controversy due to the decision of retired Marine Lt.-General Paul Van Riper, who commanded the game's Opposing (or Red) Force, to quit prematurely on the grounds that the game was scripted to ensure victory for the US (Blue) force. Before he quit, however, Van Riper's unconventional tactics created considerable difficulties for the US forces: for example, he used motorcycle messengers to transmit orders, negating Blue's high-tech eavesdropping capabilities. After broadcasting attack orders from the minarets of his country's mosques via the morning call to prayer, he launched a surprise attack that sank much of the Blue Navy with a fleet of suicide bombers in small speed boats. At this point the managers stopped the game, 'refloated' the Blue fleet, and resumed play. Van Riper later derided Blue command's central strategic concepts, such as 'effects-based operations' and 'rapid, decisive operations' as little more than slogans.[3] His memories of Vietnam shaped his critique of these concepts:

> I think they were fundamentally flawed in that they leaned heavily on technology. They leaned heavily on systems analysis of decision-making. ... What I saw in this particular exercise and the results from

it were very similar to what I saw as a young second lieutenant back in the 1960s, when we were taught the systems engineering techniques that Mr. McNamara had implemented in the American military. We took those systems, which had good if not great utility in the acquisition of weapon systems, to the battlefield, where they were totally inappropriate. The computers in Saigon said we were winning the war, while out there in the rice paddies we knew damn well we weren't. ... That's where we went astray, and I see these new concepts potentially being equally as ill-informed and equally dangerous.[4]

In creating unforeseen problems for the Blue force through his unorthodox tactics, Van Riper demonstrated that Clausewitz's concept of 'friction' was not something that could be 'transcended' by superior technology but an *inherent* dimension of warfare arising from its interactive nature.[5] Van Riper's concern that future forces would rely on these concepts although they had 'never been properly grounded in any sort of an experiment' proved prescient. For, in important respects, the Millennium Challenge episode, and Van Riper's critique of the technocratic approach to warfare that it 'tested', anticipated the course of the Iraq conflict. The Iraq War highlights a central paradox about American military culture: for it was the ultimate expression *both* of the desire to render war a precise instrument of policy, *and* of the continuing separation of political and military considerations within American strategy. While it is still too early to rule out the possibility that the Iraq intervention will ultimately result in the establishment of a stable post-Saddam regime, it is clear that the vision of Immaculate Destruction failed on its own terms. The regime was indeed decapitated with unparalleled efficiency, yet the transition to democracy that followed (the central political objective of the war) proved anything but immaculate. However, the difficulties encountered in Iraq have fostered a new period of introspection within the American military: the basic assumptions of US military culture are once again being reassessed. The very nature of the much-hyped concept of 'Military Transformation' has begun to be reconceptualized.

Regime decapitation

Immaculate Destruction as a political vision

At least during its first term, the Bush administration's basic assumptions about war were distinctive in their radical optimism with regard to the political utility of military force. This optimism extended both to the domestic and strategic dimensions of political utility: it was assumed both that military action could be made acceptable to the American public (for technology would make it humane), and that it could achieve its strategic objectives with little risk of events spiralling out of control (for technology would render the battlefield transparent and predictable). With regard to the latter dimension, a further assumption was central: that for the prosecution of grand strategy to be successful it was sufficient simply to destroy those entities, whether they be hostile regimes or terrorist networks, that threatened US security.

American military force was to be used proactively in the interests of national policy, but its proper use would not extend to the reconstruction or stabilization of other societies. Thus, despite the new recognition of the dangers posed by failing states, the lingering influence of the administration's pre-9/11 conviction that war should not be a form of international 'social work' could still be detected. During the 2000 presidential campaign, Bush declared that the United States might be the peace-*maker*, but America's European friends were more suited for the job of peace-*keeping*.[6] As Condoleezza Rice put it so scathingly on the campaign trail, 'We don't need to have the 82nd Airborne escorting kids to kindergarten'.

After 9/11, the administration appeared to perceive no contradiction between its pre-existing aversion to 'nation-building' and its new commitment to forceful 'democratic enlargement'. Perhaps because of its declared belief in historical teleology – a History moving inexorably towards Freedom – the administration appeared to believe that it was enough to remove impediments to democracy ('tyrants and terrorists'), and the 'democratic forces' unleashed would then do the rest on their own. This ideological combination also permitted the administration to deny the imperial logic of its agenda in good conscience: in Wolfowitz's words, 'It's back to the absurdity of saying we're trying to impose our ideas on other people when we want to help them become democracies. ... It's a funny empire that relies on *releasing basic human desires to be free* and prosperous and live in peace.'[7] After the war in Afghanistan, Bush invoked the memory of World War II: 'General Marshall knew our military victory had to be followed by a moral victory that resulted in better lives for individual human beings.' Yet any expectations raised by this remark were belied by the fact that, on the same day, Rumsfeld announced that the Pentagon did not envision using American troops as part of ISAF (the International Security Assistance Force).[8] A more accurate insight into the administration's true attitude was given by Rumsfeld's reply when asked during the Afghan War what responsibility the US would incur after the overthrow of the Taliban:

> I don't think it leaves us with a responsibility to try to figure out what kind of government that country ought to have. I don't know people who are smart enough from other countries to tell other countries the kind of arrangements they ought to have to govern themselves.[9]

Indeed, in a February 2003 speech entitled 'Beyond Nation-Building', Rumsfeld explicitly outlined his opposition to large-scale nation-building projects on the grounds that they created unnatural 'dependencies' in the countries concerned.[10] True to form, by August 2003, the *New York Times* calculated that Washington had spent $10 billion a year since the war on 'search-and-destroy' in Afghanistan, but less than $1 billion on reconstruction, although Congress had authorized more.[11] The military's role in post-Taliban Afghanistan was defined in *minimalist* terms: to manage the persistent risk that the country might degenerate once more into a terrorist haven. As even the administration's most noted moralist, Paul Wolfowitz, put it,

> I think the key to Afghanistan is not being seen as occupiers. And we managed to keep enough of a presence there that when there's a target that's important to us, we can go and hit it. ... Our goal has to be at a minimum to keep it from reverting to a country that harbours terrorists and, hopefully, get beyond that.[12]

The administration sought instead to outsource as much of the burdens of post-conflict stabilization as possible to others, whether they be allied powers, private military companies or local proxy forces. In this sense Immaculate Destruction as a strategic vision betrayed the continuing influence of the Vietnam Syndrome: the assumption was that the use of American military power could be confined to the destruction of adversaries without burdening the military with a broader range of messy civil and political tasks. In this sense the Pentagon hoped to have its cake and eat it: to reshape the international political environment forcibly without incurring responsibility for the political administration of defeated states. In Afghanistan, Secretary Rumsfeld and General Franks agreed on the imperative of avoiding the mistakes made by the Soviets and the British in previous Afghan conflicts. In Bob Woodward's phrase, the general rule was 'to do the opposite of the Soviets'.[13] Franks has explained that he 'wanted to avoid a cumbersome Soviet-style occupation by armoured divisions. It hadn't worked for the Soviets, and it wouldn't work for us.'[14] Describing Franks' decision to 'hire' the Northern Alliance as a 'bold act of genius', his deputy, General Michael DeLong, explained the calculus underlying General Franks' decision to offer the Northern Alliance warlords 'a stack of cash, a fortune's worth':

> The Afghans looked amazed. It was indeed a fortune. But from our perspective, it was still less than it would have cost to put even one US battalion on the ground. In that sense, it was a bargain – and more important, it would help keep thousands of US soldiers out of harm's way.[15]

It is perhaps unnecessary, in retrospect, to point out the disastrous consequences of elevating economy in the expenditure of American blood and treasure in the short-term over the long-term political stabilization of the country.

One additional factor behind the administration's reluctance to commit troops, of course, was the need to maintain strategic flexibility in the wider Global War on Terror. The apparent success of the minimalist approach in Afghanistan appears to have contributed to the assumption that a similar strategy could be employed in Iraq. In his remarks on 'Beyond Nation-Building' delivered before the Iraq War, Rumsfeld explicitly invoked the minimalist Afghan strategy as a model that would be followed if the US went to war against Iraq.[16] Iraq's more developed infrastructure and relative geopolitical importance demanded a more visible commitment to post-conflict reconstruction. Nevertheless, senior figures in the Defence Department appear to have believed that the transition to democracy would happen semi-automatically, with minimal demands on American manpower and resources.[17] Anticipating a permissive security environment and major troop contributions from allies for the occupation, the Pentagon reportedly planned to cut US forces in Iraq to no more than 70,000 and possibly as little as 30,000 troops within six months of the cessation of major combat operations.[18] In the recollection of Thomas White, then the secretary of the Army, the working budgetary assumption was that 90 days after completion of the operation, the first 50,000 troops would be withdrawn and then every 30 days another 50,000 would follow. Such a rapid withdrawal would be made possible by the precision of the attack. 'The concept,' Condoleezza Rice stated in an interview, 'was that we would defeat the Army, but the institutions would hold, everything from ministries to police forces.'[19] Franks' war plan reportedly predicted that large areas of Iraq would not require occupation by allied troops.[20] The campaign would be so immaculate that there would be *no need* for extensive post-conflict reconstruction or stability operations. Paul Wolfowitz also later admitted that the Pentagon had counted on large numbers of Iraqi military police quickly joining the nation-building effort. These assumptions were reinforced by the ideological conviction, particularly associated with influential neo-conservatives such as Wolfowitz and Richard Perle, that Iraqi support for the war would be overwhelming.[21] It was assumed, in short, that the decapitation of the regime would bring about an 'immaculate transition' to democracy.

Achieving systemic collapse: the strategy and tactics of Immaculate Destruction

In Russell Weigley's classic account of the American way of war, the distinctive American style at the *strategic* level of warfare was a preference for the annihilation of the enemy forces, as opposed to less direct means of achieving victory.[22] At the operational and tactical levels of warfare, as others have argued, the traditional American approach sought decision in battle through *attrition* as opposed to manoeuvre.[23] The strategic blueprint of Immaculate Destruction, conversely, rejects both of these preferences – for annihilation at the strategic level and attrition at the operational/tactical. In a briefing before the Iraq War, Colonel Gary L. Crowder (chief of Strategy, Concepts, and Doctrine in the Air Combat Command) explained the thinking behind the war plan. Central to his briefing was a *systemic* conception of the enemy: as a 'networked' force, the US military naturally conceived of the enemy as a network or system as well. At the core of American strategy, Crowder stated, was the notion of attacking the enemy 'as a system and ... trying to achieve systemic collapse'. In an extended metaphor, he presented the most efficient means of achieving victory as analogous to the technical process of disabling an electrical grid:

> if I neutralized electrical power by going after every [electrical power] station, it would take up all my assets. ... But the reality is, electrical power is in many ways a fairly fragile grid ... so you do not have to attack each element of that system to make the system not work. An effects-based approach might look at that system and say, 'If I looked and analyzed the enemy as a system ..., I might only need to have to take out two of those power plants.'[24]

In another technical metaphor inspired by serial and parallel electrical circuits, Crowder invoked the concept of 'parallel' as opposed to 'serial' attack. As one officer who was involved in planning the ground campaign for the Coalition Forces Land Component Command (CFLCC) has subsequently written, 'Theory was not a corollary to planning; it was a driving element ... theory is more than the stuff of academia. It was the conceptual source of virtually all of CFLCC's planning.'[25] He mentions Air Force Colonel John Warden as an important theoretical influence; indeed, all three of the strategic concepts mentioned above – systemic collapse, effects-based operations, and parallel attack – are derived from the work of Colonel Warden, the architect of the *Instant Thunder* air campaign in the first Gulf War.

Warden has argued that, 'contrary to Clausewitz', the essence of warfare lies not in the destruction of the enemy military but in compelling him to accept your will (in fact, this is a misconception: Clausewitz himself defined war precisely as 'an act of force to compel our enemy to do our will'[26]). Secondly, Warden suggested that the enemy should be conceived not as 'an independent mass of tanks, aircraft, or dope pushers' but as a *system*. It follows that the most efficient means of achieving victory is not the annihilation of the enemy armed forces, but the achievement of their 'systemic paralysis'. At the tactical and operational level, therefore, military actions should be judged not by the degree of attrition of the enemy forces but by their *effect* on the overall functioning of the enemy system. The simplest way of bringing about systemic paralysis is to 'do it very fast' through the concept of 'parallel attack', rather than attacking the enemy in a linear or 'serial' manner. Parallel attack aims to bring 'so many parts of the enemy system under near-simultaneous attack that the system simply cannot react to defend or to repair itself'. If a country is paralysed strategically, Warden concluded, it is defeated and cannot sustain its fielded forces *though they be fully intact*.[27]

Another important strategic concept invoked during the Iraq War was originally entitled Rapid Dominance, and latterly dubbed Rapid Decisive Operations.[28] Widely misunderstood in media reports due to its misleading nickname of 'Shock and Awe', Rapid Dominance also rejects a 'force on force' doctrine and attrition-based measures of success. It seeks instead to achieve such complete control of the battlefield that an enemy may be convinced or compelled 'to surrender or to accept our aims *short of imposing wide scale destruction*'.[29] It adds a psychological dimension to the technical focus of 'effects-based operations': the aim is to influence 'the thought processes and decision structures of the adversary ... in order to force, induce or convince the enemy to accept our terms and our will'. Far from relying on the threat of indiscriminate violence, the objective of 'Shock and Awe' in the Iraq campaign was, as General DeLong put it, to inspire 'shock' through *precision* and 'awe' through *reliability*, inducing a sense of hopelessness in the enemy that would bring about systemic paralysis.[30] With its mechanistic assumption that psychological reactions can be induced through the precise calibration of force, this theory is reminiscent of the 'limited war' theories tested in Vietnam.

Operation Enduring Freedom began with a textbook example of an attempt at strategic paralysis, with air strikes on the Afghan command-and-control system aimed at paralyzing Taliban forces. Unfortunately, Afghanistan did not have much of a command-and-control system to disrupt. It was a case, in George Friedman's phrase, of 'doctrine driving operations'.[31] Although the co-author of 'Shock and Awe' tried to distance himself from the Bush administration's invocation of 'Shock and Awe' during Operation Iraqi Freedom (on the grounds that it was not sufficiently 'shocking'[32]), the campaign was also conducted according to the strategic principles of Rapid Dominance and Effects-Based Operations. It began with an unsuccessful attempt to decapitate the Iraqi regime by striking Saddam Hussein himself at Dora Farms,[33] an attempt faithful to Warden's precept that, 'The obvious place to induce strategic system paralysis is at the leadership, or brain, level'.[34]

The effects that the US tried to create in the campaign that followed, Colonel Crowder explained, aimed 'to make it so apparent and so overwhelming *at the very outset* of potential military operations that the adversary *quickly* realizes that there is no real alternative here other than to fight and die or to give up'.[35] In designing his war plan, General Franks identified a list of 'slices' – pressure points which would prevent the regime from functioning.[36] Rather than relying on tactical attrition throughout the theatre of operations as employed during the 38-day air campaign of the 1991 Gulf War, the coalition focused on targeting these 'slices' – narrowly defined leadership targets, command and control systems, and the Republican Guard – without attacking population centres, civilian infrastructure, industry, or lines of communication.[37] So confident was Franks in his ability to surgically decapitate the regime, he decided not to target Iraq's electrical grid with a view to preserving it pristine and intact for the post-war phase.

This war plan deliberately rejected the Overwhelming Force paradigm: when General Franks presented his war plan to Colin Powell, the Secretary of State questioned the friendly-to-enemy force ratios, and 'made the point rather forcefully that the Coalition would have "extremely long" supply lines'. In response, Franks recounts, he explained the concept of parallel attack to Powell: by applying military mass simultaneously at key points through rapid manoeuvre, rather than trying to push a broad, slow conventional advance, the enemy would be thrown off balance.[38] In the twenty-first century, in a phrase of Rumsfeld's that encapsulated the new thinking, 'overwhelming force' was considered less important than 'overmatching power'.[39] Deputy Secretary Wolfowitz even suggested at one point an even more minimal use of American force: in his so-called enclave strategy (which Powell regarded as 'absurd'), the military would have established a foothold by seizing Iraq's southern oilfields, from which support would be given to the anti-Saddam opposition to overthrow the regime. This incident was strikingly reminiscent of a similar episode in the first Gulf War, when Wolfowitz had overseen 'Operation Scorpion', a plan to force Saddam Hussein to withdraw his forces from Kuwait by establishing a base in Iraq's Western desert, as little as sixty miles from Baghdad. Like the enclave strategy, Operation Scorpion had been dismissed as far too risky at the time by the military's orthodox planners.[40]

Despite the rejection of Wolfowitz's enclave strategy, Rumsfeld's war plan still relied on a far more minimal use of American force than that called for in the Joint Staff's traditional approach to war planning, the Time-Phased Forces Deployment List, which would have called for more support forces and in particular stronger forces to secure the rear areas and flanks of the main land advance. 'To its supporters,' James Fallows has written, 'this approach is old-school in the best sense: if you fight, you really fight. To its detractors, this approach is simply old – ponderous, inefficient, and, although they don't dare call it cowardly, risk-averse at the least.'[41] In a briefing after the war, JCS Chairman Myers explained that the campaign had been focused on the regime, and *not* the annihilation of the enemy Army.[42] Indeed, the ground campaign did not aim at seizing territory but simply at controlling it, relying on rapid manoeuvre to deliberately bypass enemy formations, fixing them in place, in a dash for the regime's 'centre of gravity' in Baghdad.[43] Rejecting the 'bully's way of war', the Pentagon sought to decapitate the Iraqi regime with the clinical efficiency of the surgeon.

Friction: American expectations and the realities of war

In his autobiography, General Tommy Franks enthusiastically welcomed the ability of the revolution in sensor technology to pierce the fog of war, giving 'today's commanders the kind of Olympian perspective that Homer had given his gods'.[44] Yet Franks' Olympian perspective did not help him foresee the political chaos and continued resistance that would follow the fall of Baghdad. As initial elation was gradually replaced by concern over the post-conflict power vacuum and the increasingly vicious insurgency, such remarks began to smack of hubris. In Afghanistan, Operation Enduring Freedom's perfection was marred by the escape of Osama bin Laden and much of the *al Qaeda* leadership from Tora Bora in December 2001 and, later, by the gradual resurgence of the Taliban. The Tora Bora episode suggested that the decision to rely almost entirely on Northern Alliance forces in lieu of American ground forces was not such a 'bold act of genius', in General DeLong's phrase, after all. Admittedly, there were logistical difficulties which made it difficult to commit large numbers of troops to Afghanistan, since no neighbouring country except Pakistan would have been a viable staging base – and Pakistan was not willing to play that role. Nevertheless, the 10th Mountain Division forces deployed at Bagram Airport and in Uzbekistan, and two Marine Corps units with more than 1,000 personnel were available in December 2001. One analyst has asserted that the CIA argued at the time that General Franks should commit these forces to Tora Bora, on the grounds (subsequently vindicated by events) that its Afghan proxy forces were unreliable.[45]

There were also elements of unforeseen resistance during Operation Iraqi Freedom. One source of friction arose from malfunctioning technology – indeed, a largely classified report by the RAND Corporation that summarized its results to *Technology Review* concluded that, at the front-line, US ground forces were victorious because of their superior weapons, greater firepower, and air support, but not because they had any real insight into enemy positions through new technology. Numerous problems prevented effective relaying of crucial data, including lengthy download times, software failures, and lack of access to high-band-width communications.[46] Technical solutions, of course, can be found to technological problems. The more intractable source of friction arose from cultural factors: the enemy's refusal to conform to American expectations or fight on American terms.

However, there is some evidence that the Iraqi insurgency was planned by regime elements *before* the 'conventional' phase of the conflict. According to the Iraq Survey Group's final report on Iraqi WMD, Saddam Hussein instructed top Iraqi ministers on the eve of the US invasion to 'resist one week, and after that I will take over'; it appears that what he had in mind was 'some form of insurgency against the coalition'.[47] US intelligence agencies have reported that the broad outlines of a guerrilla campaign were set down before the war by the Iraqi Intelligence Service; between August 2002 and January 2003, Army leaders at bases throughout Iraq were ordered to move and hide weapons and other military equipment at off-base locations, including farms and homes. According to press reports, a branch of the Iraqi Intelligence Service known as M14, the directorate for special operations, may also have overseen a highly secretive enterprise under which Iraqi intelligence officers scattered as US-led forces approached Baghdad, to lead the guerrilla insurgency and plan bombings and other attacks.[48] Saddam's decision to release 100,000 criminals from Iraqi prisons several months before the invasion also suggests that he was already thinking in terms of maximizing chaos in a post-invasion scenario. However, the evidence suggesting a pre-planned insurgency is far from conclusive, and it is equally possible that Saddam's intention in hiding weapons stockpiles around the country was to create islands of regime loyalists that could *suppress* any insurgency that rose up in support of the invasion.[49]

Yet evidence of a consciously planned 'asymmetrical' strategy on the part of insurgents soon became undeniable after President Bush announced the cessation of major combat operations on 1 May 2003. In contrast to the US concern to wage war humanely, the insurgents also reminded their adversaries that war is an interactive process by displaying a determination to make the conflict as *inhumane* as possible. To this end they deliberately targeted international and humanitarian organizations such as the UN and the Red Cross and any foreign embassies whose presence was intended to demonstrate solidarity with the Coalition. After persistently suffering heavy losses in attacks on US forces, the insurgents shifted their focus to targeting those Iraqi civilians willing to collaborate with the occupying forces, nascent Iraqi security organizations, and Shiite religious and political figures (in an effort to incite civil war). Such asymmetric tactics were very effective in hindering attempts at reconstruction, humanitarian assistance, the imposition of public order, and the multilateralization of the occupation that was essential to its legitimacy. The exploitation of horrific violence through suicide bombing attacks and the filming of hostages being beheaded, both apparently pioneered by foreign *jihadis* under the leadership of Abu Musab al Zarqawi, were deliberately intended for the consumption of the international media, in an effort to further erode the already lukewarm support of international public opinion for the occupation.

The technical bias of Immaculate Destruction

The central question raised by the aftermath of regime change in Iraq is *why* the US failed to predict either that the political vacuum might contribute to chaos, or that some Iraqis might continue to resist occupation by US forces after the collapse of conventional resistance. Both this poverty of strategic expectation, and the nature of the friction encountered in Iraq, flowed from the basic assumptions of the prevailing military discourse itself. One source of the poverty of expectation was the epistemological bias of the military culture. The concept of information dominance is central to the discourse of Immaculate Destruction: it is the prerequisite for both 'predictability' and 'efficiency' in achieving the enemy's systemic paralysis. Yet what is rarely discussed is the *type* of information that is prioritized or sought. The information technologies of the RMA can vastly increase a commander's information about enemy capabilities. Yet their limits are just as important: as John A. Gentry has warned,

> Technology has little applicability to political and many military situations for elementary reasons. Sensors track physical things and activities that have electromagnetic and other signatures. Sensors cannot identify human motives, measure human emotions, quantify the coherence of human organizations, or assess the importance of the data they gather. [50]

The RMA enthusiasts are fond of quoting Sun Tzu and in particular his statements about 'knowing your enemy';[51] yet his emphasis was on human intelligence (spies) and the psychological dimension of warfare. The technological rationality that currently dominates US military culture, conversely, betrays the same bias towards precisely quantifiable technical intelligence about enemy capabilities, over the more subjective understanding of enemy intentions, that characterized the 'science' of strategy in the Cold War. Just as the 1957 Gaither report concluded that what was important was not what the Soviets *might* do, but what they *could* do, the concept of 'capabilities-based planning' articulated in the 2001 QDR prioritized not a sophisticated political and cultural understanding of the *intentions* of America's current adversaries – the members of the 'Axis of Evil', for example – but a technocratic focus on the *capabilities* that they could acquire in the future. The burden of the 'precautionary principle' enshrined in the 2002 National Security Strategy was to suggest that the risks posed by WMD proliferation to rogue states or terrorists are so great that a subjective judgement about enemy intentions is too hazy a basis on which to base action; the only prudent course is 'to confront the worst threats before they emerge' – to deny potential enemies the acquisition of dangerous capabilities that they *might* acquire and *might* use in the future.

In the case of Iraq, the absence of reliable human intelligence assets able to penetrate Saddam Hussein's regime meant that despite all the US's high-tech monitoring, US intelligence still vastly overestimated Iraqi WMD capabilities. As the former head of the Iraq Survey Group, David Kay, candidly acknowledged, 'We were almost all wrong – and I certainly include myself here'.[52] At the root of this failure, according to his ISG successor Charles Duelfer, were unsophisticated assumptions about Iraqi *intentions*:

> Like the operating system of our computers, we have logic and assumptions that are virtually built in. ... When considering the very

different system that existed under the government of Saddam Hussein, there is a risk of not seeing the meaning and not seeing the implications of the evidence.[53]

This failure of human intelligence also had severe ramifications in the aftermath of the war: to quote one retired Navy captain, 'The huge investment in computer networks, drone aircraft, and the other high-tech gadgetry failed to provide situational awareness about the only thing that counted – which Iraqis favoured and which opposed the occupation'.[54] The tendency to derive policy and measures of success and failure from precisely quantifiable data rather than a sophisticated political and cultural analysis is also a broader feature of the Global War on Terror. In a leaked memo of October 2003, Rumsfeld noted that, 'Today we lack metrics to know if we are winning or losing the global war on terror. Are we capturing, killing or deterring and dissuading more terrorists every day than the madrassas and the radical clerics are recruiting, training and deploying against us?'[55] Reminiscent of McNamara's emphasis on body-counts during the Vietnam War, such language suggests a conception of the conflict as a war of attrition rather than a broader political and ideological struggle.

Catastrophic success: the failure of Shock and Awe

It is both tragic and paradoxical that the viciousness of the insurgency may have been *exacerbated* by the 'immaculate' nature of the US victory in the phase of major combat operations. Condoleezza Rice has put the blame for the insurgency primarily on the fact that many Iraqi forces fled during the US push to Baghdad, only to fight another day.[56] President Bush has also remarked that, 'Had we to do it over again, we would look at the consequences of *catastrophic success* – being so successful, so fast, that an enemy that should have surrendered or been done in, escaped and lived to fight another day'.[57] Yet this 'catastrophic success' was a direct result of the US pursuit of Immaculate Destruction – which aimed at achieving rapid 'systemic collapse' with minimal attrition of enemy forces and infrastructure – in favour of the traditional American strategy of 'annihilation'. As JCS Chairman General Myers told the Senate Armed Services Committee in June 2004,

> you could have gone several different ways, but we made the decision and we wanted this to be as humane as a combat operation – as war – can be. ... And so certain factors are emphasized over others if you're going to do that, and one of them was speed and precision and to let regular Iraqi divisions, while destroying equipment and some of their people, if they melted away then let them melt away because they were conscripts, after all. So if there's blame here it was making some assumptions on how the Iraqi people would react to that, and I would submit we were probably *too gracious in our victory* in hindsight.[58]

The emphasis on minimizing the number of US troops required to achieve systemic paralysis had particularly severe consequences in the war's aftermath. L. Paul Bremer (the Presidential Envoy to Iraq) remarked in October 2004 that the US did not have enough troops on the ground to prevent looting in Baghdad when he arrived in May 2003, which created an 'atmosphere of lawlessness', conditions in which the insurgency could flourish.[59] General Jay Garner, who preceded Bremer as the US 'proconsul' in Iraq, also admitted that the US did not have enough troops to seal the borders and thus was unable to prevent an influx of foreign insurgents.[60] Despite Rumsfeld's repeated statements that American troop levels were sufficient to defeat the insurgency, there were clear indications that they were not: immediately after the siege of Fallujah in November 2004, to take just one example, a Stryker brigade had to be dispatched north to Mosul to quell a fresh outbreak of violence despite the fact that it was still required to maintain the cordon around Fallujah.[61] Indeed, matching the troop levels relative to the Iraqi population that the British maintained to police the insurgencies in Malaysia and Northern Ireland (20 per 1,000) would have required 480,000 troops, which was the total authorized strength of the active US Army;[62] clearly, without a significant expansion of the all-volunteer force, a return to the draft, or large numbers of allied troops, Rumsfeld seems to have concluded that he had little choice but to deny the problem existed.[63]

James Dobbins has put the nature of the US victory into historical perspective by recalling the circumstances of Japan's defeat in World War II:

> Years of total war had wrought devastation, including the firebombing of Japanese cities and, finally, two nuclear attacks. As a result, the surviving population was weary of conflict and disinclined to contest defeat. When conflicts have ended less conclusively and destructively, or not terminated at all ... the post-conflict security challenges are more difficult. *Indeed, it seems that the more swift and bloodless the military victory, the more difficult post-conflict stabilization can be.*[64]

Harlan Ullman, the co-author of *Shock and Awe*, has protested that the Bush administration did not apply *enough* 'Shock and Awe'; but the concept's mechanistic assumption that the enemy's psychology may be manipulated through the precise calibration of violence may be flawed in a more fundamental sense. Many of the regime's security and intelligence officers who organized the insurgency may simply have concluded that they were so bound up with the regime that they had no future in a post-Saddam Iraq, and thus nothing to lose by continued resistance. To paraphrase General DeLong, the hardcore Ba'athist resistance may have been 'shocked by the precision' of US weaponry and 'awed by its reliability', but this was no substitute for the physical destruction of the Iraqi forces. Equally, as Admiral Cebrowski himself acknowledged, the psychological effect of

America's 'immaculate' victory may have been less awe-inspiring than the overwhelming force that characterized US victories in the past:

> I think we are confronted now with a new problem, in a way the kind of problem we always wanted to have, where you can achieve your initial military ends without the wholesale slaughter. ... So we're moving in the more moral direction, which is appropriate. Now we're confronted with the problem ... that, in traditional terms, *a person feels less defeated than he was before*.[65]

The separation of politics and strategy

The Bush administration's optimism with regard to the political utility of force derived from the conceit that the US could achieve complete technical control of the battlefield. The assumption that technical mastery would equal political utility, however, was not subjected to critical reflection on how military victory could be translated into political success. On the contrary, as one military historian has recently suggested, American military culture's preoccupation with the operational dimension of war since Vietnam may be regarded as 'a covert way of reintroducing the split between politics and strategy'.[66] In Afghanistan, the separation of politics and strategy was apparent in the Defence Department's unwillingness to devote significant resources to ensuring long-term political stability, at least relative to the resources devoted to hunting down Taliban and *al Qaeda* remnants.

In Iraq, the separation of political and military considerations was apparent even before the invasion. White House Chief of Staff Andrew Card told Bob Woodward that, during the prelude to the war in Iraq, he thought of the President as a circus-horse rider, with one foot on a 'diplomacy' steed and the other on a 'war' steed, struggling to steer both simultaneously in the direction of 'regime change'. Eventually, Bush had to let go of the 'diplomacy' horse.[67] Yet, if political and military considerations had been properly integrated from the outset, there would only have been one hybrid steed of 'coercive diplomacy'.

Most serious was the neglect of the transition from the conflict to the 'post-conflict' phase, and the failure to anticipate any sort of prolonged resistance after the fall of Baghdad. In his autobiography, General Franks relates how, having sketched a matrix plotting the regime's 'centres of gravity' against forms of US pressure that could be brought to bear on them, he remarked to a colleague, 'This is what you call your basic *grand strategy*'.[68] Of course, as Andrew Bacevich pointed out in his review of the book, it was nothing of the sort: the objective underlying Franks' war planning process was the narrowly *technical* one of achieving the 'systemic paralysis' of Iraqi forces, rather than the broader political goal of facilitating the smoothest possible transition to a post-Saddam regime. Indeed, Bacevich concluded,

'For Franks, war is a matter of engineering – and generalship the business of organizing and coordinating materiel'.[69] Convinced that Saddam Hussein's regime could be surgically decapitated without large-scale damage to Iraqi infrastructure or civil society, the Pentagon leadership simply assumed that a smooth transition to democracy would follow. Such optimism was not warranted on the basis of any familiarity with Iraqi political history.

This separation of political and military considerations was institutionalized in the lack of co-ordination between the Departments of State and Defence. By the end of 2003 the Army War College had assembled a report analysing likely post-conflict scenarios which foresaw much of the chaos that might follow the war and stressed that detailed post-conflict planning had to begin as soon as possible. Much of this planning had in fact already occurred in the form of the State Department's 'Future of Iraq' project set up in the spring of 2002. Regardless of how effective the project's proposed remedies would have been, it at least anticipated how disorderly Iraq would be in the aftermath of regime change, foreseeing both the power vacuum and the looting that would accompany it. It recognized that, in the short term, the occupying forces would therefore have to be prepared to impose order.[70] After the Department of Defence requested and was granted authority for planning and implementing post-conflict stabilization in early 2003, none of the senior American officials involved in the Future of Iraq Project were adopted by the Pentagon. General Garner, who headed the Office of Reconstruction and Humanitarian Assistance (ORHA), has stated that he was instructed by Rumsfeld to ignore it.[71]

While he acknowledged that the Pentagon had made errors, Paul Wolfowitz argued in his own defence that, 'it was difficult to imagine before the war that the criminal gangs of sadists and gangsters who have run Iraq for thirty-five years would continue fighting'.[72] But, on the contrary, this was not difficult to imagine at all; given the identification of Ba'athist security forces with the old regime and their bleak prospects in a post-Saddam Iraq, it was obvious that they would have very little to lose by continued resistance, despite any psychological impact of 'Shock and Awe'. Indeed, in one respected think-tank's pre-war assessment of the prospects of regime change, two scholarly specialists on Iraq predicted future resistance with a high degree of accuracy. 'Despite a probable euphoric mood among the Iraqis sparked by being rid of Saddam's tyranny,' wrote one, 'an Islamic militia supported by its ex-enemies, the nationalist remnants of the Ba'ath, could play on an apprehensive mood to wage a "war of liberation" against the imperialist infidels.'[73] Similarly, another contributor foresaw that

> a massive release [of Iraqi soldiers] from military service is fraught with dangers. These are people who know each other, have combat skills, understand discipline, have experienced commanders and share the same provenance. Last but not least, they will have hidden weapons and ammunition caches. If not stopped right away, they will almost

certainly become either a political underground organisation that will topple the regime the moment foreign armies leave, or a formidable mafia organisation, or both. Even before the foreign armies leave, they could become an underground ... organisation that could assassinate US and British soldiers and officers in Iraq.[74]

However, such considerations based on familiarity with the complexities of Iraqi politics, history, and culture were largely ignored by a military discourse that conceived of war in terms of the technical mastery of the battlefield. During the war-planning process, conceptualizations of the enemy as a *technical system* vulnerable to disruption were emphasized over the analysis of political and cultural factors that might contribute to continued resistance. Inspired by technical metaphors, the strategic concept of 'systemic collapse' was largely devoid of political content. Thus, while the preeminent concern of the vision of Immaculate Destruction was to restore the political utility of force, its technical bias rendered it politically autistic. Like the pre-Vietnam science of strategy, in neglecting those subjective political factors that resisted subordination to technical rationality, it only partially accepted that war is a true continuation of politics. Rumsfeld had begun to conceptualize war, as one senior Army officer put it, 'outside its political and human dimensions'. In a remark that summarized the administration's approach, another senior official in the ORHA later recalled, 'We did what suited us ... *on the assumption that the Iraqis would be passive*. Not only passive, but gratefully, happily passive.'[75]

Feedback: counter-insurgency and the evolution of American military culture

The US military's initial reactions to the friction encountered in Afghanistan and Iraq (in the form of political instability and persistent guerrilla resistance) were improvised responses to forms of resistance that refused to conform to American expectations. Nevertheless, as the struggle evolved, there were clear signs that the military were willing to reconsider some of their basic assumptions and doctrinal tenets. In response to forms of political instability that could neither be smashed into submission nor fixed by technical means, the US military were forced to accept more and more responsibility for imposing a political settlement on post-Saddam Iraq. The military historian John Lynn terms this process by which a military culture re-evaluates its cultural preconceptions in the harsh light of military experience 'feedback'.[76]

Initial reactions: the aversion to constabulary duties in Iraq

The reluctance to think systematically about the requirements of post-conflict stabilization and counter-insurgency was a distinctive characteristic of *both* of the competing discourses in American military culture. Proponents of the Overwhelming Force philosophy sought to restrict American political objectives to those that could be neatly achieved through the use of military force, which militated against participation in messy nation-building projects or constabulary duties where the boundary between military and political functions became inherently blurred. Visionaries of Immaculate Destruction were far more optimistic about the political utility of force, but rarely addressed the subject of how the technical mastery of the battlefield could be translated into political success. Although the concept of the 'electronic battlefield' originated as a technical solution to problems of counterinsurgency in Vietnam, the limits of the so-called Revolution in Military Affairs quickly became apparent in a conflict in which the major difficulty was distinguishing insurgents from the sea of civilians in which they swam. However transparent the battlefield had become against conventional Iraqi forces, the 'fog of war' quickly settled over the post-conflict phase.

The military culture's post-Vietnam aversion to low-intensity conflict thus left it ill-prepared for the demands of occupying Iraq. Timothy Carney, a former Ambassador who served in the ORHA immediately after Operation Iraqi Freedom, has noted that 'no lessons seem to have taken hold from the recent nation-building efforts in Bosnia or Kosovo, so we in ORHA felt as though we were reinventing the wheel'.[77] Indeed, the Army was preparing to close its Peacekeeping Institute at the Army War College until events in Afghanistan and Iraq forced it to reconsider.[78] A Joint Staff report on 'Operation Iraqi Freedom Strategic Lessons Learned' produced in August 2003 reportedly found that the US military and government viewed combat and stability operations as sequential efforts, and had not addressed stability requirements as an integrated part of combat operations planning.[79] Former Army Secretary Thomas White has explained that, 'There was kind of this mind-set ... that the post-war deal is kind of a lower form of life; it's kind of a necessary evil'.[80]

The lesser prestige in which 'operations other than war' are held within the Army was reflected in the fact that, as one officer involved in the planning for Phase IV (post-conflict stabilization) told journalist James Fallows, 'All the A-Team guys wanted to be in on Phase III (major combat operations), and the B-team guys were put on Phase IV'.[81] In response to demands from Iraqis that the United States restore order, CENTCOM spokesman Brigadier General Vincent Brooks said the military would help rebuild the civil administration but expected the Iraqis to restore public order. 'At no time,' he stated, 'do we see [the US military] becoming a police force.' In fact, Rumsfeld reportedly refused a request to send in several thousand more military policemen as it would have necessitated a further mobilization of reserves.[82] Larry Hollingworth, a former British colonel and relief specialist who briefly served with ORHA, also noted that the rigid force-protection rules were anything but appropriate to the ORHA's work: 'At the US military's insistence, we travelled out from our fortified headquarters in Saddam's old Republican Palace in armoured vehicles, wearing helmets and flak jackets, trying to convince Iraqis that peace was at hand, and that they were safe. It was ridiculous.'[83]

Christopher Varhola, a cultural anthropologist and a major in the US Army Reserve specializing in Civil Affairs, noted after his return from Iraq that US military organization was not geared towards co-ordinated civil-military operations. Civil Affairs units were 'divided piecemeal among the combat units' and their actions were 'not synchronized in a nation-wide setting'. Structurally, this subordinated Civil-Military Operations to ground combat operations. Targeting insurgents took precedence over working with the Iraqi people.[84] US units had far too few Arabic speakers and experts on Iraqi religious and cultural practices, rendering them ill-prepared to win the trust of the population.[85] As one senior CPA official explained, 'Some of these commanders have paid close attention to the lessons learned over the years [about countering insurgency] and are applying them in theatre but it is not division or battalion wide. It often is up to the individual commanders.'[86] In short, despite the lessons from more than a decade of post-conflict stability operations, post-conflict stability had still not been accepted as a core mission of the US military.[87] It conflicted with the 'warrior ethos' that was so central to the military's self-image.

First attempts at counter-insurgency: 'using a sledgehammer to crush a walnut'

Classic counter-insurgency doctrine seeks to establish a political settlement by marginalizing insurgents and winning over the wider population. In military terms, it focuses on *population control*: hindering the insurgents' access to the wider population (or of the 'fish' to the 'sea', in Chairman Mao's famous phrase) by diffusing light infantry through the main population centres in order to hold and secure territory.[88] This puts a premium on the acceptance of risk to patrolling troops, the deliberate limitation of force, and sensitivity to the political and cultural dimension of war. In counter-insurgency the most seemingly isolated tactical act – damaging a mosque, for example – may have far-reaching political consequences if it offends the cultural sensibilities of the local population. American military culture is maladapted to these requirements. For example, the over-riding emphasis on force protection, reflecting the military's conviction that American support will collapse in the face of heavy casualties, has hindered the military's ability to engage with the Iraqi population. Michael Codner of the Royal United Services Institute has contrasted this with the British approach: American commanders, he noted, are not at liberty to put their troops at risk even if the pay-off in winning hearts and minds would be substantial. The British experience in Northern Ireland and in withdrawing from empire, conversely, gave them extensive experience in reassuring a civilian community: 'They have learned that there is a fine balance between reassurance and coercion, and between force protection on the one hand and positive communication through human behaviour on the other.'[89]

The distinction in counter-insurgency doctrine could also be seen in the allies' contrasting approaches to the use of force. In 2004, the British defended compounds in Basra and Amara against heavy assaults from Moqtada al-Sadr's 'al-Mahdi Army'. Yet the British mounted no major counter-strikes, on the grounds that such 'search-and-destroy' missions would be counter-productive – the insurgents would simply disappear back into the population and pursuing them was less important than sparing neighbouring localities and limiting civilian casualties. American forces, conversely, drove al-Sadr's forces from Najaf's golden shrine with overwhelming force – tank-fire, laser-guided bombs, and armoured assaults that left much of Najaf's old city in ruins.[90] With their greater emphasis on force protection and cultural aversion to acting as a constabulary force, the American military rejected the British emphasis on 'pacification' in favour of 'search-and-destroy' tactics that more closely resembled those employed by the Israeli Defence Forces (IDF) against Palestinian terrorists.

Indeed, in late 2003, IDF specialists were reportedly engaged in the training of US units in counter-insurgency tactics at the US Special Forces base at Fort Bragg. This was followed by a series of meetings held in Israel involving a US team headed by the commander of the US Army's training and doctrine command, General Kevin Byrnes.[91] It was also reported in September 2003 that the US had asked the Israeli Army to translate its special educational software program that teaches soldiers how to behave in occupied territories, so that US forces could apply it in Iraq.[92] The US adopted a style of counter-insurgency that eschewed 'population control' in favour of a reliance on heavy firepower and precision air strikes on suspected insurgent bases and weapons caches. For example, in late 2003 suspected guerrilla positions near Tikrit were attacked with AC-130 gunships, A-10 attack planes, and Apache helicopter gunships, as well as Air Force F-16 and F-15E fighter-bombers with 500-pound bombs. The American general responsible for these tactics characterized the approach as 'using a sledgehammer to smash a walnut'.[93] During the siege of Fallujah in November 2004, US forces relied heavily on artillery: to minimize danger to ground troops, batteries, air strikes, and mortar fire struck suspected insurgent targets before the infantry went in.[94] Whatever this achieved in denying insurgents a base of activities, it also flattened much of the city and alienated 300,000 Sunnis who were driven from their homes.

The evolution of US counter-insurgency strategy

The first signs of a counter-insurgency strategy that transcended narrowly military and technical approaches appeared in Afghanistan in late 2002, when the Pentagon responded to the deterioration in the security situation by shifting the focus of US operations towards greater involvement in civil affairs and reconstruction. Although they would not perform police functions, sixty-member 'Provincial Reconstruction Teams' were deployed near major cities throughout the country to provide assistance in rebuilding local infrastructure and ensuring local security.[95] By early 2004, under the direction of Lt.-General David W. Barno, the shift from 'search-and-destroy' tactics to 'population control' became explicit. In the past, he stated, American forces typically gathered intelligence about hostile forces, carried out focused raids for several days against those targets, then returned to base to plan and prepare for their next mission. He announced that the new approach, conversely, was to move 'to a more classic counter-insurgency strategy' in Afghanistan. Large, long-range infantry sweeps would give way to more dispersed missions by smaller units with 'ownership' of the districts surrounding their bases. The objective was to give soldiers 'great depth of knowledge, understanding, and much better intelligence access to the local people in those areas by owning, as it were, those chunks of territory'. The overall aim, moreover, was to replace 'the narrow counter terrorist role that we may have started in when initial operations began' with the role of assisting 'the ongoing political, economic, and in some ways even social, development of the country'.[96]

In Iraq, the early signs of a similar re-orientation could be identified in February 2004, when the first Marine Division announced the resurrection of the counter-insurgency strategy the corps had adopted in Vietnam – the 'Combined Action Programme', or CAP. By giving select units intensive language and cultural training to live in Sunni villages alongside members of the nascent Iraqi Civil Defence Corps, the Marines hoped to build trust among the locals that might glean critical intelligence about the insurgency. Adopting a more 'British' approach, 1st Marine Division commander Major-General James Mattis ordered Marines to patrol mostly on foot in Sunni cities instead of in armoured vehicles, and to restrict use of artillery or other 'indirect fire' that might result in civilian casualties.[97] By June 2004, senior US commanders announced a major shift from offensive combat operations to protecting the new Iraqi government and parts of the economy while building up Iraq's own security forces.[98] The November 2004 fight to gain control of Fallujah, while characterized by the use of artillery and massive firepower on the US side, nevertheless reflected the reversal of the April 2004 decision – to cede control of Fallujah to an Iraqi general – in favour of a new resolve to deny insurgents a base of operations. The operations which followed extended the same strategy to other centres of insurgent activity in the Sunni Triangle.

In a more explicit acknowledgement of the need to institutionalize classic principles of counter-insurgency in Army culture, in November 2004 the Army issued its first field guide for decades focusing explicitly on unconventional warfare. As General William Wallace acknowledged, counter-insurgency 'hadn't been looked at since the post-Vietnam era'. The new manual was developed in close consultation with the Marine Corps and the British military. In a classic statement of the principles of population control and the need to integrate political and civil concerns with narrowly military operations, Lt.-Colonel Jan Horvath, who led the development of the Manual, explained that, 'Our military's role is to secure the populace from insurgent violence and intimidation, therefore, influence. In securing the people, we must separate them from the insurgents. We do this by patrolling everywhere, talking with the people, and earning a modicum of trust.'[99]

One passage of the Manual particularly illustrated how the emphasis on overwhelming force was being reconsidered:

> The American way of war has been to substitute firepower for manpower. As a result, US forces have frequently resorted to firepower in the form of artillery or air any time they make contact. This creates two negatives in a counter-insurgency. First, massive firepower causes collateral damage, thereby frequently driving the locals into the arms of the insurgents. Second, it allows insurgents to break contact after having inflicted casualties on friendly forces.[100]

However, the most heavily publicized shift from a search-and-destroy strategy to an approach based on population control was announced at the end of November 2005. The 'National Strategy for Victory in Iraq', published by the White House, described a threefold military approach:

1. Help the Iraqi Security Forces and the Iraqi government take territory out of enemy control – 'clear';
2. Keep and consolidate the influence of the Iraqi government afterwards – 'hold';
3. Establish new local institutions that advance civil society and the rule of law in areas formerly under enemy influence and control – 'build'.[101]

Thus, from an early stress on 'search-and-destroy' and force protection, US counter-insurgency doctrine gradually evolved by 2005 to lay a greater emphasis on restraint, population control, and cultural and political sensitivity. However, while these developments signalled the military's incorporation of a broader political perspective into their strategic thinking, their significance should not be over-stated. The over-riding imperative of minimizing US casualties continued to hamper the adoption of a more effective population control strategy. An equally basic underlying problem also remained: the lack of sufficient troops to impose security. The Pentagon's solution was 'Iraqization': a greater emphasis on training indigenous security forces, it was hoped, would permit Iraqis to shoulder a steadily increasing burden of responsibility for their own security. At the time of writing (early 2007), the President's decision to 'surge' more troops to Baghdad in an attempt to regain control appeared to reflect a (belated) recognition that Iraqization was, in Douglas MacArthur's words, no substitute for victory.

Conclusion: the reconceptualization of military transformation

A report on 'Transition to and from Hostilities', conducted in Summer 2004 by the influential Defence Science Board, concluded that the Pentagon and the State Department needed 'to make stabilisation and reconstruction (S&R) missions one of their core competencies. ... DOD has not yet embraced S&R operations as an explicit mission with the same seriousness as combat operations. This mind-set must be changed.' To that end, it argued that the military needed to become more culturally and politically sensitive, by developing what in effect would resemble a kind of post-modern imperial constabulary force:

> To be fully effective the United States will need to have some of its people continuously abroad for years, so they become familiar with the local scene and the indigenous people come to trust them as individuals – tours of duty that we imagine to be far longer than traditional assignments today.

The main thrust of the report was that the military could no longer afford to define its function in narrowly military terms of defeating other conventional military organizations, but would have to reconceptualize its role to encompass low-intensity conflict and a much broader array of civil and political functions.[102]

The implications of such recommendations for force planning and weapons acquisition were clearly reflected in the Pentagon's 2006 budget request, which called for a $55 billion cut in major weapons programmes (including missile defence and valuable power-projection capabilities) over the next six years while adding $25 billion to cover the costs of reorganizing the Army. 'The net effect,' concluded a *Washington Post* editorial, 'may be to shift the US military closer to preparing for the wars it has actually been fighting during the past four years rather than the ones defense theorists – among them Defense Secretary Donald H. Rumsfeld – have imagined.'[103] The 2006 Quadrennial Defense Review went so far as to acknowledge that,

> In the post-September 11 world, *irregular warfare has emerged as the dominant form of warfare* confronting the United States, its allies and its partners; accordingly, guidance must account for distributed, long-duration operations, including unconventional warfare, foreign internal defense, counterterrorism, counterinsurgency, and stabilization and reconstruction operations.[104]

Thus, the Defence Department continued to invoke the rhetoric of Military Transformation; yet in important respects the *meaning* of Transformation had begun to be redefined. Its original emphasis on technology has broadened to encompass the broader political dimension of war: its scope has widened from a narrow focus on technology, to a wider focus on the strategic circumstances in which that technology is likely to be used and, fundamentally, to the more effective use of military means to achieve political ends. The Pentagon's 'Directive 3000', issued at the end of November 2005, went so far as to state that henceforth stability operations will '*be given priority comparable to combat operations* and be explicitly addressed and integrated across all DoD activities including doctrine, organizations, training, education, exercises, materiel, leadership, personnel, facilities, and planning'.[105]

The original Transformation agenda provided a valuable insight into American military culture precisely because it set out a vision of an *idealized* future American force structure and way of war which polarized the military. For enthusiasts of Network-Centric Warfare and the Revolution in Military Affairs, it promised to realize the holy grail of Immaculate Destruction through the pioneering of a new American way of war. For those more sceptical of the potential of technology to render warfare 'immaculate', it represented a potentially dangerous departure from the philosophy of Overwhelming Force that had been institutionalized in US force structure and doctrine after Vietnam.

However, neither the enthusiasts nor the mainstream critics of the pre-Iraq Transformation agenda had much to say about unconventional warfare, counter-insurgency, stability operations, or other forms of warfare in which political and military considerations blur into one another.[106] On the contrary, both philosophies of war sought to minimize American involvement in such activities. Their assumptions about the political *utility* of force were diametrically opposed, but neither discourse fully accepted Clausewitz's insight that war is a true *continuation* of politics. The new preoccupation with translating battlefield victory into political stability has emerged gradually in response to the strategic friction encountered in Afghanistan and Iraq. There is thus much to be said for the observation of Colonel Robert B. Killebrew that, 'The most transformational influence on the Army today is war itself, which has accelerated change in ways that DoD theoreticians could not imagine. The battlefield is a tough place for theory.'[107]

Conclusion
The rise and fall of the new American way of war

> The nation appears to have reached a stage where its military learning is no longer appropriate, and so we wonder about the process of un-learning.
> John Shy, 1971[1]

Operation Iraqi Freedom was hailed after the fall of Baghdad as the triumphant validation of a new American way of war.[2] In reality, the war's chaotic aftermath revealed its failure. This controversial statement, of course, requires heavy qualification – for as a purely *technological* phenomenon, in many respects America's military transformation is revolutionizing the way that conventional and even some aspects of irregular war will be fought. As the historian of the great powers Paul Kennedy remarked after the Afghan War, 'One hears the distant rustle of military plans and feasibility studies by general staffs across the globe being torn up and dropped into the dustbin of history'.[3] However, the new American way of war was always conceived as more than a mere technological phenomenon or a revolution in operational style: it also encapsulated a broader *political* vision. The radical leap in military efficiency brought about by new technology, many enthusiasts assumed, would bring about a concomitant revolution in the political utility of force. The Revolution in Military Affairs would translate into a Revolution in *Strategic* Affairs or, in Paul Wolfowitz's phrase, a 'whole transformation of strategy and politics'.[4] In this broader political sense, the new American way of war was intimately bound up with a desire to overcome the lingering influence of the Vietnam Syndrome, which in the view of many influential figures associated with the Bush administration was only reaffirmed, rather than 'kicked', by the outcome of the first Gulf War.

This vision failed because the aftermath of the Iraq War revealed once again the timeless truth that military success and political victory are not the same thing. On the subject of the translation of the former into the latter, the discourse of Immaculate Destruction had very little to say. The new American way of war permitted American forces to dispatch both conventional Iraqi adversaries and insurgents with unprecedented lethality and precision, but it appeared incapable either of stabilizing a new political order or of keeping US casualties sufficiently low that the American public would contemplate their continued presence in Iraq with equanimity. Ironically, therefore, critics were soon arguing that the new American way of war suffered from the same defect as the old.[5] Although made three decades ago, Russell Weigley's historical generalization that American military strategists had tended to give 'little regard to the non-military consequences of what they were doing'[6] appeared to summarize with admirable concision the failures of the planning for Operation Iraqi Freedom.

One impact of the war's traumatic aftermath has been to puncture the technological hubris of the prevailing military discourse, the conceit that technology can render war predictable. Criticizing the fashionable concepts that drove the planning for the Iraq War, for example, retired Lt.-General Van Riper recently remarked that,

> Anyone who understands war would never deny the place of technology. It has a very prominent place, a very important place. ... [But] ... Worst of all would be for technology to lead the military instead of the ideas leading the development of the technology. ... The art of war and the science of war are not coequal. The art of war is clearly the most important. It's science in support of the art. Any time that science leads in your ability to think about and make war, I believe you're headed down a dangerous path.[7]

The Bush administration's radical optimism over the political utility of force has also been discredited: the President's intoxicating belief that he had 'changed the nature of how war is fought and won' has given way to a nasty hangover. The 2002 National Security Strategy's vision of forcefully confronting the worst threats to American security before they are fully formed has been supplemented by a much greater declaratory emphasis on resolving the North Korean and Iranian nuclear issues through peaceful diplomacy. There has been a backlash of criticism, moreover, from retired military elites whose voices were marginalized or ignored in the months before Operation Iraqi Freedom. Another influential figure in US military circles, former CENTCOM Commander General Anthony Zinni, has invoked the memory of Vietnam, implicitly portraying civilian strategists such as Rumsfeld, Wolfowitz, and Feith as a new generation of civilian technocrats in the mould of McNamara and his whiz kids:

> Almost everyone in this room, of my contemporaries – our feelings and our sensitivities were forged on the battlefields of Vietnam; where we heard the garbage and the lies, and we saw the sacrifice. We swore never again would we do that. We swore never again would we allow it to happen. And I ask you, is it happening again?[8]

Whether one agrees with the implication that responsibility for the mistakes made in Vietnam and Iraq can be attributed to civilians or not, Zinni's sense of history repeating itself is telling. Indeed, a central theme of this book has been the parallel between the cultural fractures of the pre- and post-Vietnam era military culture. Just as the assumption of control in the pre-Vietnam science of strategy made 'limited war' in Vietnam more *thinkable*, so the assumption of predictability in the discourse of Immaculate Destruction underpinned the decision to wage preventive war against Iraq. In both cases, more risk-averse military elites emphasizing the innate tendency of warfare to defy rational control regarded themselves as having been vindicated by the course of events. Thus, contrary to the notion of a linear transition from an 'old' to a 'new' American way of war, American military discourse on the political dimension of war has evolved in a markedly *dialectical* trajectory.

The dialectical evolution of American military culture

From the early Cold War period, US military culture was fractured by diametrically opposed discourses on both the sovereignty of the political dimension of war and the political utility of force. One effect of the Vietnam War was to resolve the debate over the *sovereignty* of politics: in the post-Vietnam period, almost without exception, the national security community at least paid lip-service to the primacy of political objectives. Yet military discourse on the political *utility* of force continued to fluctuate between extremes of scepticism, emphasizing the fragility of the public will and the unpredictability of war's peculiar 'grammar', and optimism, emphasizing the potential of science and technology to render war controllable and predictable, and thus to calibrate its conduct to the 'logic' of policy.

For much of this period, the existence of these cultural fractures meant that the 'American way of war' did not represent a behavioural expression of an internally coherent military culture (as the phrase itself tends to suggest), so much as the confused and incoherent expression of the military culture's inner contradictions. The Clinton period, in which policy-makers were caught between the risk-aversion of post-Vietnam military elites on the one hand, and the mirage of immaculate warfare on the other, is one example. At particular moments one military vision won out: the Bush administration's decision to wage preventive war against Iraq, for example, reflected the marginalization of the Overwhelming Force paradigm after 9/11. Yet the aftermath of the war has already prompted a new period of cultural revaluation, which may result in the emergence of a new cultural synthesis between the rival paradigms of Overwhelming Force and Immaculate Destruction. The obvious theoretical question raised by this historical interpretation of American military culture is *why* it evolved in this peculiar 'dialectical' fashion. If, as we suggested above, a dominant conception of warfare emerges through a military culture's attempt to reconcile the competing demands of functional (strategic) and societal imperatives, then why in the American case was this process of reconciliation so unstable, giving rise to such diametrically opposed discourses on the political utility of force? To pose the question in this way, of course, assumes that other military cultures have evolved more stable discourses on the political dimension of war, reflecting their more enduring and successful mediation of the tension between the perceived threats to the state's security on the one hand, and societal constraints on the use of force on the other.

The peculiarities of the American case may be explained simply by the unusual severity of this 'tension'. In the literature on the traditional American way of war, the most formative influence on US military culture was the period of so-called free security in which American ideas about war and peace and the ideology of American exceptionalism were nurtured. Insulated from the demands of constantly employing the threat or use of limited force in pursuit of the national interest, Americans were said to have developed, in Kissinger's phrase, a 'pure and abstract doctrine of aggression' which rejected the Clausewitzian concept of war as an instrument of policy. Thus, the most powerful societal imperative on American military culture was the United States' own republican self-image. Yet, simply by virtue of its super-power status since the end of World War II, for over half a century the strategic predicament of the United States has continually imposed the opposite strategic imperative of constantly employing force to manage the international system. Indeed, according to one influential commentator, this pressure has been such that American and European attitudes have now reversed. The US security guarantee to Western Europe enabled the states of the European Union to enter their own era of 'free security', or as Robert Kagan terms it,

> a post-historical paradise of peace and relative prosperity, the realization of Kant's 'Perpetual Peace'. The United States, meanwhile, remains mired in history, exercising power in the anarchic Hobbesian world where international laws and rules are unreliable and where true security and the defence and promotion of a liberal order still depend on the possession and use of military might. That is why on major strategic and international questions today, Americans are from Mars and Europeans are from Venus.[9]

Kagan's distinction between American and European attitudes towards war and peace may lack nuance and be drawn too starkly; but it emphasizes the point that the geopolitical condition of 'free security' that nurtured the traditional American way of war has long been absent. The ideology of American Exceptionalism, in contrast, remains a powerful force in American political culture, as is readily apparent from the rhetoric of the Bush administration. The degree to which other Western democracies can use military force is obviously also severely restricted by societal constraints, as witnessed by the deep anti-war sentiment in European public opinion in recent years. Yet few of America's Western allies have quite such an idealized view of their own virtue, and none of them has to face the global responsibilities entailed by super-power status. These tensions are nicely captured in Raymond Aron's appellation of the US as 'the Imperial Republic'.[10] The dialectical evolution of American military culture with regard to the political utility of force, therefore, ultimately reflects a deeper societal ambivalence that derives from the unique contradictions of the United States' strategic predicament: the tension between the republican ideal that war should be renounced as an instrument of state policy, and the quasi-imperial responsibility to police the international system. It seems unlikely that this tension will be resolved in the foreseeable future: the impact of globalization and the proliferation of advanced weapons technology render any return to 'isolationism' ever more unthinkable.

The fact that the fracture within US military culture over the political utility of force has often corresponded fairly closely to a civilian–military divide is also understandable. In Weigley's words, 'The great structural question throughout most of the history of American military policy was that of the proper form of military organization in a democratic society'.[11] A central preoccupation of the military has always been to maintain its republican links with the American people and to avoid involvement in unpopular limited wars for ambiguous political objectives. Even with the creation of the all-volunteer force in the post-Vietnam period, the military resisted its own transformation into an imperial constabulary force. The military's perception of the strategic imperatives on American strategy has always been conditioned by a deep sensitivity to societal imperatives. The very essence of the civilian strategists' role, in contrast, is to calibrate the use of military force to the logic of national policy, a self-image less-tempered by concern over the impact of this policy on the military's links with the wider society.

Yet, however deep the fractures over the political *utility* of force, in one respect American military discourse on the political dimension of war remained consistent throughout the Cold War and post-Cold War period. There was never widespread acceptance within American military culture of Clausewitz's most far-reaching claim that the conduct of war is *permeated* by politics: civilian strategists and military commanders alike were equally neglectful of those ambiguous political 'imponderables' that ultimately govern strategic success. Yet events in Iraq have now forced the US military to fight in a context in which they can no longer be neglected. The central question for US military culture is whether the form of warfare that the US military is now fighting in Afghanistan and Iraq – in which military and political considerations are inextricably intertwined – will increasingly be the exception or the norm. If the latter is more likely, then it is more important than ever that US military culture absorbs the full import of the assertion that war is a true *continuation* of politics. Throughout this thesis, the 'realities' of war have been considered only to explore how they deviated from the dominant military discourse of the moment. To conclude this discussion it is necessary to reverse this sequence and consider how US military discourse needs to adapt to the evolving reality of war.

The changing reality of war

All wars, Clausewitz tells us, are political. This is true even of total war – war in which the entire human and material resources of the state are mobilized in an existential struggle against an adversary. Yet the more closely it tends towards the Clausewitzian concept of war in its 'absolute' form, the less obvious the political dimension will be. As he wrote in a letter in 1827:

> The more politics serves great interests which are all-encompassing and existential ... the more politics and enmity coincide, the more the former melts into the latter, *the simpler war becomes*, the more directly it is a function of force and annihilation. ... Such a war appears quite apolitical, and for that reason has been regarded as the norm. ... But ... the political principle is not entirely absent here any more than in other wars, only it coincides so entirely with the concepts of force and annihilation that it becomes invisible to our eyes.[12]

By implication, in other forms of warfare the 'concepts of force and annihilation' may exist in constant *tension*, rather than coincide, with the political principles at stake. To paraphrase George Orwell, all wars are political, but some are more political than others. A central challenge for American military culture in the early twenty-first century is that war is becoming *more political* than ever, in this specific sense that 'the concepts of force and annihilation' are increasingly in tension with the political contexts in which they are most likely to be employed. Only if the American discourse on war adapts to this changing reality of contemporary warfare will the political utility of force be restored for the United States.

A central paradox of the American military experience over the half century since the ceasefire in Korea is that the war which most closely approximated to the kind of conflict which the military had imagined and trained for – the Gulf War of 1990–1991 – was also an aberration. It deviated from the contemporaneous trend in the sense that in the planning and execution of the war, political and military considerations could be separated from each other with unusual clarity. However, such a strategic context, in which political and military considerations could be distinguished with relative ease, was *increasingly unusual*. The trend was in the opposite direction: US military interventions tended to be increasingly conducted in complicated political contexts in which military and political concerns were inextricably intertwined. With the partial exception of the interventions in Grenada and Panama, the majority of US interventions between Vietnam and 9/11 posed problems more akin to those of Vietnam than to those of the Gulf War. In Lebanon, Somalia, and the Balkans, the US intervened in conflicts of great political ambiguity and faced adversaries that deliberately refused to fight the US on its own terms. The US was, in effect, increasingly taking upon itself the quasi-imperial responsibility of imposing order over the internal ethnic, religious, and political divisions of highly unstable parts of the world (a responsibility which, in baulking at the prospect of stabilizing a post-Saddam Iraq, it rejected in 1991). Increasingly, the United States was engaged in intervening in what scholars have variously termed 'low-intensity conflict', 'the new wars', or (most recently) 'war amongst the people'.[13]

While these scholars offer differing interpretations of the precise characteristics of the phenomena they seek to describe, they agree on certain trends in the recent evolution of warfare. Most fundamentally, it is argued that the paradigm of inter-state industrial warfare that dominated the nineteenth and the first half of the twentieth centuries increasingly deviates from the contemporary realities of war. The increasing obsolescence of inter-state industrial war is largely a direct consequence of its own destructiveness, which reached its logical culmination in the development of thermonuclear weapons. Inter-state industrial warfare became so destructive that states could perceive fewer conceivable circumstances in which it might achieve any coherent political purpose. 'Thus,' in the words of Martin van Creveld, 'the effect of nuclear weapons ... has been to push conventional war into the nooks and crannies of the international system or ... into the faults between the main tectonic plates.'[14]

This is not to rule out altogether the possibility of future US military action against another state – North Korea or Iran, for example, if relations with the US deteriorated further over their pursuit of a nuclear capability. Nevertheless, the catastrophic consequences – including the possible use of WMD – that would plausibly follow for the protagonists in most of these scenarios mean that the logic of deterrence still applies.[15] This may well remain the case however successful the United States is in revolutionizing conventional warfare: indeed, it is striking how little RMA enthusiasts have to say about the continued salience of nuclear weapons or other WMD in the hands of potential opponents of the US.[16] Some caution is necessary here: Van Creveld and the 'New Wars' theorists probably go too far in their emphasis on the redundancy of conventional inter-state war.[17] Even if they are correct, for inter-state deterrence to continue to function it must be backed up by the credible threat of force. The balance of conventional forces will thus retain its relevance: as long as incompatible political ideologies continue to sow mutual distrust between the major powers, the logic of Vegetius' injunction, 'If you want peace, prepare for war', will still apply.

However, such a view is quite compatible with the insight that the nature of *actually occurring* conflict will be increasingly unconventional. As conventional (i.e. non-nuclear inter-state) war becomes more uncommon, it is being replaced by a form of war that in many respects resembles Europe's earlier experience of endemic warfare that accompanied the process of state formation in the sixteenth and seventeenth centuries. These 'new wars', however, tend to be associated with the process of state disintegration rather than state-building.[18] They thus tend to occur in areas where a major empire once held sway but has since disintegrated, and where those state entities that sought to take their place proved too weak to contain the centrifugal pressures of ethnic, religious, or political divisions. The central defining characteristic of these wars is thus that they occur in theatres of conflict where the state has lost its monopoly of violence. As a consequence, regular armed forces – that is, organized military forces deliberately distinguishable by their dress from non-combatants, with a hierarchical structure answerable to the state, a legal right to bear arms, a separate disciplinary code, and centralized funding – have lost control over the course of conflict.[19] The battlefield, conversely, is everywhere. War is increasingly conducted 'amongst the people'. In some respects the term 'new wars' is a misleading label, since many of the features associated with this form of conflict are as old as war itself.[20] Equally, while 'low-intensity conflict' is frequently employed to describe this form of war, it is also misleading, as Martin van Creveld has pointed out. For whether this form of warfare is judged in terms of the momentous *consequences* it has helped to precipitate, which include the humiliation of colonial powers whose empires once spanned half the globe, or in terms of the numbers of casualties with which it is associated, the appendage 'low-intensity' appears grossly misconceived:

> Truth to say, what we are dealing with here is neither low-intensity nor some bastard offspring of war. Rather, it is WARRE in the elemental, Hobbesian sense of the word, by far the most important form of armed conflict in our time.[21]

Given that its defining feature is the loss of the state's monopoly of violence, perhaps a useful term to describe this form of war is 'non-Trinitarian warfare': for the Clausewitzian concept of war as a 'Remarkable Trinity' (of primordial hatred, creativity, and political rationality, corresponding to a distinction between the state, the military and the people) is increasingly inapplicable to many of the protagonists. From the perspective of American military strategy, the central concern should be the implications of the dynamic asymmetry in those cases where 'Trinitarian' and 'non-Trinitarian' forms of conflict interact. Thus, if it is accepted that American military intervention will increasingly be conducted against irregular forces in parts of the world where no state entity possesses a monopoly of violence, then the question for American military culture is how US military forces should adapt their basic assumptions about war to the non-Trinitarian challenge posed by their adversaries.

For our purposes, the most important implication will be that in those conflicts where Trinitarian face 'non-Trinitarian' forces, it will be increasingly difficult to separate military from political considerations. Political considerations will permeate the conduct of military operations to the extent that the most seemingly trivial tactical decisions may have far-flung political implications. There are several reasons why this should be so. Firstly, the US will increasingly be fighting 'non-Trinitarian' foes. It is striking how the Iraq war has mutated – a US campaign against the conventional forces of the former Iraqi regime has evolved into an intractable counter-insurgency campaign against a non-Trinitarian adversary. This illustrates the oft-noted paradox that a simple consequence of the United States' unchallengeable superiority in the conventional military sphere is that future adversaries will have little choice but to adopt asymmetrical strategies that refuse to confront the US on its own terms. Even where the US is facing the armed forces of another state, they are thus increasingly likely to adopt unconventional tactics and to mingle with civilian populations to neutralize the American technological edge.

However, it is more likely that the US will be fighting in areas like Bosnia, Afghanistan, and Iraq where no state or non-state entity has a clear monopoly of violence (either because the state was already failing or because the US has removed a hostile regime), and where the US is trying to restore it to some local proxy. The 2002 National Security Strategy acknowledged that failed states now pose as much of a danger to the security of the US as strong states:[22] there is thus a growing recognition that the US simply cannot afford to ignore unstable regions any longer. The danger posed by the potential for failed states to become havens for terrorist activity is magnified by the impact of globalization and the proliferation of WMD. Consequently, the US will have little choice but to attempt to foster political stability in areas where it intervenes, a task that will require long-term commitment and sophisticated engagement with local political complexities.

Finally, the US will increasingly be fighting 'amongst the people'. A central aim in adopting guerrilla tactics is to mingle with the non-combatant population and thus to throw the burden of indiscriminate violence on to the enemy. In such circumstances, any use of overwhelming force by the US may be counter-productive and play into enemy hands by harming non-combatants and damaging civilian infrastructure. In Richard Betts' words, the essence of counter-insurgency is defined by 'a delicate interweaving of political and military functions'.[23] This puts a premium on language skills, restraint in the use of force, sensitivity to local cultures, and, above all, political awareness. Both domestic and foreign audiences, moreover, will be watching in real time. During the first Gulf War,

CNN gave a more or less favourable coverage of the US. However, the proliferation of media networks like *al Jazeera* that are either indifferent or actively hostile to the US perspective will magnify the political impact of any American mistakes.

In summary, therefore, the contemporary reality of war is evolving in such a way that it will be increasingly difficult for the US to disentangle narrowly military tasks from their wider political implications. Neither of the rival paradigms that have dominated American military culture since Vietnam is suited to meet this challenge. In this sense, the epigraph to this chapter seems pertinent once again: the US military appears to have reached a point where its military learning *is no longer appropriate*. To quote General Zinni once again:

> we're going to be doing things like humanitarian operations, consequence management, peacekeeping, and peace enforcement. ... And do you know what? We're going to bitch and moan about it. We're going to dust off the Weinberger Doctrine and the Powell Doctrine and throw them in the face of our civilian leadership. The truth is that military conflict has changed and we have been reluctant to recognize it. Defeating nation-state forces in conventional battle is not the task for the twenty-first century. ... We all know it, but we won't acknowledge it.[24]

The question, then, is how successfully will American military culture adapt to the changing realities of war?

The future of American military culture

It is dangerous to use cultural arguments to make predictions about future patterns of thought and behaviour. Nevertheless, it may be possible to delineate some plausible trajectories for the future evolution of US military discourse by extrapolating from current trends. In accounting for the evolution of military culture, it was suggested that US military discourse has emerged from the attempt to *reconcile* perceived societal imperatives – 'arising from the social forces, ideologies, and institutions dominant within the society' – with perceived functional (strategic) imperatives stemming from the threats to the society's security. Any discourse that is widely perceived as over-emphasizing one imperative at the expense of the other will be regarded as dysfunctional, and will therefore either have to adapt or lose influence to a rival discourse that seems to redress the balance.

Applying these considerations to the contemporary debate on American strategy, a pervasive concern can already be discerned that the American military needs to re-orient itself towards the 'societal imperative'. There is deep anxiety within the military that the scandals surrounding the mistreatment of prisoners of war in Guantanamo Bay and Abu Ghraib have severely tarnished the positive image so painfully restored in the decades after Vietnam. Equally, there is a widespread perception that the Bush administration's grand strategy has over-stretched the military and its links with American society. A particularly forceful expression of this concern was the leaked memo of January 2005 in which Lt.-General James Helmly, the Chief of the Army Reserves, declared that the reserves were 'rapidly degenerating into a broken force'.[25] The evolution of American military discourse in the near future is thus likely to be marked by a renewed orientation towards the 'societal imperative'. It will probably express, therefore, a renewed sensitivity to the limits of public support and a renewed concern to rebuild the military's links with American society. Such an emphasis could resemble a new attempt to formulate a set of conditions for going to war that would harmonize with the limits of public support, analogous to the Powell and Weinberger doctrines.

One expression of this renewed emphasis on societal constraints may already be discerned in attitudes towards the political *utility* of force. The hubris of the Bush administration has been deflated – with comparisons between Iraq and Vietnam becoming increasingly commonplace in scholarly and media commentary, the pendulum has clearly swung back towards a more sceptical view of the utility of force. The assumption that the technical mastery of the battlefield automatically translates into political utility is no longer accepted uncritically. The Iraq insurgency has underlined the limits of technology, and the ubiquity of friction, deriving from the quintessential human capacity to respond creatively and thus unpredictably. The capacity of technology to overcome the constraints American society imposes on the use of force has been cast into doubt: insurgents found ways of negating the American technological advantage and inflicting casualties on US troops through asymmetric tactics that refused to confront the US military on their own terms.

Despite Rumsfeld's goal of 'changing the psychology of how Americans view war', a poll conducted in late 2004 found that although 58 per cent of Americans believed that US troops should remain in Iraq, 70 per cent already believed that any gains had come at the cost of 'unacceptable' losses in casualties; 56 per cent believed, moreover, that the war wasn't 'worth fighting'.[26] A return to the casualty tolerance levels of pre-Vietnam days seems highly unlikely. Niall Ferguson has calculated, for example, that between April and October 2003 just over 350 US service personnel lost their lives, while there was a 29 per cent drop in the popularity of the Iraq war; during the Vietnam War it took about three years and more than 30,000 killed in action for popular support to reduce by a comparable amount.[27] Such comparisons which correlate casualty levels with public support are obviously reductionist: in Iraq, the issue is complicated in particular by the failure to find WMD or proof of Iraqi links to *al Qaeda*. Nevertheless, the comparison is still suggestive. If Eric Larson is correct in his hypothesis that American casualty tolerance is partly a function of the degree of consensus between elites over the necessity of military intervention, then there are signs that such elite consensus may already be past the point of collapse: the widely publicized speech by Congressman John Murtha in November 2005 calling for an American withdrawal from Iraq was described by the *Washington Post* as 'the week when President Bush lost control over the Iraq war debate'.[28]

The War on Terror may yet bring about the opposite result to that hoped for by Rumsfeld: rather than 'changing the psychology' of American casualty aversion, a withdrawal from Iraq that then spiralled into total chaos would surely exacerbate it. Within the military culture, Iraq would join Vietnam, the Lebanon, and Somalia as another episode illustrating the fragility of popular support for drawn-out foreign interventions. Indeed, Lawrence Freedman has already suggested that Rumsfeld's ultimate legacy will be a new version of the Vietnam Syndrome:

> whenever Rumsfeld finally packs up his office at the Pentagon, he will leave behind an even more burdensome Iraq syndrome – the renewed, nagging and sometimes paralyzing belief that any large-scale US military intervention abroad is doomed to practical failure and moral iniquity.[29]

While this is certainly a plausible scenario, it may be premature: the *intensity* of any such Iraq Syndrome will largely depend on how events unfold in Iraq itself. Perhaps the greatest source of the Vietnam Syndrome was the retrospective sense of the war's futility: despite the massive sacrifice of American lives and resources, South Vietnam still fell. In contrast, the future of Iraq is still unclear. American pessimism with regard to the utility of force would certainly be mitigated if the intervention eventually results in the establishment of a stable democratic government able to deal with the insurgency. If, conversely, Iraq is perceived as a complete failure – either because the insurgency is successful in forcing an American withdrawal, or the country descends further into civil war while the troops are there or after they are withdrawn – then Freedman's pessimism may prove justified.

Whether one regards the renewed scepticism towards the political utility of force prompted by Iraq as a positive or negative development, a related outcome has been a wider acceptance of Clausewitz's insight that war is a true *continuation* of politics. The central lesson of Iraq for many observers both inside and outside the military has been that success in war is ultimately about the achievement of stable political outcomes. War is about the peace that it leaves behind. To quote General Zinni a final time,

> There's a difference between winning battles, or defeating the enemy in battle, and winning the war. ... What strikes me is that we are

constantly redesigning the military to do something it already does pretty well. ... If we're talking about the future, we need to talk about not how you win the peace as a separate part of the war, but you've got to look at this thing from start to finish. ... The military does a damn good job of killing people and breaking things. ... But that is not the problem [30]

Zinni's view is now more widely shared. Not only have such insights been reflected in recent strategy documents such as the 2006 QDR, but perhaps more importantly a generation of mid-level American military officers has had its baptism of fire in the attempt to win hearts and minds in the face of a vicious insurgency. This process of cultural feedback has been reflected both in the gradual evolution of US counter-insurgency strategy and in the reconceptualization of the very meaning of 'Military Transformation'.

However, it remains to be seen whether such rhetoric will result in real change.[31] A historical *caveat* is in order here. As Russell Weigley pointed out, many times in its history the US Army has had to relearn strategic doctrines suitable to the conduct of highly politicized unconventional conflicts, only to forget them again after the termination of hostilities on the assumption that such conflicts represented aberrations.[32] The case of Vietnam is particularly relevant: it is frequently forgotten that when General Creighton Abrams replaced William Westmoreland as US commander in Vietnam, he abandoned the latter's emphasis on search-and-destroy in favour of a 'clear-and-hold' strategy that soon achieved tangible results (albeit too late to alter the outcome of the war).[33] Yet the Army's willed amnesia in the decades following the war, and its decision to focus once again on conventional conflict in Europe meant that these lessons were never institutionalized in its training, force structure, or military doctrine. Thus, the historical record does not give grounds for optimism.

However, one factor appears different in the current case. In the past, the US military's cultural disinterest in conflict against unconventional opponents – in which the distinctions between military and political tasks are inherently blurred – has been rationalized by the need to concentrate on the more pressing threat posed by conventional opponents, such as the Axis powers or the Soviet Union. Yet in the War on Terror, unconventional opponents are perceived – for the first time in US military history – as *the* main adversary. Thus if, as seems likely, American military culture is moving towards a wider sensitivity towards the interpenetration of political and military considerations, then one effect of the failures of American strategy in Iraq will have been a convergence between US expectations and the reality of war in the twenty-first century. One reflection of this shift could be discerned in the recent re-branding of the War on Terror as 'the Long War' in the 2006 QDR, with its greater emphasis on the broader political tasks that must accompany the military battle of attrition against Islamist terrorists. The QDR committed the US to the truly grand project of employing military force to export political stability and freedom throughout the world:

> Victory will come when the enemy's extremist ideologies are discredited in the eyes of their host populations and tacit supporters, becoming unfashionable, and following other discredited creeds, such as Communism and Nazism, into oblivion. This requires the creation of a global environment inhospitable to terrorism. It requires legitimate governments with the capacity to police themselves and to deny terrorists the sanctuary and the resources they need to survive. It also will require support for the establishment of effective representative civil societies around the world, since the appeal of freedom is the best long-term counter to the ideology of the extremists.[34]

It remains to be seen, however, whether the military can sustain the long-term support of the American people for such an ambitious *Mission Civilisatrice*, which could strain the services themselves to breaking point. The greatest challenge for American military culture in the twenty-first century will be to reconcile this breathtakingly expansive conception of the imperatives on American strategy, with the constraints deriving from the nature of American society itself.

Notes

Introduction: American ways of war, old and new

1 Russell F. Weigley, *The American Way of War: A History of United States Military Strategy and Policy*, Bloomington: Indiana University Press, 1977, pp. xviii–xix.
2 Samuel P. Huntington, *The Soldier and the State: The Theory and Politics of Civil–Military Relations*, Cambridge, MA: Belknap Press, 1957, p. 151.
3 James Reston, Jr, *Sherman's March and Vietnam*, (New York: Macmillan, 1984), p. 51. My emphasis.
4 See, for example, Norman Friedman, *Terrorism, Afghanistan, and America's New Way of War*, Annapolis: Naval Institute Press, 2003; Arthur C. Cebrowski with Thomas P. M. Barnett, 'The American Way of War', *Proceedings of the US Naval Institute*, Vol. 129 No. 1, January 2003; and Max Boot, 'The New American Way of War', *Foreign Affairs*, Vol. 82 No. 4, July/August 2003.
5 Bob Woodward, *Plan of Attack: The Road To War*, London: Simon & Schuster, 2004, p. 425.
6 State Department, 'President Bush Outlines Progress in Operation Iraqi Freedom', 16 April 2003 – www.state.gov/p/nea/rls/rm/19709.htm. Accessed 12 August 2005.
7 Department of Defense, 'Deputy Secretary Wolfowitz Interview with Sam Tannenhaus', *Vanity Fair*, 9 May 2003 – www.defenselink.mil/transcripts/2003/tr20030509-depsecdef0223.html. Accessed 1 July 2005.
8 Department of Defense, 'Deputy Secretary Wolfowitz Remarks at the Aspen Institute,' 16 July 2004 – www.defenselink.mil/transcripts/2004/tr20040716-secdef1041.html. Accessed 12 August 2005.
9 Department of Defense, 'Strategy and the Idea of Freedom', Lecture by Douglas J. Feith at the Heritage Foundation, 24 November 2003 – www.defenselink.mil/speeches/2003/sp20031124-0703.html. Accessed 3 February 2005.
10 Antulio J. Echevarria, *Toward an American Way of War* (Carlisle: US Army War College Strategic Studies Institute, 2004) – www.strategicstudiesinstitute.Army.mil/pdffiles/PUB374.pdf. Accessed 19 January 2006.
11 See, for example, General Anthony Zinni, Address to the Marine Corps Association and US Naval Institute Forum, Arlington, Virginia, 4 September 2003 – www.mca-usniforum.org/forum03zinni.htm. Accessed 12 August 2005. See also PBS, *Frontline* interview with retired General Paul Van Riper for *Rumsfeld's War*, conducted 8 July 2004. – www.pbs.org/wgbh/pages/frontline/shows/pentagon/interviews/vanriper.html. Accessed 12 August 2005.
12 Carl von Clausewitz, *On War*, edited and translated by Michael Howard and Peter Paret, Princeton; Guildford: Princeton University Press, 1976, Book VIII, chapter VI, p. 605.

13 Russell F. Weigley, *The American Way of War: A History of United States Military Strategy and Policy*, 1977. Originally published in 1973.
14 Brian McAllister Linn, 'The American Way of War Revisited', *Journal of Military History*, Vol. 66 No. 2, April 2002, p. 502.
15 Russell F. Weigley, 'American Strategy from Its Beginnings through the First World War', in Peter Paret, ed., *Makers of Modern Strategy: From Machiavelli to the Nuclear Age*, Princeton: Princeton University Press, 1986, p. 408.
16 Weigley, *The American Way of War*, p. xxii. For a comprehensive critique of Weigley's argument, including his distinction between strategies of 'annihilation' and 'attrition', see Linn, 'The American Way of War Revisited', *Journal of Military History*, Vol. 66 No. 2, April 2002.
17 Weigley, *The American Way of War*, p. xviii.
18 See, for example, Alvin and Heidi Toffler, *War and Anti-war: Survival at the Dawn of the 21st Century*, Boston; London: Little, Brown, 1993; and George and Meredith Friedman, *The Future of War: Power, Technology and American World Dominance in the 21st Century*, New York: Crown, 1996.
19 For accounts of the reception of Clausewitz in the United States, see Christopher Bassford, *Clausewitz in English: The Reception of Clausewitz in Britain and America, 1815–1945*, New York: Oxford University Press, 1994; and Beatrice Heuser, *Reading Clausewitz*, London: Pimlico, 2002, chapter 7.
20 Heuser, *Reading Clausewitz*, p. 7.
21 Clausewitz, *On War*, p. 605.
22 Clausewitz, *On War*, pp. 87–88.
23 Colin S. Gray, *Modern Strategy*, Oxford: Oxford University Press, 1999, pp. 93–94.
24 On Clausewitz's views on war's tendency to defy rational control, see Alan Beyerchen, 'Clausewitz, Nonlinearity and the Unpredictability of War', *International Security*, Vol. 17 No. 3, Winter 1992.
25 Clausewitz, *On War*, pp. 87–88.
26 Chris Hables Gray, *Postmodern War: The New Politics of Conflict*, London: Routledge, 1997, p. 138.
27 John Keegan, *A History of Warfare*, London: Pimlico, 1994, pp. 11–12.
28 Clausewitz, *On War*, p. 593.
29 Robert B. Bathurst, *Intelligence and the Mirror: On Creating an Enemy*, London: Sage, 1993, p. 121.
30 For early contributions to this debate see John Shy, 'The American Military Experience: History and Learning', *Journal of Interdisciplinary History*, Vol. 1 No. 2, Winter 1971; Jack Snyder, *The Soviet Strategic Culture: Implications for Limited Nuclear Operations*, Santa Monica: RAND R-2154-AF, 1977; Colin S. Gray, 'National Style in Strategy: The American Example', *International Security*, Vol. 6 No. 2, Fall 1981; Jack Snyder, 'The Concept of Strategic Culture: Caveat Emptor', in Carl Jacobsen, ed., *Strategic Power: USA/USSR*, London: Macmillan, 1990. For the important debate on the nature of strategic culture between Alistair Iain Johnston and Colin S. Gray, see Johnston, 'Thinking about Strategic Culture', *International Security*, Vol. 19 No. 4, Spring 1995; Gray, 'Strategic culture as context: the first generation of theory strikes back', *Review of International Studies*, Vol. 25 No. 1, January 1999, pp. 49–69; Johnston, 'Strategic Cultures Revisited: Reply to Colin Gray', *Review of International Studies*, Vol. 25 No. 3, July 1999; Stuart Poore, 'What is the Context? A Reply to the Gray–Johnston Debate on Strategic Culture', *Review of International Studies*, Vol. 29 No. 2, April 2003. For other cultural approaches to the study of warfare, see John Keegan, *A History of Warfare*, London: Pimlico, 1994; Victor Davis Hanson, *Why the West Has Won: Carnage*

and Culture from Salamis to Vietnam, London: Faber and Faber, 2001; Isabel V. Hull, *Absolute Destruction: Military Culture and the Practices of War in Imperial Germany*, Ithaca: Cornell University Press, 2005; and John A. Lynn, *Battle: A History of Combat and Culture*, Boulder: Westview Press, Revised and Updated Edition, 2004.
31 Thankfully, however, Lynn strips the concept of 'discourse' of the radical subjectivism of post-structuralist literary theory with which it is sometimes associated.
32 Lynn, *Battle: A History of Combat and Culture*, pp. xx–xxi.
33 Lynn, *Battle*, p. 361.
34 Lynn, *Battle*, p. 360.
35 Samuel P. Huntington, *The Soldier and the State: The Theory and Politics of Civil–Military Relations*, Cambridge, MA: Belknap Press, 1957, p. 2.

1 No substitute for victory: the separation of politics and strategy in the American military tradition

1 Russell F. Weigley, *The American Way of War*, p. 281.
2 George F. Kennan, *American Diplomacy: Expanded Edition*, Chicago; London: University of Chicago Press, 1984, p. 100.
3 Walter Lippmann, *Public Opinion and Foreign Policy in the United States*, London: George Allen and Unwin, 1952, pp. 25–26.
4 This notion came to be associated with the term 'free security', which was coined in an article by C. Vann Woodward in 1960. C. Vann Woodward, 'The Age of Reinterpretation', *American Historical Review*, Vol. 66 No. 1, October 1960, pp. 2–8.
5 Samuel P. Huntington, *The Soldier and the State: The Theory and Politics of Civil–Military Relations*, p. 151.
6 Henry A. Kissinger, *Nuclear Weapons and Foreign Policy*, New York: Harper, 1957, chapter 1.
7 Robert Endicott Osgood, *Limited War: The Challenge to American Strategy*, Chicago: University of Chicago Press, 1957, p. 10.
8 Lippmann, *Public Opinion and Foreign Policy in the United States*, pp. 15, 28–29.
9 James Reston, Jr, *Sherman's March and Vietnam*, Macmillan, 1984, p. 51.
10 See the critique of 'War is Hell' as a moral doctrine in Michael Walzer, *Just and Unjust Wars*, New York: Basic Books, 2000, pp. 32–33.
11 John W. Brinsfield, 'The Military Ethics of General William T. Sherman', in Lloyd J. Matthews and Dale E. Brown, *The Parameters of Military Ethics*, Washington; London: Pergamon-Brassey's, 1989, p. 164.
12 Reston, *Sherman's March and Vietnam*, pp. 50–51.
13 Walter Russell Mead, *Special Providence: American Foreign Policy and How It Changed the World*, New York; London: Routledge, 2002, p. 253.
14 Michael S. Sherry, *The Rise of American Air Power: The Creation of Armageddon*, New Haven: Yale University Press, 1987, p. 288.
15 John Lewis Gaddis, *Strategies of Containment: A Critical Appraisal of Postwar American National Security Policy*, New York: Oxford University Press, 1982, p. 251.
16 Michael Howard, 'Constraints on Warfare', in Michael Howard, George J. Andreopoulos, and Mark R. Shulman, eds, *The Laws of War: Constraints on Warfare in the Western World*, New Haven: Yale University Press, 1994, p. 3.
17 David B. Rivkin and Lee A. Casey, 'Leashing the Dogs of War', *The National Interest*, No. 73, Fall 2003, p. 64.

18 Michael D. Pearlman, *Warmaking and American Democracy: The Struggle over Military Strategy, 1700 to the Present*, Lawrence: University Press of Kansas, 1999, pp. 20–21.
19 Christopher Bassford, *Clausewitz in English: The Reception of Clausewitz in Britain and America, 1815–1945*, Oxford: Oxford University Press, 1994, pp. 160, 199.
20 Beatrice Heuser, *Reading Clausewitz*, London: Pimlico, 2002, p. 56.
21 T. Harry Williams, *Americans at War: The Development of the American Military System*, Baton Rouge: Louisiana State University Press, 1960, p. 79.
22 Russell F. Weigley, *The American Way of War*, p. 133.
23 Eliot Cohen, 'Kosovo and the new American Way of War', in Andrew J. Bacevich and Eliot Cohen, eds, *War Over Kosovo: Politics and Strategy in a Global Age*, New York: Columbia University Press, 2001, p. 38.
24 Weigley, *The American Way of War*, pp. 475–476.
25 Christopher M. Gacek, *The Logic of Force: The Dilemma of Limited War in American Foreign Policy*, New York: Columbia University Press, 1994, p. 135.
26 Richard K. Betts, *Soldiers, Statesmen, and Cold War Crises*, Cambridge, MA: Harvard University Press, 1977, pp. 20–21.
27 I have adopted the term 'absolutism' from Morris Janowitz's discussion of 'absolutist' versus 'pragmatic' schools in American military thought. What he terms the 'pragmatic' school corresponds roughly to the scientific preoccupation with *efficiency* discussed in the following chapter. Morris Janowitz, *The Professional Soldier: A Social and Political Portrait*, Glencoe: The Free Press, 1960, pp. 264–277.
28 Mark S. Watson, *Chief of Staff: Pre-War Plans and Preparations (US Army in World War II)*, Washington, DC: USGPO, 1950, p. 12; quoted in Harry G. Summers, *On Strategy: A Critical Analysis of the Vietnam War*, Novato: Presidio Press, 1982, p. 51.
29 Gacek, *The Logic of Force: The Dilemma of Limited War in American Foreign Policy*, p. 64.
30 John Shy, 'The American Military Experience: History and Learning', *Journal of Interdisciplinary History*, Vol. 1 No. 2, Winter 1971, p. 216.
31 See, for example, Ken Booth, 'American Strategy: The Myths Revisited', in Booth and Wright, eds, *American Thinking about Peace and War*, Hassocks: Harvester Press, 1978, p. 7; and Peter Maslowski, 'To the edge of greatness: The United States, 1783–1865', in Williamson Murray, MacGregor Knox, and Alvin Bernstein, eds, *The Making of Strategy: Rulers, States, and War*, Cambridge; New York: Cambridge University Press, 1994, p. 226.
32 Maslowski, 'To the edge of greatness: The United States, 1783–1865', p. 225.
33 James Chace, 'In Search of Absolute Security', in A. J. Bacevich, ed., *The Imperial Tense: Prospects and Problems of American Empire*, Chicago: Ivan R. Dee, 2002, p. 123.
34 David Mayers, *Wars and Peace: The Future Americans Envisioned 1861–1991*, New York: St. Martin's Press, 1999, p. 5.
35 Williams, *Americans at War*, p. 87.
36 Walter A. McDougall, *Promised Land, Crusader State: The American Encounter with the World Since 1776*, Boston: Houghton Mifflin Company, 1997, p. 42.
37 Mayers, *Wars and Peace*, p. 75.
38 Anatol Rapoport, 'Changing Conceptions of War in the United States', in Booth and Wright, eds, *American Thinking about Peace and War*, p. 61.
39 Paul Johnson, *A History of the American People*, London: Phoenix Giant, 1997, pp. 20–21.
40 Jürgen Heideking, 'The Image of an English Enemy during the American Revolution', in Fiebig-von Hase and Lehmkuhl, eds, *Enemy Images in American History*, Providence: Berghahn Books, 1997, p. 98.

41 Reginald C. Stuart, *War and American Thought: From the Revolution to the Monroe Doctrine*, Kent: Kent State University Press, 1982.
42 George E. Hopkins, 'Bombing and the American Conscience during World War II', *The Historian*, Vol. 28 No. 3, May 1966, p. 463.
43 Sherry, *The Rise of American Air Power*, pp. 122, 139.
44 Hopkins, 'Bombing and the American Conscience during World War II', pp. 451, 463.
45 Walzer, *Just and Unjust Wars*, p. 264.
46 Jonathan Lewis and Ben Steele, *Hell in the Pacific*, London: Channel 4 Books, 2001, p. 215.
47 Weigley, *The American Way of War*, p. xx.
48 Lawrence Delbert Cress, *Citizens in Arms: The Army and the Militia in American Society to the War of 1812*, Chapel Hill: University of North Carolina Press, 1982, p. 12.
49 Cress, *Citizens in Arms*, chapters 5 and 6.
50 William C. Banks and Jeffrey D. Straussman, 'A New Imperial Presidency? Insights from US Involvement in Bosnia', in Demetrios James Caraley, ed., *The New American Interventionism*, New York: Columbia University Press, 1999, p. 41.
51 Robert B. Zoellick, 'Congress and the Making of US Foreign Policy', *Survival*, Vol. 41 No. 4, Winter 1999–2000, p. 25.
52 Pearlman, *Warmaking and American Democracy*, p. 215.
53 Mead, *Special Providence*, p. 257.
54 Sam C. Sarkesian, *America's Forgotten Wars: The Counterrevolutionary Past and Lessons for the Future*, Westport: Greenwood Press, 1984, p. 122.
55 Cohen, 'Kosovo and the new American Way of War', p. 44.
56 Avant, Deborah D., *Political Institutions and Military Change: Lessons from Peripheral Wars*, Ithaca: Cornell University Press, 1994, p. 26.
57 Russell F. Weigley, *History of the United States Army*, New York: Macmillan, 1967, p. 281.
58 Pearlman, *Warmaking and American Democracy*, p. 21.
59 Sarkesian, *America's Forgotten Wars*, pp. 135–136.
60 Avant, *Political Institutions and Military Change*, pp. 39–40. For some interesting parallels of the American case with the Imperial German Army's tendency to exclude political considerations from military consideration, see Isabel V. Hull, *Absolute Destruction: Military Culture and the Practices of War in Imperial Germany*, Ithaca: Cornell University Press, 2005, Part II.
61 Weigley, *The American Way of War*, p. 178.
62 Brian McAllister Linn, 'The American Way of War Revisited', p. 507.
63 Carol Reardon, *Soldiers and Scholars: The US Army and the Uses of Military History, 1865-1920*, Lawrence: University Press of Kansas, 1990, pp. 26–27.
64 Mark A. Stoler, *Allies and Adversaries: The Joint Chiefs of Staff, The Grand Alliance, and US Strategy in World War II*, Chapel Hill: University of North Carolina Press, 2000, pp. 9–10, 12–13.
65 Weigley, *The American Way of War*, p. 128.
66 Pearlman, *Warmaking and American Democracy*, pp. 224, 241, 254.
67 Stoler, *Allies and Adversaries*, p. 270.
68 Jeffrey Record and W. Andrew Terrill, *Iraq and Vietnam: Differences, Similarities and Insights*, Carlisle Barracks: Strategic Studies Institute, May 2004, p. 56.
69 Pearlman, *Warmaking and American Democracy*, p. 359.
70 Stoler, *Allies and Adversaries*, p. 269.
71 As Brian Linn has pointed out, some episodes in American military history, such as the Spanish-American War, seem to pose particularly severe problems for Weigley's dichotomy – Linn, 'The American Way of War Revisited',

pp. 515–516. The issue is further complicated by the fact that many analysts have argued that at the *operational* (as opposed to the strategic) level of warfare, the American style was defined precisely by its reliance on 'attrition' rather than 'manoeuvre'. See Carnes Lord, 'American Strategic Culture', in Fred E. Baumann and Kenneth M. Jensen, eds, *American Defense Policy and Liberal Democracy*, Charlottesville: University Press of Virginia, 1989, p. 52; Edward N. Luttwak, 'The Operational Level of War', *International Security*, Vol. 5 No. 3, Winter 1980–1981; and Colin S. Gray, 'National Style in Strategy: The American Example', *International Security*, Vol. 6 No. 2, Fall 1981, p. 32. In an important reply to Linn's critique of his theory, moreover, Weigley himself noted towards the end of his life that, 'Almost from the moment of its publication, I have regretted characterizing the two main strategic categories in American (and other) history as a strategy of annihilation and a strategy of attrition. It would have been better to designate the latter throughout as a strategy of erosion. ... Beyond the confusion nourished by my choice of the word attrition over erosion, I plead guilty to placing too much emphasis on only two categories of strategy and trying to shoehorn practically everything into one or another of these limited concepts.' – Russell F. Weigley, 'Response to Brian McAllister Linn', *The Journal of Military History*, Vol. 66 No. 2, April 2002, p. 531.
72 Weigley, *The American Way of War*, chapters 2–8.
73 Pearlman, *Warmaking and American Democracy*, p. 188.
74 Janowitz, *The Professional Soldier*, p. 268.
75 Mark E. Grotelueschen, *Doctrine Under Trial: American Artillery Employment in World War I*, Westport: Greenwood Press, 2001, pp. 145–151.
76 Shy, 'The American Military Experience: History and Learning', p. 221.
77 Eliot A. Cohen, 'The strategy of innocence? The United States, 1920–1945', in Murray, Knox, and Bernstein, eds, *The Making of Strategy*, p. 434.
78 Weigley, *The American Way of War*, chapter 14; Shy, 'The American Military Experience: History and Learning', p. 221.
79 Bernard Brodie, *War and Politics*, New York: Macmillan, 1973, chapter 2; Gray, 'National Style in Strategy: The American Example', p. 30.
80 F. G. Hoffman, *Decisive Force: The New American Way of War*, Westport: Praeger, 1996, p. 8.
81 Pearlman, *Warmaking and American Democracy*, pp. 19–20.
82 Cohen, 'The Strategy of Innocence?', pp. 458–459.
83 Stoler, *Allies and Adversaries*, pp. 103–105.
84 Betts, *Soldiers, Statesmen, and Cold War Crises*, pp. 4–5.
85 Hoffman, *Decisive Force*, p. 9. My emphasis.
86 Pearlman, *Warmaking and American Democracy*, p. 21.
87 Andrew J. Krepinevich, Jr, *The Army and Vietnam*, Baltimore; London: Johns Hopkins University Press, 1986, p. 16.
88 Weigley, *The American Way of War*, p. 394.
89 Gacek, *The Logic of Force*, pp. 87, 178.
90 Weigley, *The American Way of War*, pp. 451, 458, 464.
91 Fred Kaplan, *The Wizards of Armageddon*, New York: Touchstone, 1984, pp. 43–44, 271.
92 Henry Kissinger, *Nuclear Weapons and Foreign Policy*, New York: Harper, 1957, p. 12.
93 Janowitz, *The Professional Soldier*, p. 143.
94 Betts, *Soldiers, Statesmen, and Cold War Crises*, p. 130.
95 Max Boot, *The Savage Wars of Peace: Small Wars and the Rise of American Power*, New York: Basic Books, 2002, pp. xiv–xv, 283–285.
96 Max Boot, *The Savage Wars of Peace*, preface and chapter 13.

97 Avant, *Political Institutions and Military Change*, p. 26.
98 Russell F. Weigley, 'American strategy from its beginnings through the First World War', in Peter Paret, ed., *Makers of Modern Strategy: From Machiavelli to the Nuclear Age*, 1986, p. 411.
99 Brian McAllister Linn, *Guardians of Empire: The US Army and the Pacific, 1902–1940*, Chapel Hill: University of North Carolina Press, 1997, pp. 47–48.
100 John T. Correll, 'Basic Beliefs', *Air Force Magazine*, Vol. 87 No. 6, June 2004, pp. 42–47.
101 Betts, *Soldiers, Statesmen, and Cold War Crises*, p. 13.
102 Krepinevich, *The Army and Vietnam*, chapter 2; Boot, *The Savage Wars of Peace*, p. 293.
103 Boot, *The Savage Wars of Peace*, pp. 293–295.
104 Gaddis, *Strategies of Containment*, pp. 262–263.
105 Krepinevich, *The Army and Vietnam*, pp. 37, 164.
106 George J. Andreopoulos, 'The Age of National Liberation Movements', in Michael Howard, George J. Andreopoulos, and Mark R. Shulman, eds, *The Laws of War: Constraints on Warfare in the Western World*, New Haven: Yale University Press, 1994, p. 194, footnote 16.
107 Boot, *The Savage Wars of Peace*, p. 303.
108 Mark Clodfelter, *The Limits of Air Power: The American Bombing of North Vietnam*, New York: The Free Press, 1989, p. 36.
109 Wray R. Johnson, 'War, Culture and the Interpretation of History: The Vietnam War Reconsidered', *Small Wars and Insurgencies*, Vol. 9 No. 2, Autumn 1998, p. 84.
110 Avant, *Political Institutions and Military Change*, p. 22.
111 Niall Ferguson, *Colossus: The Rise and the Fall of the American Empire*, London: Allen Lane, 2004, especially chapter 2, 'The Imperialism of Anti-Imperialism'.
112 Linn, *Guardians of Empire*, p. 77.
113 Samuel P. Huntington, *The Soldier and the State: The Theory and Politics of Civil–Military Relations*, 1957, p. 3.
114 Andrew J. Bacevich, *American Empire: The Realities and Consequences of US Diplomacy*, Cambridge, MA: Harvard University Press, 2002, p. 121.
115 Michael S. Sherry, *In the Shadow of War: The United States Since the 1930s*, New Haven: Yale University Press, 1995, pp. 32–33.
116 National Security Council, *NSC 68, United States Objectives and Programs for National Security*, 14 April 1950. Full text available online at www.fas.org/irp/offdocs/nsc-hst/nsc-68.htm. Accessed 19 January 2006.
117 Carnes Lord, 'American Strategic Culture in Small Wars', *Small Wars and Insurgencies*, Vol. 3 No. 3, Winter 1992, p. 210.
118 Hoffman, *Decisive Force*, pp. 8, 28.
119 Kaplan, *The Wizards of Armageddon*, p. 271.

2 The science of strategy: war as a political instrument in the nuclear age

1 Arthur Herzog, *The War Peace Establishment*, New York: Harper and Row, 1965, p. 74.
2 Arthur Herzog, *The War Peace Establishment*, pp. 32–33.
3 Gregg Herken, *Counsels of War*, New York: Alfred A. Knopf, 1985, pp. 31, 81–82.
4 Herzog, *The War Peace Establishment*, pp. 36, 60.
5 J. C. Garnett, 'Herman Kahn', in John Baylis and John Garnett, eds, *Makers of Nuclear Strategy*, London: Pinter Publishers, 1991, pp. 72, 87, 93.
6 Herken *Counsels of War*, p. 208.

7 Fred Kaplan, *The Wizards of Armageddon*, p. 231.
8 Herken, *Counsels of War*, pp. 78–79, 83, 86, 138–139,143.
9 Beatrice Heuser, *Reading Clausewitz,* London: Pimlico, 2002, pp. 162–164.
10 Phil Williams, 'Thomas Schelling', in Baylis and Garnett, eds, *Makers of Nuclear Strategy*, p. 123.
11 Herken, *Counsels of War*, p. 51.
12 Heuser, *Reading Clausewitz,* p. 166.
13 Williams, 'Thomas Schelling', p. 121.
14 Garnett, 'Herman Kahn', in John Baylis and John Garnett, eds, *Makers of Nuclear Strategy*, p. 88.
15 Herzog, *The War Peace Establishment*, pp. 76, 81.
16 Garnett, 'Herman Kahn', pp. 88–89.
17 Paul N. Edwards, *The Closed World: Computers and the Politics of Discourse in Cold War America*, Cambridge: MIT Press, 1996, p. 126.
18 Herken, *Counsels of War*, p. 78.
19 Michael S. Sherry, *The Rise of American Air Power: The Creation of Armageddon*, New Haven: Yale University Press, 1987, p. 235.
20 Russell F. Weigley, *The American Way of War*, p. 446.
21 Colin S. Gray, 'Strategic culture as context: the first generation of theory strikes back', *Review of International Studies*, Vol. 25 No. 1, January 1999, p. 58.
22 Thomas P. Hughes, *Human-Built World: How to Think about Technology and Culture*, Chicago: University of Chicago Press, 2004, pp. 68–73.
23 Huntington, *The Soldier and the State*, pp. 195–203. Its 'technicist' educational bias continues to this day, as the journalist David Lipsky noted in his 2003 book about West Point. Observing that the academy compared itself to the best engineering schools in the country, including the Ivy League and MIT, Lipsky remarked that, 'At a time when the military is reassessing its global role ... it is surprising to learn that the Department of Military Instruction does not offer a major. In fact, in a school of four thousand students, only thirty even minor in the actual study of the art and science of warmaking. The department offers courses on Low-Intensity Conflict, Battlefield Operating Systems and Strategy; the most popular course is Public Speaking.' David Lipsky, *Absolutely American: Four Years at West Point*, New York: Houghton Mifflin, 2003, pp. 66–67.
24 See Merritt Roe Smith, 'Army Ordnance and the "American System" of Manufacturing, 1815–1861', in Roe Smith, ed., *Military Enterprise and Technological Change: Perspectives on the American Experience*, Cambridge, MA: MIT Press, 1985.
25 Ellis, John, *A Social History of the Machine Gun*, Baltimore: Johns Hopkins University Press, 1986, pp. 29, 41, 74–76.
26 Samuel P. Huntington, *The Soldier and the State*, p. 228.
27 Howard P. Segal, *Technological Utopianism in American Culture*, Chicago: University of Chicago Press, 1985, p. 1.
28 Carroll Pursell, *The Machine in America: A Social History of Technology*, Baltimore: Johns Hopkins University Press, 1995, p. 204.
29 Pursell, *The Machine in America*, pp. 210–211; Hounshell, David A., *From the American System to Mass Production 1800–1932*, Baltimore: Johns Hopkins University Press, 1984, p. 249.
30 Pursell, *The Machine in America*, pp. 92, 210–211.
31 Hounshell, *From the American System to Mass Production 1800–1932*, p. 249. My emphasis.
32 Azar Gat, *A History of Military Thought: From the Enlightenment to the Cold War*, Oxford: Oxford University Press, 2001, pp. 288–289.

33 Weigley, *The American Way of War*, pp. 82–83.
34 Carol Reardon, *Soldiers and Scholars: The US Army and the Uses of Military History, 1865–1920*, Lawrence: University Press of Kansas, 1990, pp. 9–10.
35 Weigley, *The American Way of War*, p. 213.
36 Brian McAllister Linn, 'The American Way of War Revisited', *Journal of Military History*, Vol. 66 No. 2, April 2002, p. 527.
37 Martin Van Creveld, *Fighting Power: German and US Army Performance, 1939-1945*, Westport: Greenwood Press, 1982, p. 167.
38 Eliot A. Cohen, 'The strategy of innocence? The United States, 1920–1945', in Williamson Murray, MacGregor Knox, and Alvin Bernstein, eds, *The Making of Strategy: Rulers, States, and War*, Cambridge; New York: Cambridge University Press, 1994, p. 464.
39 Sherry, *The Rise of American Air Power*, p. 230.
40 James William Gibson, *The Perfect War: Technowar in Vietnam*, New York: The Atlantic Monthly Press, 2000, p. 358.
41 Michael D. Pearlman, *Warmaking and American Democracy*, p. 191.
42 Sherry, *The Rise of American Air Power*, p. 118.
43 H. Bruce Franklin, *War Stars: The Superweapon and the American Imagination*, New York; Oxford: Oxford University Press, 1988, p. 72.
44 Kennedy, David M., *Freedom from Fear: The American People in Depression and War, 1929–1945*, New York: Oxford University Press, 1999, pp. 469, 619.
45 Sherry, *The Rise of American Air Power*, p. 121.
46 Cohen, 'The strategy of innocence? The United States, 1920–1945', p. 447.
47 Kennedy, *Freedom from Fear*, pp. 244, 647–648, 654.
48 Sherry, *The Rise of American Air Power*, p. 192.
49 Kennedy, *Freedom from Fear*, p. 361.
50 Robert B. Bathurst, *Intelligence and the Mirror: On Creating an Enemy*, London: Sage, 1993, p. 62.
51 Cohen, 'The strategy of innocence? The United States, 1920–1945', p. 465.
52 Pearlman, *Warmaking and American Democracy*, p. 267.
53 Kennedy, *Freedom from Fear*, p. 668.
54 Sherry, *The Rise of American Air Power*, p. 177.
55 Pursell, *The Machine in America*, p. 271.
56 Kaplan, *The Wizards of Armageddon*, p. 80.
57 National Security Council, *NSC 68, United States Objectives and Programs for National Security*, 14 April 1950. Full text available online at www.fas.org/irp/offdocs/nsc-hst/nsc-68.htm. Accessed 19 January 2006.
58 Herken, *Counsels of War*, p. 51.
59 Pearlman, *Warmaking and American Democracy*, p. 127.
60 Michael Lind, *Vietnam: The Necessary War: a Reinterpretation of America's Most Disastrous Military Conflict*, New York: Free Press, 1999, epigraph to prologue.
61 Bernard Brodie, 'War in the Atomic Age', in Brodie, ed., *The Absolute Weapon: Atomic Power and World Order*, New York: Harcourt, Brace and Company, 1946, p. 76.
62 Herken, *Counsels of War*, pp. xii, 38.
63 Chris Hables Gray, *Postmodern War: The New Politics of Conflict*, London: Routledge, 1997, p. 138.
64 Kaplan, *The Wizards of Armageddon*, p. 197.
65 Williamson Murray, 'Clausewitz Out, Computers In: Military Culture and Technological Hubris', *The National Interest*, No. 48, Summer 1997, p. 60.
66 Michael Howard, *Clausewitz*, Oxford; New York: Oxford University Press, 1983, p. 31.

67 'For two decades, from the early 1940s until the early 1960s, the armed forces of the United States were the single most important driver of digital computer development.' Edwards, *The Closed World*, p. 43.
68 Paul N. Edwards, 'The Closed World: Systems Discourse, Military Policy and post-World War II US Historical Consciousness', in Les Levidow and Kevin Robins, *Cyborg Worlds: The Military Information Society*, London: Free Association Books, 1989, p. 156.
69 George and Meredith Friedman, *The Future of War*, New York: Crown, 1996, p. 10.
70 Weigley, *The American Way of War*, pp. 406–407; Kaplan, *The Wizards of Armageddon*, p. 121; Herken, *Counsels of War*, p. 100; Edwards, *Closed World: Computers and the Politics of Discourse*, p. 150.
71 Friedmans, *The Future of War*, pp. 52–59.
72 Herken, *Counsels of War*, p. 100.
73 Ken Booth, 'Bernard Brodie', in Baylis and Garnett, eds, *Makers of Nuclear Strategy*, p. 38, 43.
74 Michael T. Klare, *War Without End: American Planning for the Next Vietnams*, New York: Knopf, 1972, p. 65.
75 Kaplan, *The Wizards of Armageddon*, p. 257.
76 Herzog, *The War Peace Establishment*, pp. 47–48, 62.
77 Sharon Ghamari-Tabrizi, *The Worlds of Herman Kahn: The Intuitive Science of Thermonuclear War*, Cambridge, MA: Harvard University Press, 2005, pp. 48–49, 59.
78 Herzog, *The War Peace Establishment*, p. 34.
79 Kaplan, *The Wizards of Armageddon*, p. 246.
80 Christopher M. Gacek, *The Logic of Force: The Dilemma of Limited War in American Foreign Policy*, New York: Columbia University Press, 1994, p. 150.
81 John Lewis Gaddis, *Strategies of Containment: A Critical Appraisal of Postwar American National Security Policy*, New York: Oxford University Press, 1982, p. 84.
82 Kaplan, *The Wizards of Armageddon*, p. 142. This technicist bias would also be reflected, as the Cold War progressed, in progressively larger spending on *technical* intelligence-gathering focused on enemy capabilities at the expense of 'human intelligence', which sought to impart an insight into enemy intentions. Bathurst, *Intelligence and the Mirror*, p. 108.
83 Kaplan, *The Wizards of Armageddon*, p. 92.
84 Gaddis, *Strategies of Containment,* chapters 2 and 3.
85 Kaplan, *The Wizards of Armageddon,* p. 101.
86 Kaplan, *The Wizards of Armageddon,* pp. 109, 172.
87 Robert H. Johnson, *Improbable Dangers: US Conceptions of Threat in the Cold War and After*, Basingstoke: Macmillan, 1994, p. 90.
88 Herken, *Counsels of War*, p. 156.
89 Gibson, *The Perfect War*, p. 80.
90 Herken, *Counsels of War*, pp. 209–210.
91 Gibson, *The Perfect War*, p. ix.
92 Gibson, *The Perfect War*, pp. 97, 323.
93 Friedmans, *The Future of War,* p. 64.
94 Walter A. McDougall, *Promised Land, Crusader State: The American Encounter with the World Since 1776*, Boston: Houghton Mifflin, 1997, p. 189.
95 Gibson, *The Perfect War*, pp. 305–306.
96 Klare, *War Without End*, p. 113.
97 Heuser, *Reading Clausewitz*, p. 159.
98 Sherry, *The Rise of American Air Power*, p. 234.

99 Lawrence Freedman, *The Evolution of Nuclear Strategy*, London: Macmillan, 1989, p. 181.
100 Edwards, 'The Closed World: Systems Discourse', p. 155.
101 Kaplan, *The Wizards of Armageddon*, pp. 214, 317.
102 Herken, *Counsels of War*, p. 197.
103 Garnett, 'Herman Kahn', p. 90.
104 Gaddis, *Strategies of Containment*, footnote, p. 255.
105 Edwards, *Closed World: Computers and the Politics of Discourse*, p. 128.
106 Gaddis, *Strategies of Containment*, p. 252.
107 Wray R. Johnson, 'War, Culture and the Interpretation of History: the Vietnam War Reconsidered', *Small Wars and Insurgencies*, Vol. 9 No. 2, Autumn 1998.
108 Gibson, *The Perfect War*, p. 98. My emphasis.
109 Alton Frye, 'The American Character and the Formation of US Foreign Policy', in Michael P. Hamilton, ed., *American Character and Foreign Policy*, Grand Rapids: W. B. Eerdmans Pub. Co., 1986, p. 153.
110 Jeffrey Record, 'Vietnam in Retrospect: Could We Have Won?', *Parameters: US Army War College Quarterly*, Vol. 26 No. 4, Winter 1996–1997 – http://carlisle-www.Army.mil/usawc/Parameters/96winter/record.htm. Accessed 19 January 2006.
111 Sherry, *The Rise of American Air Power*, p. 177.
112 Gaddis, , *Strategies of Containment*, p. 238.
113 Herken, *Counsels of War*, pp. 219–224.
114 Kaplan, *The Wizards of Armageddon*, p. 336.
115 Herken, *Counsels of War*, p. 224.
116 Weigley, *The American Way of War*, p. 477.
117 Edwards, 'The Closed World: Systems Discourse', pp. 152–153.

3 Overwhelming force: the American military and the memory of Vietnam

1 Michael D. Pearlman, *Warmaking and American Democracy*, p. 397.
2 Philip Windsor, *Strategic Thinking: An Introduction and Farewell*, London: Lynne Rienner, 2002, p. 181.
3 According to Brian Holden Reid, the first reference appeared in either the *Washington Post* or the *New York Times*. Brian Holden Reid, 'The Influence of the Vietnam Syndrome on the Writing of Civil War History', *RUSI Journal*, Vol. 147 No. 1, February 2002, p. 44. The coining of the phrase 'Vietnam Syndrome' has alternatively been attributed to President Carter's national security adviser, Zbigniew Brzezinski – Pearlman, *Warmaking and American Democracy*, p. 397.
4 Andrew J. Bacevich, *The New American Militarism*, New York: Oxford University Press, 2005, p. 74.
5 Holden Reid, 'The Influence of the Vietnam Syndrome on the Writing of Civil War History', p. 45.
6 Christopher M. Gacek, *The Logic of Force: The Dilemma of Limited War in American Foreign Policy*, New York: Columbia University Press, 1994, p. 241.
7 Richard K. Betts, *Soldiers, Statesmen, and Cold War Crises*, Cambridge, MA: Harvard University Press, 1977, pp. 4-5.
8 This conclusion is reinforced by recent survey data included in Peter D. Feaver and Christopher Gelpi, *Choosing Your Battles: American Civil–Military Relations and the Use of Force*, Princeton: Princeton University Press, 2004.
9 Jeffrey Record, *Making War, Thinking History: Munich, Vietnam, and Presidential Uses of Force from Korea to Kosovo*, Annapolis: Naval Institute Press, 2002, p. 29.

10 Max Boot, *The Savage Wars of Peace: Small Wars and the Rise of American Power*, New York: Basic Books, 2002, p. 319.
11 Michael Handel, *Masters of War*, London: Frank Cass, 1992, p. 13; see also Williamson Murray, 'Clausewitz Out, Computers In: Military Culture and Technological Hubris', p. 61, for a similar argument.
12 Donald M. Snow and Dennis M. Drew, *From Lexington to Desert Storm: War and Politics in the American Experience*, Armonk: M. E. Sharpe, 1994, p. 319.
13 In identifying the Remarkable Trinity with the triangle of government, military, and people, Summers reinforced a common misconception. Clausewitz in fact wrote that war was dominated by a trinity composed of 'the primordial violence of its nature, the hatred and enmity which must be regarded as a blind natural instinct'; 'the interplay of probability and chance, which make war a free activity of the soul'; and 'the subordinate nature of a political tool, through which war becomes subject to reason'. The first of these three sides, he argued, 'is turned towards the people, the second towards the military commander and his Army, the third towards the government'. However, it is this 'second trinity' of government, military, and people that has attracted more attention amongst scholars. Beatrice Heuser, *Reading Clausewitz*, p. 53.
14 It is interesting to note in this regard that Russell Weigley, author of the classic account of the American way of war, expressed his concern in 2002 that his earlier work 'may have contributed to a continuing American military propensity to require the application of overwhelming force as the only acceptable American way of war'. Russell F. Weigley, 'Response to Brian McAllister Linn', *The Journal of Military History*, Vol. 66 No. 2, April 2002, p. 532.
15 James Mann, *The Rise of the Vulcans: The History of Bush's War Cabinet*, New York: Viking, 2004, p. 221.
16 James Kitfield, *Prodigal Soldiers*, Washington; London: Brassey's, 1997, p. 121.
17 Lawrence J. Korb, 'Fixing the Mix', *Foreign Affairs*, Vol. 83 No. 2, March/April 2004, pp. 2–3.
18 Richard Lock-Pullan, 'An Inward-Looking Time: The United States Army, 1973–1976', *The Journal of Military History*, Vol. 67 No. 2, April 2003, p. 487.
19 Robin Toner, 'Trust in the Military Heightens Among Baby Boomers' Children', *New York Times*, 27 May 2003.
20 Harry G. Summers, Jr, *On Strategy: A Critical Analysis of the Vietnam War*, Novato: Presidio, 1982, pp. 11–12.
21 Stephen Peter Rosen, 'Vietnam and the American Theory of Limited War', *International Security*, Vol. 7 No. 2, Fall 1982, p. 95.
22 Kenneth J. Campbell, 'Once Burned, Twice Cautious: Explaining the Weinberger–Powell Doctrine', *Armed Forces and Society*, Vol. 24 No. 3, Spring 1998, p. 364.
23 F. G. Hoffman, *Decisive Force: The New American Way of War*, Westport: Praeger, 1996, p. 22.
24 Bacevich, *The New American Militarism*, p. 41.
25 Harry G. Summers, Jr, *On Strategy II: A Critical Analysis of the Gulf War*, New York: Dell, 1992, pp. 113–114.
26 Hoffman, *Decisive Force: The New American Way of War*, p. 28.
27 Michael Lind, *Vietnam: The Necessary War: A Reinterpretation of America's Most Disastrous Military Conflict*, New York: Free Press, 1999, p. 81.
28 Al Santoli, *Leading the Way: How Vietnam Veterans Rebuilt the US Military*, New York: Ballantine Books, 1993, p. 55.
29 Stanley I. Kutler, 'The Long Shadow: the Third Indochina War, 1975–1995', in David K. Adams and Cornelis A. Van Minnen, eds, *Aspects of War in American History*, Keele: Keele University Press, 1997, pp. 241, 244.

30 Santoli, *Leading the Way*, p. 417.
31 Boot, *The Savage Wars of Peace*, p. 318.
32 Mann, *The Rise of the Vulcans*, p. 185.
33 Russell F. Weigley, 'The American Military and the Principle of Civilian Control from McClellan to Powell', *The Journal of Military History*, Vol. 57 No. 5, October 1993, p. 56.
34 Harvey M. Sapolsky and Jeremy Shapiro, 'Casualties, Technology and America's Future Wars', *Parameters: US Army War College Quarterly*, Vol. 26 No. 2, Summer 1996 – http://carlisle-www.Army.mil/usawc/Parameters/96summer/sapolsky.htm. Accessed 19 January 2006.
35 Eliot A. Cohen, 'Twilight of the Citizen Soldier', *Parameters: US Army War College Quarterly*, Vol. 31 No. 2, Summer 2001 – http://carlisle-www.Army.mil/usawc/Parameters/01summer/cohen.htm. Accessed 19 January 2006.
36 George A. Brinegar, 'The Abrams Doctrine: Has it been abused in the Global War on Terror?', in Williamson Murray, ed., *A Nation at War in an Era of Strategic Change*, Carlisle Barracks: Strategic Studies Institute, September 2004, p. 178.
37 Kitfield, *Prodigal Soldiers*, pp. 149–151.
38 Lock-Pullan, 'An Inward-Looking Time: The United States Army, 1973–1976', p. 502.
39 Summers, *On Strategy*, p. 11.
40 Meirion and Susie Harries, *Soldiers of the Sun: The Rise and Fall of the Imperial Japanese Army*, New York: Random House, 1991, p. vii.
41 Pearlman, *Warmaking and American Democracy*, p. 224.
42 Boot, *The Savage Wars of Peace*, p. 303.
43 Richard A. Lacquement, 'The Casualty-aversion Myth', *Naval War College Review*, Vol. 57 No. 1, Winter 2004, www.Army.mil/professionalwriting/volumes/volume2/march_2004/3_04_2.html. Accessed 24 September 2007.
44 Edward N. Luttwak, 'Toward Post-Heroic Warfare', *Foreign Affairs*, Vol. 74 No. 3, May/June 1995.
45 Eric V. Larson, *Casualties and Consensus: The Historical Role of Casualties in Domestic Support for US Military Operations*, Santa Monica: RAND, 1996; James Burk, 'Public Support for Peacekeeping in Lebanon and Somalia: Assessing the Casualties Hypothesis', *Political Science Quarterly*, Vol. 114 No. 1, Spring 1999. Some who have seized on this evidence in support of a claim that casualty-aversion is a 'myth' (e.g. Lacquement, 'The Casualty-aversion Myth') arguably miss the point – for the single most enduring political legacy of the Vietnam War is precisely the shattering of consensus within the political elite over the nature and purpose of America's role in the world. As the most influential author of the 'elite consensus' explanation of casualty-aversion himself concluded, 'Until US leaders arrive at a new bipartisan consensus on the role of military force in the post-Cold War world ... The absence of a larger foreign policy consensus will contribute to support that is often shallow and highly responsive to the costs in casualties,' Larson, *Casualties and Consensus*, pp. 102–103.
46 Boot, *The Savage Wars of Peace*, chapter 14; Peter D. Feaver and Christopher Gelpi, 'A Look At Casualty Aversion: How Many Deaths Are Acceptable? A Surprising Answer', *Washington Post*, 7 November 1999; Lacquement, 'The Casualty-aversion Myth'; Charles K. Hyde, 'Casualty Aversion: Implications for Policymakers and Senior Military Officers', *Aerospace Power Journal*, Vol. 14 No. 2, Summer 2000 – www.airpower.maxwell.af.mil/airchronicles/apj/apj00/sum00/hyde.pdf. Accessed 19 January 2006.
47 Bacevich, *The New American Militarism*, p. 65.

48 Karl W. Eikenberry, 'Take No Casualties', *Parameters: US Army War College Quarterly,* Vol. 26 No. 2, Summer 1996 – http://carlisle-www.Army.mil/usawc/Parameters/96summer/eiken.htm. Accessed 19 January 2006.
49 Hoffman, *Decisive Force: The New American Way of War,* p. xi.
50 Andrew J. Krepinevich, Jr, *The Army and Vietnam,* Baltimore; London: Johns Hopkins University Press, 1986, pp. 260, 272.
51 Carnes Lord, 'American Strategic Culture in Small Wars', *Small Wars and Insurgencies,* Vol. 3 No. 3, Winter 1992, p. 211.
52 Robert M. Cassidy, 'Prophets or Praetorians? The Uptonian Paradox and the Powell Corollary', *Parameters: US Army War College Quarterly,* Vol. 33 No. 3, Autumn 2003, p. 138.
53 Lock-Pullan, 'An Inward-Looking Time: The United States Army, 1973–1976', p. 497.
54 Mark Clodfelter, *The Limits of Air Power: The American Bombing of North Vietnam,* New York: The Free Press, 1989, p. 209.
55 Boot, *The Savage Wars of Peace,* p. 314.
56 Stephen D. Wrage, 'Conclusion: Prospects for Precision Air Power', in Wrage, ed., *Immaculate Warfare: Participants Reflect on the Air Campaigns over Kosovo, Afghanistan, and Iraq,* Westport: Praeger, 2003, p. 74.
57 Summers, *On Strategy,* p. 25. My emphasis.
58 David H. Petraeus, 'Military Influence and the Post-Vietnam Use of Force', *Armed Forces and Society,* Vol. 15 No. 4, Summer 1989, p. 491.
59 David Halberstam, *War in a Time of Peace: Bush, Clinton, and the Generals,* London: Bloomsbury, 2003, p. 265.
60 Michael R. Gordon and Bernard E. Trainor, *The Generals' War,* Boston: Little Brown, 1995, pp. 33, 149.
61 Campbell, 'Once Burned, Twice Cautious: Explaining the Weinberger-Powell Doctrine', p. 366.
62 Petraeus, 'Military Influence and the Post-Vietnam Use of Force', p. 494.
63 Halberstam, *War in a Time of Peace,* p. 42.
64 Mann, *The Rise of the Vulcans,* p. 118.
65 Bacevich, *The New American Militarism,* p. 49.
66 Halberstam, *War in a Time of Peace,* pp. 38–42.
67 James Der Derian, *Virtuous War,* Boulder: Westview Press, 2001, pp. 192–193.
68 Richard H. Shultz, Jr, 'Showstoppers', *The Weekly Standard,* 26 *January 2004.*
69 Carnes Lord, 'American Strategic Culture in Small Wars', p. 209.
70 Gordon and Trainor, *The Generals' War,* pp. xii, 154.
71 Hoffman, *Decisive Force: The New American Way of War,* p. 83.
72 Pearlman, *Warmaking and American Democracy,* p. 397.
73 Gordon and Trainor, *The Generals' War,* p. 439.
74 Gordon and Trainor, *The Generals' War,* pp. 447–448.
75 Dan Goodgame, '1990: The Two George Bushes', *Time Magazine,* 2 January 1990.
76 Gordon and Trainor, *The Generals' War,* p. xv.
77 Record, *Making War, Thinking History,* pp. 134–135.
78 Alvin and Heidi Toffler, *War and Anti-war: Survival at the Dawn of the 21st Century,* London: Little, Brown, and Co, 1993, pp. 82–83; Gordon and Trainor, *The Generals' War,* pp. 76–80.
79 Halberstam, *War in a Time of Peace,* pp. 51–52, 69–70.
80 Gordon and Trainor, *The Generals' War,* pp. 134, 321, 178.
81 Dana Priest, *The Mission: Waging War and Keeping Peace With America's Military,* New York; London: W. W. Norton & Co, 2003, p. 52.
82 Halberstam, *War in a Time of Peace,* p. 40, 42.

83 Priest, *The Mission*, p. 53.
84 Bacevich, *The New American Militarism*, p. 21.
85 Stephen D. Wrage, 'Introduction: The Promise of Immaculate Warfare', in Wrage, ed., *Immaculate Warfare*, p. 10.
86 Wrage, 'Conclusion', in Wrage, ed., *Immaculate Warfare*, p. 104.
87 Douglas Porch, *Wars of Empire*, London: Cassell, 2000; Andrew J. Bacevich, *American Empire: The Realities and Consequences of US Diplomacy*, Cambridge, MA: Harvard University Press, 2002, p. 165.
88 Robert M. Perito, *Where is the Lone Ranger When We Need Him? America's Search for a Postconflict Stability Force*, Washington, DC: United States Institute of Peace, 2004, p. 28.
89 Lawrence Freedman, 'Victims and victors: reflections on the Kosovo War', *Review of International Studies*, Vol. 26 No. 3, 2000.
90 Halberstam, *War in a Time of Peace*, p. 457.
91 Halberstam, *War in a Time of Peace*, p. 464.
92 Eliot A. Cohen, 'Why the Gap Matters', *The National Interest*, No. 61, Fall 2000, pp. 41, 45.
93 Robert H. Johnson, *Improbable Dangers: US Conceptions of Threat in the Cold War and After*, Basingstoke: Macmillan, 1994, pp. 47, 231.
94 For the argument that Western approaches to warfare are increasingly influenced by concepts of 'risk management', see Yee Kuang-Heng, *War as Risk Management*, Unpublished PhD Thesis, London School of Economics and Political Science, 2004. For a complementary argument focused specifically on NATO, see Christopher Coker, *Globalisation and Insecurity: NATO and the Management of Risk*, IISS Adelphi Paper 345, (Oxford University Press, 2002).
95 Heng, *War as Risk Management*, p. 96.
96 Priest, *The Mission*, p. 97.
97 Heng, *War as Risk Management*, pp. 48, 124–125.

4 Immaculate Destruction: the impact of 9/11 on American military culture

1 Eliot A. Cohen, 'Kosovo and the New American Way of War', in Cohen and Bacevich, eds, *War Over Kosovo: Politics and Strategy in a Global Age*, New York: Columbia University Press, 2001, p. 59.
2 For analyses of the role of such cultural reference points in conditioning the construction of national security policy, see Jeffrey Record, *Making War, Thinking History, Munich, Vietnam, and Presidential Uses of Force from Korea to Kosovo*, Annapolis: Naval Institute Press, 2002; and Yuen Foong Khong, *Analogies at War: Korea, Munich, Dien Bien Phu, and the Vietnam decisions of 1965*, Princeton: Princeton University Press, 1992.
3 This was the central conclusion of Richard H. Schultz, who was commissioned by the Pentagon's Department of Special Operations and Low-Intensity Conflict after 9/11 to investigate why the military's elite counter-terrorism units had never been used for their intended purpose during the 1990s. See Richard H. Shultz, Jr, 'Showstoppers', *The Weekly Standard*, 26 January 2004.
4 Consider, for example, these remarks of Condoleezza Rice: 'I really think this period is analogous to 1945 to 1947, in that the events so clearly demonstrated that there is a big global threat, and that it's a big global threat to a lot of countries that you would not have normally thought of as being in the coalition. That has started shifting the tectonic plates in international politics. And it's important to try to seize on that and position American interests and institutions and all of that before they harden again.' Nicholas Lemann, 'The Next World Order', *The New Yorker*, 1 April 2004.

5 Williamson Murray, 'Clausewitz Out, Computers In: Military Culture and Technological Hubris', *The National Interest*, No. 48, Summer 1997, p. 62.
6 Harlan K. Ullman and James P. Wade, Jr, *Rapid Dominance, A Force for all Seasons: Technologies and Systems for Achieving Shock and Awe*, (London: RUSI, 1998), pp. 18–19.
7 Martin Libicki, *www.USDoD.com: Virtual Diplomacy Report 7*, (United States Institute of Peace, February 1999) – www.usip.org/virtualdiplomacy/publications/reports/libickiISA99.html. Accessed 3 February 2006.
8 Interview with Lt.-General Liu Yazhou of the Chinese Air Force by Dai Xu, for *Dongfang Wang* (Shanghai), 31 May 2004 – online translation www.eveningpost.org/blog/_archives/2005/1/8. Accessed 12 August 2005.
9 James Der Derian, *Virtuous War*, Boulder: Westview Press, 2001, p. 113.
10 William A. Owens with Ed Offley, *Lifting the Fog of War*, Baltimore; London: Johns Hopkins University Press, 2001, pp. 14–15.
11 John A. Warden III, 'Air Theory for the Twenty-first Century', in Karl P. Magyar, ed., *Challenge and Response: Anticipating US Military Security Concerns*, Maxwell AFB: Air University Press, 1994. My emphasis.
12 GlobalSecurity.Org, 'Global Strike Task Force', 26 April 2005 – www.globalsecurity.org/military/agency/usaf/gstf.htm. Accessed 12 August 2005.
13 Williamson Murray, 'Introduction', in Williamson Murray, ed., *A Nation at War in an Era of Strategic Change*, Carlisle Barracks: Strategic Studies Institute, September 2004, pp. 2–3. For Cebrowski's statement see House Armed Services Committee, 'Statement of Arthur K. Cebrowski before the Subcommittee on Terrorism, Unconventional Threats and Capabilities', 26 February 2004 – www.house.gov/hasc/openingstatementsandpressreleases/108thcongress/04-02-26cebrowski.pdf. Accessed 12 August 2005.
14 On the Western attempt to humanize war see Christopher Coker, *Humane Warfare*, London and New York: Routledge, 2002.
15 F. G. Hoffman, *Decisive Force: The New American Way of War*, Westport: Praeger, 1996, p. 89.
16 Brad Knickerbocker, 'The Pentagon's Quietest Calculation: the Casualty Count', *Christian Science Monitor*, 28 January 2003.
17 Harvey M. Sapolsky and Jeremy Shapiro, 'Casualties, Technology and America's Future Wars', *Parameters: US Army War College Quarterly*, Vol. 26 No. 2, Summer 1996 – http://carlisle-www.Army.mil/usawc/Parameters/96summer/sapolsky.htm. Accessed 1 December 2005.
18 Nicholas Wheeler, 'Dying for "Enduring Freedom": Accepting Responsibility for Civilian Casualties in the War against Terrorism', *International Relations*, Vol. 16 No. 2, August 2002, p. 217.
19 Michael R. Gordon, 'US Attacked Iraqi Defenses Starting in 2002', *New York Times*, 20 July 2003. According to one estimate, one civilian died for every twelve munitions dropped during the Afghan air war; and one for every thirty-five munitions dropped in Iraq: Williamson Murray and Robert H. Scales, Jr, *The Iraq War: A Military History*, Cambridge, MA; London: Harvard University Press, 2003, pp. 179–180.
20 William A. Arkin, 'Spiralling Ahead', *Armed Forces Journal*, February 2006.
21 Tim Weiner, 'Lockheed and the Future of Warfare', *New York Times*, 28 November 2004.
22 The White House, *The National Security Strategy of the United States of America*, 2002 – www.whitehouse.gov/nsc/nss.html. Accessed 3 February 2006.
23 Department of Defense, 'Deputy Secretary Wolfowitz Remarks at the Aspen Institute', 16 July 2004 – www.defenselink.mil/transcripts/2004/tr20040716-secdef1041.html. Accessed 12 August 2005.

24 According to Bob Woodward, the President made this request to Rumsfeld on 21 November 2001; General Franks states that Rumsfeld relayed this request to CENTCOM on 27 November. Bob Woodward, *Plan of Attack: The Road To War*, London: Simon & Schuster, 2004, p. 11; Tommy Franks with Malcolm McConnell, *American Soldier*, New York: Harper Collins, 2004, p. 315.
25 Frederick W. Kagan, 'War and Aftermath', *Policy Review*, No. 120, August/September 2003, www.policyreview.org/aug03/kagan.html. Accessed on 1 December 2005.
26 Woodward, *Plan of Attack*, p. 425.
27 State Department, 'President Bush Outlines Progress in Operation Iraqi Freedom', 16 April 2003 – www.state.gov/p/nea/rls/rm/19709.htm. Accessed 12 August 2005.
28 Albert Wohlstetter, 'On Vietnam and Bureaucracy', July 1968, available online in 'The Writings of Albert Wohlstetter' – www.rand.org/publications/classics/wohlstetter/D17276.1/D17276.1.html. Accessed 1 December 2005.
29 Peter Brush, 'The Story Behind the McNamara Line', *Vietnam Magazine*, February 1996, pp. 18–24.
30 Paul Dickson, *The Electronic Battlefield*, London: Boyars, 1976, p. 21.
31 Michael T. Klare, *War Without End: American Planning for the Next Vietnams*, New York: Knopf, 1972, pp. 166, 188, 202, 209.
32 Paul N. Edwards, *The Closed World: Computers and the Politics of Discourse in Cold War America*, Cambridge: MIT Press, 1996, p. 114.
33 General William Westmoreland, 'The Battlefield of the Future', Speech to the Association of the United States Army, Washington, DC, 14 October 1969.
34 Klare, *War Without End*, p. 203.
35 Dickson, *The Electronic Battlefield*, p. 159.
36 Lawrence Freedman, *The Revolution in Strategic Affairs*, Adelphi Paper 318 Oxford: Oxford University Press, 1998, p. 11, 21.
37 Neil Swidey, 'The Analyst', *The Boston Globe*, 18 May 2003.
38 Andrew W. Marshall, J. J. Martin, and Henry S. Rowen, eds, *On Not Confusing Ourselves: Essays on National Security Strategy in Honour of Albert and Roberta Wohlstetter*, Boulder: Westview Press, 1991, p. 11.
39 Albert Wohlstetter, 'Between an Unfree World and None: Increasing Our Choices', *Foreign Affairs*, Vol. 63 No. 5, Summer 1985, p. 992.
40 Stefan Halper and Jonathan Clarke, *America Alone: The Neo-Conservatives and the Global Order*, Cambridge: Cambridge University Press, 2004, p. 64.
41 William A. Owens, 'Creating a US Military Revolution', in Theo Farrell and Terry Terriff, eds, *The Sources of Military Change: Culture, Politics, Technology*, Boulder: Lynne Rienner, 2002, pp. 207–209.
42 Andrew F. Krepinevich, 'Cavalry to Computer: The Pattern of Military Revolutions', *The National Interest*, No. 37, Fall 1994, p. 30.
43 Karl W. Eikenberry, 'Take No Casualties', *Parameters: US Army War College Quarterly*, Vol. 26 No. 2, Summer 1996; Gene I. Rochlin, *Trapped in the Net: The Unanticipated Consequences of Computerization*, Princeton: Princeton University Press, 1997, pp. 140–142.
44 For a concise survey of different schools of thought within the RMA debate, see Michael O'Hanlon, *Technological Change and the Future of Warfare*, Washington, DC: Brookings Institution Press, 2000, chapter 2.
45 Bill Keller, 'The Fighting Next Time', *New York Times Magazine*, 10 March 2002.
46 Perle dated Wohlstetter's daughter as a teenager in Los Angeles, and was later recruited (with Wolfowitz) for his first job in Washington by Wohlstetter. Perle dedicated the book he co-wrote with David Frum, *An*

166 Notes

      End to Evil, to Wohlstetter's memory. Wohlstetter was also Wolfowitz's PhD supervisor and mentor at the University of Chicago. James Mann, *The Rise of the Vulcans: The History of Bush's War Cabinet*, New York: Viking, 2004, pp. 29–34.
47. Donald Mackenzie, *Inventing Accuracy: A Historical Sociology of Nuclear Missile Guidance*, Cambridge, MA: The MIT Press, 1990, p. 393.
48. George and Meredith Friedman, *The Future of War*, New York: Crown, 1996, p. 72.
49. Kagan, 'War and Aftermath'.
50. Wohlstetter, 'Between an Unfree World and None', p. 992.
51. These implications were not lost on Wohlstetter – in the early 1990s, for example, he became a passionate advocate for early US military intervention in Bosnia against the Serbs. Swidey, The Analyst'.
52. Department of Defense, 'Deputy Secretary Wolfowitz Interview with Sam Tannenhaus', *Vanity Fair*, 9 May 2003 –www.defenselink.mil/transcripts/2003/tr20030509-depsecdef0223.html. Accessed on 1 July 2005.
53. Les Aspin, Address to the Jewish Institute for National Security Affairs, Washington, DC, 21 September 1992.
54. Westmoreland, 'The Battlefield of the Future'.
55. Dickson, *The Electronic Battlefield*, p. 120.
56. Rochlin, *Trapped in the Net: The Unanticipated Consequences of Computerization*, p. 131.
57. Rowan Scarborough, *Rumsfeld's War*, Washington, DC: Regnery, 2004, p. 15. My emphasis.
58. Andrew Krepinevich, 'Skipping "Skipping a Generation?"', CSBA Backgrounder, January 5, 2002 – www.csbaonline.org/4Publications/Archive/B.20020501.Skipping__Skipping/B.20020501.Skipping__Skipping.htm. Accessed 19 January 2006.
59. Scarborough, *Rumsfeld's War*, p. 119.
60. Woodward, *Plan of Attack*, p. 19.
61. Bob Woodward, *Bush at War*, London: Pocket Books, 2003, pp. 23, 320.
62. Department of Defense, *Quadrennial Defense Review Report*, 2001 – www.defenselink.mil/pubs/qdr2001.pdf. Accessed 1 December 2005.
63. Anthony J. Blinken, 'From Pre-emption to Engagement', *Survival*, Vol. 45 No. 4, Winter 2003–2004, p. 35.
64. The White House, *The National Security Strategy of the United States of America*, 2002 –www.whitehouse.gov/nsc/nss.html. Accessed 3 February 2006.
65. The White House, 'President Bush Delivers Graduation Speech at West Point', 1 June 2002 – www.whitehouse.gov/news/releases/2002/06/print/20020601-3.html. Accessed 1 December 2005.
66. Yee Kuang-Heng, *War as Risk Management*, p. 101.
67. Philip H. Gordon, 'Bush's Middle East Vision', *Survival*, Vol. 45 No. 1, Spring 2003, p. 135. My emphasis.
68. 'Bush tries to deflect criticism of prewar intelligence on Iraq', *New York Times*, 9 July 2003. My emphasis.
69. For a summary of the Powell Doctrine see above, chapter 5, p. 154.
70. Andrew J. Bacevich, *American Empire: The Realities and Consequences of US Diplomacy*, Cambridge, MA: Harvard University Press, 2002, p. 226.
71. Michael Ignatieff, *Empire Lite: Nation-Building in Afghanistan, Kosovo, and Bosnia*, London: Vintage, 2003, p. 5.
72. Woodward, *Plan of Attack*, p. 26.
73. Scarborough, *Rumsfeld's War*, p. 127.

74 Thomas G. Mahnken and James R. Fitzsimonds, 'Tread-Heads or Technophiles? Army Officer Attitudes Toward Transformation', *Parameters: US Army War College Quarterly*, Vol. 34 No. 2, Summer 2004, pp. 60, 63.
75 Department of Defense, *Quadrennial Defense Review Report,* Washington, DC, 2006, p. 44 – www.defenselink.mil/qdr/report/Report20060203.pdf. Accessed 9 February 2006.
76 Jennifer D. Kibbe, 'The Rise of the Shadow Warriors', *Foreign Affairs*, Vol. 83 No. 2, March/April 2004, p. 110.
77 Scarborough, *Rumsfeld's War*, p. 27.
78 Woodward, *Plan of Attack*, pp. 35, 207.
79 James Fallows, 'Blind Into Baghdad', *The Atlantic Monthly*, January/February 2004.
80 Scarborough, *Rumsfeld's War*, p. 142.
81 PBS, *Frontline* interview with Former Secretary of the Army Thomas White for *Rumsfeld's War*, conducted 12 August 2004 – www.pbs.org/wgbh/pages/frontline/shows/pentagon/interviews/white.html. Accessed 19 January 2006.
82 Woodward, *Plan of Attack*, pp. 80, 148–151, 272.
83 Woodward, *Bush at War*, p. 61.
84 Peter D. Feaver and Christopher Gelpi, *Choosing your Battles: American Civil–Military Relations and the Use of Force*, Princeton: Princeton University Press, 2004, p. 1.
85 PBS, *Frontline* interview with Colonel Douglas MacGregor for *Rumsfeld's War*, conducted 23 July 2004 – www.pbs.org/wgbh/pages/frontline/shows/pentagon/interviews/macgregor.html. Accessed 19 January 2006.
86 Franks, *American Soldier*, pp. 367, 441.
87 Anthony H. Cordesman, *The Iraq War: Strategy, Tactics, and Military Lessons*, Washington, DC: CSIS Press, 2003, pp. 209–210.
88 Thom Shanker, 'Officials Debate Whether to Seek a Bigger Military', *New York Times*, 21 July 2003.
89 Thom Shanker, 'Officials Debate Whether to Seek a Bigger Military'; Eric Schmitt, 'Its Recruitment Goals Pressing, the Army Will Ease Some Standards', *New York Times*, 1 October 2004; Andrew Buncombe, 'Pentagon forces 6,500 troops to return to Army service', *The Independent*, 1 July 2004.
90 Maxim Kniazkov, 'US Army Reserve Becoming "Broken Force",', DefenseNews.com, 6 January 2005 – www.defensenews.com/story.php?F=586113&C=landwar. Accessed 1 December 2005.
91 Lawrence J. Korb, 'Fixing the Mix', *Foreign Affairs*, Vol. 83 No. 2, March/April 2004.
92 Paul Kennedy, 'Washington's Pax Americana smacks of Roman power game', *The Australian*, 4 August 2003.
93 Willem Steenkamp, 'The Multi-Battalion Regiment: an Old Concept with a New Relevance', in J. Cilliers and B. Sass, eds, *Get on parade: Restructuring South Africa's Part-time Military Force for the 21st Century*, South Africa: Institute for Defence Policy, 1996, web version – www.iss.co.za/Pubs/Monographs/No1/Steenkamp.html. Accessed 1 December 2005.
94 Reginald P. Rogers, 'Army changes from divisions to brigade units of action', TRADOC News Service, Department of Defense, 5 April 2004 – www.tradoc.Army.mil/pao/TNSarchives/April04/040604.htm. Accessed 19 January 2006; Eric Schmitt and Thom Shanker, 'Rumsfeld Seeks Broad Review of Iraq Policy', *New York Times*, 7 January 2005; Eric Schmitt, 'Army Retraining Soldiers to Meet Its Shifting Needs', *New York Times,* 11 March 2004. Department of Defense, *Quadrennial Defense Review Report,* Washington, DC,

2006, p. 43 – www.defenselink.mil/qdr/report/Report20060203.pdf. Accessed 9 February 2006.
95. Mary H. Cooper, 'Private Affair: A New Reliance on America's Other Army', *Congressional Quarterly Weekly Report 2194* (2004).
96. Department of Defense, News Briefing with Secretary Rumsfeld and General Myers, 23 December 2002 – www.defenselink.mil/transcripts/2002/t12232002_t1223sd.html. Accessed 6 February 2006.
97. The White House, 'Radio Address of the President to the Nation', 15 September 2001 – www.whitehouse.gov/news/releases/2001/09/20010915.html. Accessed 1 December 2005.
98. The White House, 'Presidential Address to a Joint Session of Congress and the American People', 20 September 2001 – www.whitehouse.gov/news/releases/2001/09/20010920-8.html. Accessed 1 December 2005.
99. Greg Jaffe, 'Rumsfeld's Vindication Promises a Change in Tactics, Deployment', *Wall Street Journal*, 10 April 2003; Toby Harnden, 'Fight Light Theory Advances', *Daily Telegraph*, 14 April 2003.
100. Mann, *The Rise of the Vulcans*, p. 221.
101. Scarborough, *Rumsfeld's War*, p. 126.
102. Department of Defense, 'Secretary Rumsfeld Speaks on "21st Century Transformation" of US Armed Forces', 31 January 2002 – www.defenselink.mil/speeches/2002/s20020131-secdef.html. Accessed 12 August 2005.
103. Jaffe, 'Rumsfeld's Vindication Promises a Change in Tactics, Deployment'.
104. PBS, *Frontline* interview with Former Secretary of the Army Thomas White for *Rumsfeld's War*, conducted 12 August 2004 – www.pbs.org/wgbh/pages/frontline/shows/pentagon/interviews/white.html. Accessed 19 January 2006.
105. Scarborough, *Rumsfeld's War*, p. 164.
106. Arthur C. Cebrowski with Thomas P. M. Barnett, 'The American Way of War', *Proceedings*, January 2003.
107. Defense Advanced Research Projects Agency, Statement by DARPA Director Dr Anthony Tether to the Subcommittee on Emerging Threats and Capabilities, Senate Armed Services Committee, 10 April 2002 – www.darpa.mil/body/news/2002/DARPAtestim.pdf. Accessed 3 February 2006.
108. Dana Priest, *The Mission: Waging War and Keeping Peace With America's Military*, New York; London: W. W. Norton & Co, 2003, p. 143.
109. Chris C. Demchak, 'Complexity and Theory of Networked Militaries', in Farrell and Terriff, *Sources of Military Change*, pp. 233, 237.
110. Der Derian, *Virtuous War*, p. 133.
111. 'Statement by DARPA Director Dr Anthony Tether', p. 4. My emphases.
112. Transcript of the second Presidential Candidates' Debate, 8 October 2004 – www.debates.org/pages/trans2004c.html. Accessed 19 January 2006.
113. Michael DeLong and Noah Lukeman, *Inside CentCom*, Washington, DC: Regnery, 2004, p. 70.
114. Scarborough, *Rumsfeld's War*, p. 25.
115. James Dao and Andrew C. Revkin, 'Machines are Filling in for Troops', *New York Times*, 16 April 2002.
116. David Talbot, 'The Ascent of the Robotic Attack Jet', TechnologyReview.com, March 2005 – www.technologyreview.com/articles/05/03/issue/feature_jet.asp?p=0. Accessed 12 August 2005.
117. Dao and Revkin, 'Machines are Filling in for Troops'.
118. Christopher Coker, *The Future of War: The Re-Enchantment of War in the Twenty-First Century*, Oxford: Blackwell, 2004, p. 130.
119. www.globeandmail.com, 'More cash flowing to robotics research', 11 May 2004 – www.globetechnology.com/servlet/story/RTGAM.20040412.gtrobots-apr12/BNStory/Technology. Accessed 19 January 2006.

5 The new American way of war: vision and reality in Afghanistan and Iraq

1 Carl von Clausewitz, *On War*, Book 2, chapter 3, cited in Alan Beyerchen, 'Clausewitz, Nonlinearity and the Unpredictability of War', International Security, Vol. 17 No. 3, Winter 1992.
2 A full transcript of this letter, supposedly written by Abu Musab al Zarqawi to Ayman al Zawahiri and intercepted by the Coalition Provisional Authority (CPA) in January 2004, is available on the CPA website at www.cpa-iraq.org/transcripts/20040212_zarqawi_full.html. Accessed 12 August 2005.
3 Sean D. Naylor, 'War games rigged?', Army Times, 16 August 2002.
4 PBS, 'The Immutable Nature of War', NOVA interview with Paul Van Riper, conducted 17 December 2003 – www.pbs.org/wgbh/nova/wartech/nature.html. Accessed 12 August 2005.
5 Beyerchen, 'Clausewitz, Nonlinearity and the Unpredictability of War'. For a discussion of the theoretical implications of this unpredictability for the enterprise of strategy, see Colin S. Gray, Strategy for Chaos: Revolutions in Military Affairs and the Evidence of History, London: Frank Cass, 2002, chapter 4.
6 Robert M. Perito, *Where is the Lone Ranger When We Need Him? America's Search for a Postconflict Stability Force*, Washington, DC: United States Institute of Peace, 2004, p. 247.
7 Radek Sikorski, 'Interview with Paul Wolfowitz', Prospect, December 2004, p. 26. My emphasis.
8 Perito, *Where is the Lone Ranger When We Need Him?*, p. 293.
9 Bob Woodward, *Bush at War*, London: Pocket Books, 2003, p. 220.
10 Department of Defense, 'Beyond Nation-Building', Remarks as Delivered by Donald Rumsfeld, 11th Annual Salute to Freedom, Intrepid Sea-Air-Space Museum, New York City, Friday, 14 February 2003 – www.defenselink.mil/speeches/2003/sp20030214-secdef0024.html. Accessed 26 February 2004.
11 'Belated help for Afghanistan', New York Times, Editorial, 9 August 2003.
12 Department of Defense, News Briefing with Deputy Secretary of Defense Paul Wolfowitz, 24 July 2004 – www.defenselink.mil/transcripts/2004/tr20040724-depsecdef1081.html. Accessed 5 December 2005.
13 Bob Woodward, *Bush at War*, p. 115.
14 Tommy Franks with Malcolm McConnell, *American Soldier*, New York: Harper Collins, 2004, p. 271.
15 Michael DeLong and Noah Lukeman, *Inside CentCom*, Washington, DC: Regnery, 2004, p. 25.
16 Rumsfeld, 'Beyond Nation-Building'.
17 James Fallows, 'Blind Into Baghdad', The Atlantic Monthly, January/February 2004.
18 Jeffrey Record, *Bounding the Global War on Terrorism*, Carlisle Barracks: Strategic Studies Institute, December 2003, p. 39.
19 Michael R. Gordon, 'How the Postwar Situation in Iraq Went Awry', New York Times, 19 October 2004.
20 Rowan Scarborough, *Rumsfeld's War*, Washington, DC: Regnery, 2004, p. 46.
21 Anthony H. Cordesman, *The Iraq War: Strategy, Tactics, and Military Lessons*, Washington, DC: CSIS Press, 2003, p. 498.
22 Russell F. Weigley, *The American Way of War: A History of United States Military Strategy and Policy*, Bloomington: Indiana University Press, 1977, p. xxii.
23 Carnes Lord, 'American Strategic Culture', in Fred E. Baumann and Kenneth M. Jensen, eds, *American Defense Policy and Liberal Democracy*, Charlottesville: University Press of Virginia, 1989, p. 52; Edward N. Luttwak,

'The Operational Level of War', International Security, Vol. 5 No. 3, Winter 1980–1981; and Colin S. Gray, 'National Style in Strategy: The American Example', International Security, Vol. 6 No. 2, Fall 1981, p. 32.
24 Cordesman, *The Iraq War*, p. 261.
25 Steven W. Peterson, *Central but Inadequate: The Application of Theory in Operation Iraqi Freedom*, National Defense University, 2004 – www.ndu.edu/library/n4/n045602I.pdf. Accessed 12 August 2005.
26 Carl von Clausewitz, *On War*, edited and translated by Michael Howard and Peter Paret, Princeton; Guildford: Princeton University Press, 1976, p. 75.
27 John A. Warden III, 'Air Theory for the Twenty-first Century', in Karl P. Magyar, ed., *Challenge and Response: Anticipating US Military Security Concerns*, Maxwell AFB: Air University Press, 1994. This chapter is available online at www.airpower.maxwell.af.mil/airchronicles/battle/chp4.html. Accessed 12 August 2005.
28 John D. Nelson, 'Swiftly defeat the efforts, then what? The "New American Way of War" and the Transition from Decisive Combat Operations to Post-Conflict Security Operations', in Williamson Murray, ed., *A Nation at War in an Era of Strategic Change*, Carlisle Barracks: Strategic Studies Institute, September 2001, p. 43.
29 Harlan K. Ullman and James P. Wade, Jr, *Rapid Dominance, A Force for all Seasons: Technologies and Systems for Achieving Shock and Awe*, London: RUSI, 1998, pp. 19–20. My emphasis.
30 DeLong, *Inside CentCom*, p. 106.
31 George Friedman, *America's Secret War*, London: Little, Brown, 2004, p. 169.
32 See, for example, Ullman's remarks in Paul Sperry, 'No Shock, No Awe: It Never Happened', WorldNetDaily.com, 3 April 2003 – wnd.com/news/article.asp?ARTICLE_ID=31858. Accessed 5 February 2006.
33 Franks, *American Soldier*, p. 459.
34 Warden, 'Air Theory for the Twenty-first Century'.
35 Fred Kaplan, 'The Flaw in Shock and Awe', *Slate Magazine*, 26 March 2003 – http://slate.msn.com/id/2080745/. Accessed 12 August 2005.
36 Franks, *American Soldier*, pp .337–341.
37 Cordesman, *The Iraq War*, p. 76.
38 Franks, *American Soldier*, pp. 397, 480.
39 Cordesman, *The Iraq War*, p. 2.
40 Bob Woodward, *Plan of Attack: The Road To War*, London: Simon & Schuster, 2004, p. 22; James Mann, *The Rise of the Vulcans: The History of Bush's War Cabinet*, New York: Viking, 2004, p. 189.
41 Fallows, 'Blind Into Baghdad'; Cordesman, *The Iraq War*, p. 151.
42 Scarborough, *Rumsfeld's War*, p. 49.
43 Williamson Murray and Robert H. Scales, Jr, *The Iraq War: A Military History*, London: Harvard University Press, 2003, p. 94; Franks, *American Soldier*, p. 476.
44 Franks, *American Soldier*, p. 175.
45 Michael O'Hanlon, 'A Flawed Masterpiece', *Foreign Affairs*, Vol. 81 No. 3, May/June 2002, pp. 56–58; Friedman, *America's Secret War*, p. 198.
46 David Talbot, 'How Technology Failed in Iraq', www.TechnologyReview.com, November 2004 – www.techreview.com/articles/04/11/talbot1104.asp?p=1. Accessed 12 August 2005.
47 Central Intelligence Agency, Comprehensive Report of the Special Advisor to the DCI on Iraq's WMD, 30 September 2004, Volume 1, 'Regime Strategic Intent', – www.cia.gov/cia/reports/iraq_wmd_2004/chap1.html#sect1. Accessed 3 February 2006.

48 Douglas Jehl, 'Saddam's Real Secret Weapon: An Insurgency', *The International Herald Tribune*, 8 October 2004; Toby Dodge, Iraq's Future: The Aftermath of Regime Change, IISS Adelphi Paper 372, London: Routledge, 2005, p. 15.
49 Michael Gordon and Bernard Trainor, *Cobra II: The Inside Story of the Invasion and Occupation of Iraq*, London: Atlantic Books, 2006, pp. 504–506.
50 John A. Gentry, 'Doomed to Fail: America's Blind Faith in Military Technology', Parameters: US Army War College Quarterly, Vol. 32 No. 4, Winter 2002/2003. – http://carlisle-www.Army.mil/usawc/Parameters/02winter/gentry.htm. Accessed 12 August 2005.
51 See, for example, William A. Owens with Ed Offley, *Lifting the Fog of War*, Baltimore; London: Johns Hopkins University Press, 2001, pp. 10–11.
52 CBSNews.com, 'Kay: "We were almost all wrong"', 28 January 2004 – www.cbsnews.com/stories/2004/01/29/iraq/main596595.shtml. Accessed 19 January 2006.
53 Central Intelligence Agency, Comprehensive Report of the Special Advisor to the DCI on Iraq's WMD, 30 September 2004, 'Transmittal Message' – www.cia.gov/cia/reports/iraq_wmd_2004/transmittal.html. Accessed 3 February 2006.
54 Brad Knickerbocker, 'How Iraq will change US military doctrine', Christian Science Monitor, 2 July 2004, – www.csmonitor.com/2004/0702/p02s01-usmi.html. Accessed 12 August 2005.
55 www.globalsecurity.org, 'Memo by US Secretary of Defense Donald Rumsfeld on the Global War on Terrorism', 16 October 2003 – www.globalsecurity.org/military/library/policy/dod/rumsfeld-d20031016sdmemo.htm. Accessed 12 August 2005.
56 Gordon, 'How the Postwar Situation in Iraq Went Awry'.
57 Roy Eccleston, 'Iraq Success "Catastrophic": Bush', The Australian, 30 August 2004.
58 Department of Defense, Richard B. Myers Testimony to the Senate Armed Services Committee on the Transition in Iraq, 25 June 2004 – www.defenselink.mil/speeches/2004/sp20040625-depsecdef0541.html. Accessed 3 February 2006. My emphasis.
59 L. Paul Bremer, 'What I really said about Iraq', *New York Times*, 8 October 2004.
60 Gordon, 'How the Postwar Situation in Iraq Went Awry'.
61 Dan Murphy, 'As Smoke Clears, Next Battles are Political', The Christian Science Monitor, 16 November 2004. – www.csmonitor.com/2004/1116/p01s04-woiq.html. Accessed 12 August 2005.
62 Daniel Smith, 'Iraq: Descending Into a Quagmire', Foreign Policy in Focus Policy Report, June 2003 – www.fpif.org/papers/quagmire2003-upd.html. Accessed 12 August 2005.
63 Larry Jay Diamond, a senior advisor to the CPA on the transition to democracy in Iraq, has stated that during his time in the country he did not meet a single military officer who felt, privately, that the US troop presence was large enough. Larry Jay Diamond, *Squandered Victory: The American Occupation and the Bungled Effort to Bring Democracy to Iraq*, New York: Times Books, 2005, p. 241.
64 James F. Dobbins, 'America's Role in Nation-Building: From Germany to Iraq', *Survival*, Vol. 45 No. 4, Winter 2003–2004, pp. 99–102. My emphasis.
65 PBS, 'Transforming Warfare', NOVA interview with Admiral Arthur Cebrowski, conducted 15 January 2004 – www.pbs.org/wgbh/nova/wartech/transform.html. Accessed 12 August 2005. My emphasis.
66 Hew Strachan, 'The Lost Meaning of Strategy', *Survival*, Vol. 47 No. 3, Autumn 2005, p. 47.

67 Woodward, *Plan of Attack*, p. 273.
68 Franks, *American Soldier*, p. 34.
69 Andrew J. Bacevich, 'A Modern Major General', New Left Review, No. 29, September/October 2004 – www.newleftreview.net/NLR26307.shtml. Accessed 12 August 2005.
70 Fallows, 'Blind Into Baghdad'.
71 David Rieff, 'Blueprint for a Mess', *New York Times Magazine*, 2 November 2003.
72 Scarborough, *Rumsfeld's War*, p. 53.
73 Isam al Khafaji, 'A Few Days After: State and Society in a post-Saddam Iraq', in Toby Dodge and Steven Simon, eds, *Iraq at the Crossroads: State and Society in the Shadow of Regime Change*, IISS Adelphi Paper 354, London: Routledge, 2003, p. 85.
74 Amatzia Baram, 'Saddam's Power Structure: the Tikritis Before, During and After the War', in Dodge and Simon, eds, *Iraq at the Crossroads*, p. 109.
75 Diamond, *Squandered Victory*, p. 35–36, 285. My emphasis.
76 John Lynn, Battle: *A History of Combat and Culture*, Boulder: Westview Press, 2003, p. 360.
77 Rieff, 'Blueprint for a Mess'.
78 Anthony J. Blinken, 'From Pre-emption to Engagement', *Survival*, Vol. 45 No. 4, Winter 2003–2004, p. 53.
79 Scarborough, *Rumsfeld's War*, p. 54.
80 PBS, Frontline interview with Former Secretary of the Army Thomas White for Rumsfeld's War, conducted 12 August 2004 – www.pbs.org/wgbh/pages/frontline/shows/pentagon/interviews/white.html. Accessed 19 January 2006.
81 Fallows, 'Blind Into Baghdad'.
82 Diamond, *Squandered Victory*, p. 286.
83 Rieff, 'Blueprint for a Mess'.
84 Christopher H. Varhola, 'American Challenges in Postwar Iraq', Foreign Policy Research Institute E-Notes, 27 May 2004 – www.fpri.org/enotes/20040527.americawar.varhola.iraqchallenges.html. Accessed 12 August 2005.
85 Cordesman, *The Iraq War*, p. 364. The Pentagon has sought a technological fix to the language problem, equipping thousands of troops with the 'Phraselator', a hand-held electronic gadget marketed as 'a complete solution for cross-cultural awareness' that allows soldiers to deliver hundreds of phrases, pre-recorded in Arabic, to the Iraqis they encounter. Unfortunately, it cannot translate anything said in response. Robert Mackey, 'The Phraselator', *New York Times Magazine*, 12 December 2004.
86 Bruce Hoffman, *Insurgency and Counter-insurgency in Iraq*, Santa Monica: RAND, 2004, p. 9.
87 Perito, *Where is the Lone Ranger When We Need Him?*, pp. 314, 320.
88 Andrew J. Krepinevich, Jr, *The Army and Vietnam*, Baltimore and London: Johns Hopkins University Press, 1986, pp. 10–16.
89 Michael Codner, 'The Battle for Hearts and Minds', www.rusi.org/iraq/. Accessed 28 April 2004.
90 John F. Burns, 'Drawing From Its Past Wars, Britain Takes a Tempered Approach to Iraqi Insurgency', *New York Times*, 17 October 2004.
91 Paul Rogers, 'Between Fallujah and Palestine', OpenDemocracy, 22 April 2004 – www.opendemocracy.net/themes/article-2-1858.jsp. Accessed 12 August 2005.
92 Israel Beach, 'IDF Training Software to go to US Forces in Iraq', The Jerusalem Post, 17 September 2003.
93 Joel Brinkley, 'Few signs of infiltration by foreign fighters in Iraq', *New York Times*, 19 November 2003.
94 Jackie Spinner, 'Fallujah Battered And Mostly Quiet After the Battle', *Washington Post*, 16 November 2004.

95 Perito, *Where is the Lone Ranger When We Need Him?*, p. 297.
96 Eric Schmitt, 'US General Maps New Tactic to Pursue Taliban and Qaeda', New York Times, 18 February 2004; Ann Scott Tyson, 'A US "Proconsul" in Afghanistan', Christian Science Monitor, 29 July 2004.
97 Mark Mazzetti, 'Good Marines Make Good Neighbours', *Slate Magazine*, 25 February 2004 – http://slate.msn.com/id/2096027/. Accessed 12 August 2005; Michael R. Gordon, 'Marines Plan to Use Velvet Glove More Than Iron Fist in Iraq', New York Times, 12 December 2003.
98 Thom Shanker, 'US Shifts Focus in Iraq to Aiding New Government', New York Times, 1 June 2004.
99 DefenseTech.org, 'Army's insurgent manual author speaks', 17 November 2004 – www.defensetech.org/archives/2004_11.html. Accessed 6 February 2006; Douglas Jehl and Thom Shanker, 'For the First Time Since Vietnam, the Army Prints a Guide to Fighting Insurgents', *New York Times*, 13 November 2004.
100 Department of Defense, FMI 3-07.22 Counterinsurgency Operations, October 2004, p. 3/10, full text available online at www.fas.org/irp/doddir/Army/fmi3-07-22.pdf. Accessed 6 February 2006.
101 The White House, National Strategy for Victory in Iraq, 30 November 2005 – www.whitehouse.gov/infocus/iraq/iraq_strategy_nov2005.html. Accessed 6 December 2005. The apparent adoption of this classic 'expanding ink spot' counter-insurgency strategy reportedly reflected the lobbying efforts of Colonel Andrew Krepinevich of Washington's Center for Strategic and Budgetary Assessments, whose Foreign Affairs article on US strategy in Iraq influenced the White House and the US ambassador in Iraq, Zalmay Khalilzad. See Andrew Krepinevich, 'How to Win in Iraq', *Foreign Affairs*, Vol. 84 No. 5, September/October 2005; Alec Russell, 'Bush adopts British colonial model for Iraq', *The Daily Telegraph*, 3 December 2005. A second reported influence was Lewis Sorley's analysis of the final years of the US presence in Vietnam, A Better War New York: Harcourt Brace, 1999, which emphasized the successes of the 'clear-and-hold' strategy adopted by General Creighton Abrams in preference to General Westmoreland's earlier emphasis on 'search-and-destroy'. First published in 1999, the book appeared on the reading lists of many high-ranking administration and military figures in 2005, including General John Abizaid, Commander of US forces in Iraq, and State Department Counsellor Philip Zelikow. See David Ignatius, 'A Better Strategy for Iraq', *Washington Post*, 4 November 2005; Kirk Semple, 'US Forces Try New Approach: Raid And Dig In', *New York Times*, 5 December 2005.
102 Department of Defense, Defense Science Board 2004 Summer Study on Transition to and from Hostilities, December 2004, pp. vi–x – www.acq.osd.mil/dsb/reports/2004-12-DSB_SS_Report_Final.pdf. Accessed 3 February 2006.
103 Editorial, 'The Pentagon's Cuts', *Washington Post*, 10 January 2005.
104 Department of Defense, Quadrennial Defense Review Report, Washington, DC, 2006, p. 36 – www.defenselink.mil/qdr/report/Report20060203.pdf. Accessed 9 February 2006. My emphasis.
105 Department of Defense, Directive No. 3000.05: Military Support for Stability, Security, Transition, and Reconstruction Operations, 28 November 2005 – www.dtic.mil/whs/directives/corres/pdf/d300005_112805/d300005p.pdf. Accessed 19 January 2006. My emphasis.
106 There was no mention of any of these topics, for example, in Donald Rumsfeld's 2002 Foreign Affairs manifesto on Transformation: Donald Rumsfeld, 'Transforming the Military', *Foreign Affairs*, Vol. 81 No. 3, May/June 2002.

107 Robert P. Killebrew, 'It is a Daunting Time to be a Soldier', Proceedings of the US Naval Institute, Vol. 130 No. 6, June 2004, www.usni.org/proceedings/Articles04/PRO06killebrew.htm. Accessed 7 February 2006.

Conclusion: the rise and fall of the new American way of war

1 John Shy, 'The American Military Experience: History and Learning', *Journal of Interdisciplinary History*, Vol. 1 No. 2, Winter 1971, p. 227.
2 Max Boot, 'The New American Way of War', *Foreign Affairs*, Vol. 82 No. 4, July/August 2003.
3 Paul Kennedy, 'The Eagle has Landed', *Weekend Financial Times*, 2 February 2002.
4 Department of Defense, 'Deputy Secretary Wolfowitz Interview with Sam Tannenhaus, *Vanity Fair*', 9 May 2003 – www.defenselink.mil/transcripts/2003/tr20030509-depsecdef0223.html. Accessed on 1 July 2005.
5 Antulio J. Echevarria, *Toward an American Way of War*, Carlisle Barracks: Strategic Studies Institute, 2004 – www.strategicstudiesinstitute.Army.mil/pdf-files/PUB374.pdf. Accessed 19 January 2006.
6 Russell F. Weigley, *The American Way of War: A History of United States Military Strategy and Policy*, Bloomington: Indiana University Press, 1977, pp. xviii–xix.
7 PBS, 'The Immutable Nature of War', *NOVA* interview with Paul Van Riper, conducted 17 December 2003 – www.pbs.org/wgbh/nova/wartech/nature.html. Accessed 12 August 2005.
8 General Anthony Zinni, Address to the Marine Corps Association and US Naval Institute Forum, Arlington, Virginia, 4 September 2003 – www.mca-usniforum.org/forum03zinni.htm. Accessed 12 August 2005.
9 Robert Kagan, 'Power and Weakness', *Policy Review*, No. 113, June/July 2002. Online version at www.policyreview.org/JUN02/kagan.html. Accessed 19 January 2006.
10 Raymond Aron, *The Imperial Republic: The United States and the World, 1945-1973*, translated by Frank Jellinek, London: Weidenfeld & Nicholson, 1975.
11 Weigley, *The American Way of War*, p. xx.
12 Beatrice Heuser, *Reading Clausewitz*, London: Pimlico, 2002, pp. 31–32.
13 Martin van Creveld uses the term 'low-intensity conflict' in his prophetic work *The Transformation of War*, New York: Free Press, 1991, which anticipated many of the arguments that would later be associated with the 'new wars' thesis by several years. On 'new wars', see Mary Kaldor, *New and Old Wars: Organized Violence in a Global Era*, (Cambridge: Polity Press, 1999); and Herfried Münkler, *The New Wars,* translated by Patrick Camiller, Oxford: Polity Press, 2005. On 'War amongst the People', see Rupert Smith, *The Utility of Force*, London: Allen Lane, 2005.
14 Van Creveld, *The Transformation of War*, p. 11.
15 War games exploring American military options with regard to Iran and North Korea sponsored by the *Atlantic Monthly* are discussed respectively in James Fallows, 'Will Iran be Next?', *The Atlantic Monthly*, December 2004; and Scott Stossel, 'North Korea: the War Game', *The Atlantic Monthly*, July/August 2005. Both exercises pointed to the conclusion that the US currently has no plausible military options for either 'rogue state' that would not bring about potentially catastrophic consequences.
16 For an elaboration of this point see Martin van Creveld, *The Art of War: War and Military Thought*, London: Cassell, 2000, p. 213.
17 For a more pessimistic verdict on the possibility of future inter-state war, see Colin S. Gray, *Another Bloody Century: Future Warfare*, London: Weidenfeld & Nicholson, 2005.

Notes 175

18 Munkler, *The New Wars*, p. 8.
19 This definition of 'regular' armed forces is taken from Smith, *The Utility of Force*, p. 8. It should be noted here that the 2006 *Quadrennial Defense Review* acknowledges both that, 'irregular warfare has emerged as the dominant form of warfare confronting the United States' (p. 36) and that, 'Today, warfare is increasingly characterized by intra-state violence rather than conflict between states' (p. 83). Department of Defense, *Quadrennial Defense Review Report*, Washington, DC, 2006.
20 See the critical discussion of the 'new wars' thesis in Paul Hirst, *War and Power in the 21st Century*, Oxford: Polity Press, 2001, pp. 82–88.
21 Van Creveld, *The Transformation of War*, p. 21.
22 The White House, *The National Security Strategy of the United States of America*, 2002 – www.whitehouse.gov/nsc/nss.html. Accessed 3 February 2006.
23 Richard K. Betts, *Soldiers, Statesmen, and Cold War Crises*, p. 130.
24 Tom Clancy with Tony Zinni, *Battle Ready*, New York: Putnam Publishing Group, 2004, p. 424.
25 Maxim Kniazkov, 'US Army Reserve Becoming "Broken Force"', DefenseNews. com, 6 January 2005 – www.defensenews.com/story.php?F=586113&C=landwar. Accessed 1 December 2005.
26 Frank Rich, 'Washington's New Year War Cry: "Party On!"', *New York Times*, 2 January 2005.
27 Niall Ferguson, *Colossus: The Rise and the Fall of the American Empire*, London: Allen Lane, 2004, p. 214.
28 Eric V. Larson, *Casualties and Consensus*; E. J. Dionne, 'An Iraq Deadline for Bush', *Washington Post*, 18 November 2005.
29 Lawrence Freedman, 'Rumsfeld's legacy: the Iraq Syndrome?', *Washington Post*, 9 January 2005.
30 Zinni, 'Address to the Marine Corps Association'.
31 Sceptical voices were immediately heard: for instance, Max Boot pointed out that the rhetoric of the 2006 *QDR* was not reflected in the economic priorities of the 2007 defence budget request. To take just one example, 'The entire budget for language and cultural training – $181 million – comes to less than the cost of one F-35'. Max Boot, 'The Wrong Weapons for the Long War', *Los Angeles Times*, 9 February 2006 – www.latimes.com/news/opinion/commentary/la-oe-boot8feb08,0,7903755.column?coll=la-news-comment-opinions. Accessed 9 February 2006. Frederick W. Kagan has also criticized the contradiction implicit in the *QDR* between the grand strategic objectives it sets out and the means it identifies as necessary to achieve them, most seriously with regard to the size of the army: 'The review recommends increasing only the special forces component of the ground forces – and recommends reducing the programmed number of active Army brigade combat teams by one to pay for the growth. The president's budget proposes eliminating the temporary addition of 30,000 soldiers to the Active Army within a few years, to bring the force down to the level of 482,000 troops.' Frederick W. Kagan, 'A strategy for heroes', *Weekly Standard*, 20 February 2006.
32 Russell F. Weigley, 'American strategy from its beginnings through the First World War', p. 411.
33 Lewis Sorley, *A Better War: The Unexamined Victories and the Final Tragedy of America's Last Years in Vietnam*, New York: Harcourt Brace, 1999.
34 Department of Defense, *Quadrennial Defense Review Report*, Washington, DC, 2006, p. 22 – www.defenselink.mil/qdr/report/Report20060203.pdf. Accessed 9 February 2006.

Bibliography

Books and Journal Articles

Andreopoulos, George J., 'The Age of National Liberation Movements', in Michael Howard, George J. Andreopoulos, and Mark R. Shulman, eds, *The Laws of War: Constraints on Warfare in the Western World*, New Haven: Yale University Press, 1994, pp. 191–213.

Aron, Raymond, *The Imperial Republic: The United States and the World, 1945–1973*, translated by Frank Jellinek, London: Weidenfeld & Nicholson, 1975.

Avant, Deborah D., *Political Institutions and Military Change: Lessons from Peripheral Wars*, Ithaca: Cornell University Press, 1994.

Bacevich, Andrew J., 'Neglected Trinity: Kosovo and the Crisis in US Civil–Military Relations', in Andrew J. Bacevich and Eliot Cohen, eds, *War Over Kosovo: Politics and Strategy in a Global Age*, New York: Columbia University Press, 2001, pp. 155–188.

——*American Empire: The Realities and Consequences of U.S. Diplomacy*, Cambridge, MA: Harvard University Press, 2002.

——*The New American Militarism: How Americans Are Seduced by War*, New York: Oxford University Press, 2005.

Bailyn, Bernard, *The Ideological Origins of the American Revolution*, Cambridge, MA: Belknap Press, 1967.

Banks, William C. and Jeffrey D. Straussman, 'A New Imperial Presidency? Insights from U.S. Involvement in Bosnia', in Demetrios James Caraley, ed., *The New American Interventionism,* New York: Columbia University Press, 1999, pp. 39–62.

Baram, Amatzia, 'Saddam's Power Structure: the Tikritis Before, During and After the War', in Toby Dodge and Steven Simon, eds, *Iraq at the Crossroads: State and Society in the Shadow of Regime Change*, IISS Adelphi Paper 354, London: Routledge, 2003.

Bassford, Christopher, *Clausewitz in English: The Reception of Clausewitz in Britain and America, 1815–1945*, New York: Oxford University Press, 1994.

Bathurst, Robert B., *Intelligence and the Mirror: On Creating an Enemy,* London: Sage, 1993.

Benedict, Ruth, *The Chrysanthemum and the Sword: Patterns of Japanese Culture*, Boston: Houghton Mifflin, 1989, originally published 1946.

Betts, Richard K., *Soldiers, Statesmen, and Cold War Crises*, Cambridge, MA: Harvard University Press, 1977.

Beyerchen, Alan, 'Clausewitz, Nonlinearity and the Unpredictability of War', *International Security*, Vol. 17 No. 3, Winter 1992, pp. 59–90.

Blinken, Anthony J., 'From Pre-emption to Engagement', *Survival*, Vol. 45 No. 4, Winter 2003–2004, pp. 33–60.
Boot, Max, *The Savage Wars of Peace: Small Wars and the Rise of American Power*, New York: Basic Books, 2002.
——'The New American Way of War', *Foreign Affairs*, Vol. 82 No. 4, July/August 2003, pp. 41–58.
Booth, Ken, 'American Strategy: The Myths Revisited', in Booth and Moorhead Wright, eds, *American Thinking about Peace and War*, Hassocks: Harvester Press, 1978, pp. 1–35.
——'Bernard Brodie', in John Baylis and John Garnett, eds, *Makers of Nuclear Strategy*, London: Pinter Publishers, 1991, pp. 19–56.
Booth, Ken, Alan MacMillan and Russell Trood, 'Strategic Culture', in Ken Booth and Russell Trood, eds, *Strategic Cultures in the Asia-Pacific Region*, London: Macmillan, 1999, pp. 3–26.
Brinegar, George A., 'The Abrams Doctrine: Has it been abused in the Global War on Terror?', in Williamson Murray, ed., *A Nation at War in an Era of Strategic Change*, Carlisle Barracks: Strategic Studies Institute, September 2004, pp. 173–181.
Brinsfield, John W., 'The Military Ethics of General William T. Sherman', in Lloyd J. Matthews and Dale E. Brown, *The Parameters: US Army War College Quarterly of Military Ethics*, Washington; London: Pergamon-Brassey's, 1989, pp. 36–48
Brodie, Bernard, 'War in the Atomic Age', in Brodie, ed., *The Absolute Weapon: Atomic Power and World Order*, New York: Harcourt, Brace and Company, 1946, pp. 1–69.
——*War and Politics*, New York: Macmillan, 1973.
Brown, Chris, Terry Nardin and Nicholas Rengger, eds, *International Relations in Political Thought*, Cambridge: Cambridge University Press, 2002.
Builder, Carl H., *The Masks of War: American Military Styles in Strategy and Analysis*, Baltimore; London: Johns Hopkins University Press, 1989.
Burk, James, 'Public Support for Peacekeeping in Lebanon and Somalia: Assessing the Casualties Hypothesis', *Political Science Quarterly*, Vol. 114 No. 1, Spring 1999, pp. 53–78.
——'The Military Obligations of Citizens Since Vietnam', *Parameters: US Army War College Quarterly*, Vol. 114 No. 1, Summer 2001, pp. 48–60.
Campbell, Kenneth J., 'Once Burned, Twice Cautious: Explaining the Weinberger-Powell Doctrine', *Armed Forces and Society*, Vol. 24 No. 3, Spring 1998, pp. 357–374.
Cassidy, Robert M., 'Prophets or Praetorians? The Uptonian Paradox and the Powell Corollary', *Parameters: US Army War College Quarterly*, Vol. 33 No. 3, Autumn 2003, pp. 130–143.
Cebrowski, Arthur C., with Thomas P. M. Barnett, 'The American Way of War', *Proceedings of the US Naval Institute*, Vol. 129 No. 1, January 2003, pp. 42–43.
Chace, James, 'In Search of Absolute Security', in A. J. Bacevich, ed., *The Imperial Tense: Prospects and Problems of American Empire*, Chicago: Ivan R Dee, 2002.
Clancy, Tom, with Tony Zinni, *Battle Ready*, New York: Putnam Publishing Group, 2004.
Clausewitz, Carl von, *On War*, edited and translated by Michael Howard and Peter Paret, Princeton; Guildford: Princeton University Press, 1976.
Clodfelter, Mark, *The Limits of Air Power: The American Bombing of North Vietnam*, New York: The Free Press, 1989.

Cohen, Eliot A., 'Kosovo and the new American Way of War', in Andrew J. Bacevich and Eliot Cohen, eds, *War Over Kosovo: Politics and Strategy in a Global Age*, New York: Columbia University Press, 2001, pp. 38–62.
—— 'The strategy of innocence? The United States, 1920–1945', in Williamson Murray, MacGregor Knox, and Alvin Bernstein, eds, *The Making of Strategy: Rulers, States, and War*, Cambridge; New York: Cambridge University Press, 1994.
—— 'Why the Gap Matters', *The National Interest*, No. 61, Fall 2000, pp. 38–48.
—— 'Twilight of the Citizen Soldier', *Parameters: US Army War College Quarterly*, Vol. 31 No. 2, Summer 2001, pp. 23–28.
Coker, Christopher, *Humane Warfare*, London and New York: Routledge, 2001.
—— *Globalisation and Insecurity: NATO and the Management of Risk*, IISS Adelphi Paper 345, Oxford: Oxford University Press, 2002.
—— *Waging War Without Warriors: The Changing Culture of Military Conflict*, Boulder; London: Lynne Rienner, 2002.
—— *The Future of War: The Re-Enchantment of War in the Twenty-First Century*, Oxford: Blackwell, 2004.
Cooper, Mary H., 'Private Affair: A New Reliance on America's Other Army', *Congressional Quarterly Weekly Report*, 2194 (2004).
Cordesman, Anthony H., *The Iraq War: Strategy, Tactics, and Military Lessons*, Washington, DC: CSIS Press, 2003.
Cress, Lawrence Delbert, *Citizens in Arms: The Army and the Militia in American Society to the War of 1812*, Chapel Hill: University of North Carolina Press, 1982.
DeLong, Michael and Noah Lukeman, *Inside CentCom*, Washington, DC: Regnery, 2004.
Demchak, Chris C., 'Complexity and Theory of Networked Militaries', in Farrell and Terriff, *Sources of Military Change: Culture, Politics, Technology*, Boulder: Lynne Rienner, 2002, pp. 221–264.
Der Derian, James, *Virtuous War*, Boulder: Westview Press, 2001.
Diamond, Larry Jay, *Squandered Victory: The American Occupation and the Bungled Effort to Bring Democracy to Iraq*, New York: Times Books, 2005.
Dickson, Paul, *The Electronic Battlefield*, London: Boyars, 1976.
Dobbins, James F., 'America's Role in Nation-Building: From Germany to Iraq', *Survival*, Vol. 45 No. 4, Winter 2003–2004, pp. 87–109.
Dodge, Toby, *Iraq's Future: The Aftermath of Regime Change*, IISS Adelphi Paper 372, London: Routledge, 2005.
Dower, John, *War Without Mercy: Race and Power in the Pacific War*, New York: Pantheon, 1986.
Echevarria, Antulio J., *Toward an American Way of War*, Carlisle: Strategic Studies Institute, 2004 – www.strategicstudiesinstitute.Army.mil/pdffiles/PUB374.pdf. Accessed 19 January 2006.
Edwards, Paul N., 'The Closed World: Systems Discourse, Military policy and post-World War II US Historical Consciousness', in Les Levidow and Kevin Robins, *Cyborg Worlds: The Military Information Society*, London: Free Association Books, 1989, pp. 135–158.
—— *The Closed World: Computers and the Politics of Discourse in Cold War America*, Cambridge: MIT Press, 1996.

Eikenberry, Karl W., 'Take No Casualties', *Parameters: US Army War College Quarterly,* Vol. 26 No. 2, Summer 1996, pp. 109–118.

Ellis, John, *A Social History of the Machine Gun,* Baltimore: Johns Hopkins University Press, 1986.

Feaver, Peter D., and Christopher Gelpi, *Choosing Your Battles: American Civil–Military Relations and the Use of Force,* Princeton: Princeton University Press, 2004.

Ferguson, Eugene S., 'The American-ness of American Technology', *Technology and Culture,* Vol. 20 No. 1, 1979, pp. 3–24.

Ferguson, Niall, *Colossus: The Rise and the Fall of the American Empire,* London: Allen Lane, 2004.

Franklin, H. Bruce, *War Stars: The Superweapon and the American Imagination,* New York; Oxford: Oxford University Press, 1988.

Franks, Tommy, with Malcolm McConnell, *American Soldier,* New York: Harper Collins, 2004.

Freedman, Lawrence, *The Evolution of Nuclear Strategy,* London: Macmillan, 1989.

—— *The Revolution in Strategic Affairs,* Adelphi Paper 318, Oxford: Oxford University Press, 1998.

——'Victims and victors: reflections on the Kosovo War', *Review of International Studies,* Vol. 26 No. 3, 2000, pp. 335–358.

Friedman, George, and Meredith Friedman, *The Future of War: Power, Technology and American World Dominance in the 21st Century,* New York: Crown, 1996.

Friedman, Norman, *Terrorism, Afghanistan, and America's New Way of War,* Annapolis: Naval Institute Press, 2003.

Frye, Alton, 'The American Character and the Formation of U.S. Foreign Policy', in Michael P. Hamilton, ed., *American Character and Foreign Policy,* Grand Rapids: W. B. Eerdmans Pub Co, 1986.

Gacek, Christopher M., *The Logic of Force: The Dilemma of Limited War in American Foreign Policy,* New York: Columbia University Press, 1994.

Gaddis, John Lewis, *Strategies of Containment: A Critical Appraisal of Postwar American National Security Policy,* New York: Oxford University Press, 1982.

Garnett, John C., 'Herman Kahn', in John Baylis and John Garnett, eds, *Makers of Nuclear Strategy,* London: Pinter Publishers, 1991, pp. 70–97.

Gat, Azar, *A History of Military Thought: From the Enlightenment to the Cold War,* Oxford: Oxford University Press, 2001.

Geertz, Clifford, *The Interpretation of Cultures,* New York: Basic Books, 1973.

Gellner, Ernest, 'Concepts and Society', in Brian R. Wilson, ed., *Rationality,* Oxford: Blackwell, 1970, pp. 18–49.

Gentry, John A., 'Doomed to Fail: America's Blind Faith in Military Technology', *Parameters: US Army War College Quarterly,* Vol. 32 No. 4, Winter 2002–2003, pp. 88–103.

Ghamari-Tabrizi, Sharon, *The Worlds of Herman Kahn: The Intuitive Science of Thermonuclear War,* Cambridge, MA: Harvard University Press, 2005.

Gibson, James William, *The Perfect War: Technowar in Vietnam,* New York: The Atlantic Monthly Press, 2000.

Giddens, Anthony, *The Constitution of Society: Outline of the Theory of Structuration,* Cambridge: Polity Press, 1986.

Bibliography

Gordon, Michael R., and Bernard E. Trainor, *The Generals' War*, Boston: Little Brown, 1995.

——*Cobra II: The Inside Story of the Invasion and Occupation of Iraq*, London: Atlantic Books, 2006.

Gordon, Philip H., 'Bush's Middle East Vision', *Survival*, Vol. 45 No. 1, Spring 2003, pp. 155–165.

Gray, Colin S., 'National Style in Strategy: The American Example', *International Security*, Vol. 6 No. 2, Fall 1981, pp. 21–47.

——'Strategic Culture as Context: The First Generation of Theory Strikes Back', *Review of International Studies*, Vol. 25 No. 1, January 1999, pp. 49–69.

——*Modern Strategy*, Oxford: Oxford University Press, 1999.

——*Strategy for Chaos: Revolutions in Military Affairs and the Evidence of History*, London: Frank Cass, 2002.

——*Another Bloody Century: Future Warfare*, London: Weidenfeld & Nicholson, 2005.

Grotelueschen, Mark E., *Doctrine Under Trial: American Artillery Employment in World War I*, Westport: Greenwood Press, 2001.

Hables Gray, Chris, *Postmodern War: The New Politics of Conflict*, London: Routledge, 1997.

Halberstam, David, *War in a Time of Peace: Bush, Clinton, and the Generals*, London: Bloomsbury, 2003.

Halliday, Fred, *The World at 2000: Perils and Promises*, Basingstoke: Palgrave, 2001.

Halper, Stefan, and Jonathan Clarke, *America Alone: The Neo-Conservatives and the Global Order*, Cambridge: Cambridge University Press, 2004.

Handel, Michael I., *Masters of War: Classical Strategic Thought*, London: Frank Cass, 1996.

Hanson, Victor Davis, *Why the West Has Won: Carnage and Culture from Salamis to Vietnam*, London: Faber and Faber, 2001.

Harries, Meirion and Susie, *Soldiers of the Sun: The Rise and Fall of the Imperial Japanese Army*, New York: Random House, 1991.

Heideking, Jürgen, 'The Image of an English Enemy during the American Revolution', in Fiebig-von Hase and Lehmkuhl, eds, *Enemy Images in American History*, Providence, RI: Berghahn Books, 1997, pp. 91–107.

Herken, Gregg, *Counsels of War*, New York: Alfred A. Knopf, 1985.

Herzog, Arthur, *The War Peace Establishment*, New York: Harper and Row, 1965.

Heuser, Beatrice, *Reading Clausewitz*, London: Pimlico, 2002.

Hirst, Paul, *War and Power in the 21st Century*, Oxford: Polity Press, 2001.

Hoffman, F. G., *Decisive Force: The New American Way of War*, Westport: Praeger, 1996.

Holden Reid, Brian, 'Tensions in the Supreme Command: Anti-Americanism in the British Army, 1939–45', in Brian Holden Reid and John White, eds, *American Studies: Essays in Honour of Marcus Cunliffe*, Basingstoke: MacMillan, 1991.

——'The Influence of the Vietnam Syndrome on the Writing of Civil War History', *RUSI Journal*, Vol. 147 No. 1, February 2002, pp. 44–52.

Hopkins, George E., 'Bombing and the American Conscience during World War II', *The Historian*, Vol. 28 No. 3, May 1966, pp. 451–473.

Hounshell, David A., *From the American System to Mass Production 1800–1932*, Baltimore: Johns Hopkins University Press, 1984.

Howard, Michael, *Clausewitz*, Oxford; New York: Oxford University Press, 1983.
——'Constraints on Warfare', in Michael Howard, George J. Andreopoulos, and Mark R. Shulman, eds, *The Laws of War: Constraints on Warfare in the Western World*, New Haven: Yale University Press, 1994, pp. 1–34.
Hughes, Thomas P., *Human-Built World: How to Think about Technology and Culture*, Chicago: University of Chicago Press, 2004.
Hull, Isabel V., *Absolute Destruction: Military Culture and the Practices of War in Imperial Germany*, Ithaca: Cornell University Press, 2005.
Huntington, Samuel P., *The Soldier and the State: The Theory and Politics of Civil–Military Relations*, Cambridge, MA: Belknap Press, 1957.
Hyde, Charles K., 'Casualty Aversion: Implications for Policymakers and Senior Military Officers', *Aerospace Power Journal*, Vol. 14 No. 2, Summer 2000, pp. 17–27.
Ignatieff, Michael, *Empire Lite: Nation-Building in Afghanistan, Kosovo, and Bosnia*, London: Vintage, 2003.
Inoguchi, Rikihei, and Tadashi Nakajima, *The Divine Wind: Japan's Kamikaze Force in World War II*, Annapolis: Naval Institute Books, reprint, 1994.
Jandora, John W., 'War and Culture: A Neglected Relation', *Armed Forces & Society*, Vol. 25 No. 4, Summer 1999, pp. 541–556.
Janowitz, Morris, *The Professional Soldier: A Social and Political Portrait*, Glencoe: The Free Press, 1960.
Johnson, Paul, *A History of the American People*, London: Phoenix Giant, 1997.
Johnson, Robert H., *Improbable Dangers: U.S. Conceptions of Threat in the Cold War and After*, Basingstoke: Macmillan, 1994.
Johnson, Wray R., 'War, Culture and the Interpretation of History: the Vietnam War Reconsidered', *Small Wars and Insurgencies*, Vol. 9 No. 2, Autumn 1998, pp. 83–113.
Johnston, Alistair Iain, 'Thinking about Strategic Culture', *International Security*, Vol. 19 No. 4, Spring 1995, pp. 33–64.
——'Strategic Cultures Revisited: Reply to Colin Gray', *Review of International Studies*, Vol. 25 No. 3, July 1999, pp. 519–523.
Kagan, Frederick W., 'War and Aftermath', *Policy Review*, No. 120, August/September 2003, www.policyreview.org/aug03/kagan.html. Accessed 1 December 2005.
Kagan, Robert, 'Power and Weakness', *Policy Review*, No. 113, June/July 2002, www.hoover.org/publications/policyreview/3460246.html. Accessed 21 August 2007.
Kaldor, Mary, *New and Old Wars: Organized Violence in a Global Era*, Cambridge: Polity Press, 1999.
Kaplan, Fred, *The Wizards of Armageddon*, New York: Touchstone, 1984.
Katzenstein, Peter J., *Cultural Norms and National Security: Police and Military in Postwar Japan*, Ithaca: Cornell University Press, 1996.
Keegan, John, *A History of Warfare*, London: Pimlico, 1994.
Kennan, George F., *American Diplomacy: Expanded Edition*, Chicago; London: University of Chicago Press, 1984.
Kennedy, David M., *Freedom from Fear: The American People in Depression and War, 1929–1945*, New York: Oxford University Press, 1999.
Khafaji, Isam al, 'A Few Days After: State and Society in a post-Saddam Iraq', in Toby Dodge and Steven Simon, eds, *Iraq at the Crossroads: State and Society in the Shadow of Regime Change*, IISS Adelphi Paper 354, London: Routledge, 2003.

Khong, Yuen Foong, *Analogies at War: Korea, Munich, Dien Bien Phu, and the Vietnam decisions of 1965*, Princeton: Princeton University Press, 1992.

Kibbe, Jennifer D., 'The Rise of the Shadow Warriors', *Foreign Affairs*, Vol. 83 No. 2, March/April 2004, pp. 102–115.

Killebrew, Robert P., 'It is a Daunting Time to be a Soldier', *Proceedings of the US Naval Institute*, Vol. 130 No. 6, June 2004, pp. 75–78.

Kincade, William, 'American National Style and Strategic Culture', in Carl G. Jacobsen, ed., *Strategic Power: USA/USSR*, Basingstoke: Macmillan, 1990.

Kissinger, Henry A., 'Reflections on American Diplomacy', *Foreign Affairs*, October 1956; reprinted in James F. Hoge and Fareed Zakaria, eds, *The American Encounter: The United States and the Making of the Modern World: Essays from 75 years of Foreign Affairs*, New York: Basic Books, 1997, pp. 170–186.

——*Nuclear Weapons and Foreign Policy*, New York: Harper, 1957.

Kitfield, James, *Prodigal Soldiers: How the Generation of Officers Born of Vietnam Revolutionized the American Style of War*, Washington; London: Brassey's, 1997.

Klare, Michael T., *War Without End: American Planning for the Next Vietnams*, New York: Knopf, 1972.

Korb, Lawrence J., 'Fixing the Mix', *Foreign Affairs*, Vol. 83 No. 2, March/April 2004, pp. 2–7.

Krepinevich, Andrew, *The Army and Vietnam*, Baltimore; London: Johns Hopkins University Press, 1986.

——'Cavalry to Computer: The Pattern of Military Revolutions', *The National Interest*, No. 37, Fall 1994, pp. 30–42.

——'How to Win in Iraq', *Foreign Affairs*, Vol. 84 No. 5, September/October 2005, pp. 87–104.

Kuang-Heng, Yee, *War as Risk Management*, Unpublished PhD Thesis, London School of Economics and Political Science, 2004.

Kuper, Adam, *Culture: The Anthropologists' Account*, Cambridge, MA: Harvard University Press, 1999.

Kutler, Stanley I., 'The Long Shadow: The Third Indochina War, 1975–1995', in David K. Adams and Cornelis A. Van Minnen, eds, *Aspects of War in American History*, Keele: Keele University Press, 1997, pp. 239–256.

Lacquement, Richard A., 'The Casualty-Aversion Myth', *Naval War College Review*, Vol. 57 No. 1, Winter 2004, pp. 39–57.

Larson, Eric V., *Casualties and Consensus: The Historical Role of Casualties in Domestic Support for U.S. Military Operations*, Santa Monica: RAND, 1996.

Lewis, Jonathan, and Ben Steele, *Hell in the Pacific*, London: Channel 4 Books, 2001.

Liddell Hart, Basil, *The British Way in Warfare: Adaptability and Mobility*, Harmondsworth: Penguin, 1942.

Lind, Michael, *Vietnam: The Necessary War: A Reinterpretation of America's Most Disastrous Military Conflict*, New York: Free Press, 1999.

Linn, Brian McAllister, *Guardians of Empire: The U.S. Army and the Pacific, 1902–1940*, Chapel Hill: University of North Carolina Press, 1997.

——'The American Way of War Revisited', *Journal of Military History*, Vol. 66 No. 2, April 2002, pp. 501–533.

Lippmann, Walter, *Public Opinion and Foreign Policy in the United States*, London: George Allen and Unwin, 1952.

Lipsky, David, *Absolutely American: Four Years at West Point*, New York: Houghton Mifflin, 2003.

Lock-Pullan, Richard, 'An Inward-Looking Time: The United States Army, 1973–1976', *The Journal of Military History*, Vol. 67 No. 2, April 2003, pp. 483-511.

Lord, Carnes, 'American Strategic Culture', in Fred E. Baumann and Kenneth M. Jensen, eds, *American Defense Policy and Liberal Democracy*, Charlottesville: University Press of Virginia, 1989, pp. 44–63.

——'American Strategic Culture in Small Wars', *Small Wars and Insurgencies*, Vol. 3 No. 3, Winter 1992, pp. 205–216.

Luttwak, Edward N., 'The Operational Level of War', *International Security*, Vol. 5 No. 3, Winter 1980–1981, pp. 61–79.

——'Toward Post-Heroic Warfare', *Foreign Affairs*, Vol. 74 No. 3, May/June 1995, pp. 109–122.

Lynn, John A., *Battle: A History of Combat and Culture*, Boulder: Westview Press, revised and updated edition, 2004.

McDougall, Walter A., *Promised Land, Crusader State: The American Encounter with the World Since 1776*, Boston: Houghton Mifflin, 1997.

Mackenzie, Donald, *Inventing Accuracy: A Historical Sociology of Nuclear Missile Guidance*, Cambridge, MA: The MIT Press, 1990.

Mahnken, Thomas G., and James R. Fitzsimonds, 'Tread-Heads or Technophiles? Army Officer Attitudes Toward Transformation', *Parameters: US Army War College Quarterly*, Vol. 34 No. 2, Summer 2004, pp. 57–72.

Mann, James, *The Rise of the Vulcans: The History of Bush's War Cabinet*, New York: Viking, 2004.

Marshall, Andrew W., J. J. Martin, and Henry S. Rowen, eds, *On Not Confusing Ourselves: Essays on National Security Strategy in Honour of Albert and Roberta Wohlstetter*, Boulder: Westview Press, 1991.

Maslowski, Peter, 'To the edge of greatness: The United States, 1783–1865', in Williamson Murray, MacGregor Knox, and Alvin Bernstein, eds, *The Making of Strategy: Rulers, States, and War*, Cambridge; New York: Cambridge University Press, 1994.

Mayers, David, *Wars and Peace: The Future Americans Envisioned 1861–1991*, New York: St. Martin's Press, 1999.

Mead, Margaret, *And Keep Your Powder Dry: An Anthropologist Looks at America*, New York: Horrow, 1943.

Mead, Walter Russell, *Special Providence: American Foreign Policy and How It Changed the World*, New York; London: Routledge, 2002.

Münkler, Herfried, *The New Wars*, translated by Patrick Camiller, Oxford: Polity Press, 2005.

Murray, Williamson, 'Clausewitz Out, Computers In: Military Culture and Technological Hubris', *The National Interest*, No. 48, Summer 1997, pp. 57–64.

——'Introduction', in Williamson Murray, ed., *A Nation at War in an Era of Strategic Change*, Carlisle Barracks: Strategic Studies Institute, September 2004, pp. 1–20.

Murray, Williamson, and Robert H. Scales, Jr, *The Iraq War: A Military History*, Cambridge, MA; London: Harvard University Press, 2003.

Nelson, John D., 'Swiftly defeat the efforts, then what? The "New American Way of War" and the Transition from Decisive Combat Operations to Post-Conflict Security Operations', in Williamson Murray, ed., *A Nation at War in an Era of Strategic Change*, Carlisle Barracks: Strategic Studies Institute, September 2001, pp. 43–68.

O'Hanlon, Michael, *Technological Change and the Future of Warfare*, Washington, DC: Brookings Institution Press, 2000.

——'A Flawed Masterpiece', *Foreign Affairs*, Vol. 81 No. 3, May/June 2002, pp. 47–63.

Osgood, Robert Endicott, *Limited War: The Challenge to American Strategy*, Chicago: University of Chicago Press, 1957.

Owens, William A., 'Creating a U.S. Military Revolution', in Theo Farrell and Terry Terriff, eds, *The Sources of Military Change: Culture, Politics, Technology*, Boulder: Lynne Rienner, 2002, pp. 205–219.

Owens, William A., with Ed Offley, *Lifting the Fog of War*, Baltimore; London: Johns Hopkins University Press, 2001.

Pearlman, Michael D., *Warmaking and American Democracy: The Struggle over Military Strategy, 1700 to the Present*, Lawrence: University Press of Kansas, 1999.

Perito, Robert M., *Where is the Lone Ranger When We Need Him? America's Search for a Postconflict Stability Force*, Washington, DC: United States Institute of Peace, 2004.

Petraeus, David H., 'Military Influence and the Post-Vietnam Use of Force', *Armed Forces and Society*, Vol. 15 No. 4, Summer 1989, pp. 489–505.

Pick, Daniel, *War Machine: The Rationalisation of Slaughter in the Modern Age*, New Haven; London: Yale University Press, 1993.

Poore, Stuart, 'What is the Context? A Reply to the Gray-Johnston Debate on Strategic Culture', *Review of International Studies*, Vol. 29 No. 2, April 2003, pp. 279–284.

Porch, Douglas, *Wars of Empire*, London: Cassell, 2000.

Priest, Dana, *The Mission: Waging War and Keeping Peace with America's Military*, New York; London: W. W. Norton & Co, 2003.

Pursell, Carroll, *The Machine in America: A Social History of Technology*, Baltimore: Johns Hopkins University Press, 1995.

Rapoport, Anatol, 'Changing Conceptions Of War in the United States', in Booth and Wright, eds, *American Thinking about Peace and War*, Hassocks: Harvester Press, 1978, pp. 59–82.

Reardon, Carol, *Soldiers and Scholars: The U.S. Army and the Uses of Military History, 1865–1920*, Lawrence: University Press of Kansas, 1990.

Record, Jeffrey, 'Vietnam in Retrospect: Could We Have Won?', *Parameters: US Army War College Quarterly*, Vol. 26 No. 4, Winter 1996–1997, pp. 51–65.

——'Collapsed Countries, Casualty Dread, and the New American Way of War', *Parameters: US Army War College Quarterly*, Vol. 32 No. 2, Summer 2002, pp. 4-23.

——*Making War, Thinking History: Munich, Vietnam, and Presidential Uses of Force from Korea to Kosovo*, Annapolis: Naval Institute Press, 2002.

——*Bounding the Global War on Terrorism*, Carlisle Barracks: Strategic Studies Institute, December 2003.

Record, Jeffrey, and W. Andrew Terrill, *Iraq and Vietnam: Differences, Similarities and Insights*, Carlisle Barracks: Strategic Studies Institute, May 2004.

Reston, James, *Sherman's March and Vietnam*, New York: Macmillan, 1984.

Rivkin, David B., and Lee A. Casey, 'Leashing the Dogs of War', *The National Interest*, No. 73, Fall 2003, pp. 57–69.

Rochlin, Gene I., *Trapped in the Net: The Unanticipated Consequences of Computerization*, Princeton: Princeton University Press, 1997.

Roe Smith, Merritt, 'Army Ordnance and the "American System" of Manufacturing, 1815–1861', in Roe Smith, ed., *Military Enterprise and Technological Change: Perspectives on the American Experience*, Cambridge, MA: MIT Press, 1985, pp. 39–86.

Rosen, Stephen Peter, 'Vietnam and the American Theory of Limited War', *International Security*, Vol. 7 No. 2, Fall 1982, pp. 83–113.

Rumsfeld, Donald, 'Transforming the Military', *Foreign Affairs*, Vol. 81 No. 3, May/June 2002, pp. 19–32.

Santoli, Al, *Leading the Way: How Vietnam Veterans Rebuilt the U.S. Military*, New York: Ballantine Books, 1993.

Sapolsky, Harvey M., and Jeremy Shapiro, 'Casualties, Technology and America's Future Wars', *Parameters: US Army War College Quarterly*, Vol. 26 No. 2, Summer 1996, pp. 119–127.

Sarkesian, Sam C., *America's Forgotten Wars: The Counterrevolutionary Past and Lessons for the Future*, Westport: Greenwood Press, 1984.

Scarborough, Rowan, *Rumsfeld's War*, Washington, DC: Regnery, 2004.

Segal, Howard P., *Technological Utopianism in American Culture*, Chicago: University of Chicago Press, 1985.

Sherry, Michael S., *The Rise of American Air Power: The Creation of Armageddon*, New Haven: Yale University Press, 1987.

——*In the Shadow of War: The United States Since the 1930s*, New Haven: Yale University Press, 1995.

Shy, John, 'The American Military Experience: History and Learning', *Journal of Interdisciplinary History*, Vol. 1 No. 2, Winter 1971, pp. 205–228.

Smith, Rupert, *The Utility of Force*, London: Allen Lane, 2005.

Snow, Donald M., and Dennis M. Drew, *From Lexington to Desert Storm: War and Politics in the American Experience*, Armonk: M. E. Sharpe, 1994.

Snyder, Jack, *The Soviet Strategic Culture: Implications for Limited Nuclear Operations*, Santa Monica: RAND R-2154-AF, 1977.

——'The Concept of Strategic Culture: Caveat Emptor', in Carl Jacobsen, ed., *Strategic Power: USA/USSR*, London: Macmillan, 1990, pp. 3–9.

Sorley, Lewis, *A Better War: The Unexamined Victories and the Final Tragedy of America's Last Years in Vietnam*, New York: Harcourt Brace, 1999.

Steenkamp, Willem, 'The Multi-Battalion Regiment: an Old Concept with a New Relevance', in J. Cilliers and B. Sass, eds, *Get on parade: Restructuring South Africa's part-time military force for the 21st century*, South Africa: Institute for Defence Policy, 1996.

Stoler, Mark A., *Allies and Adversaries: The Joint Chiefs of Staff, The Grand Alliance, and U.S. Strategy in World War II*, Chapel Hill: University of North Carolina Press, 2000.

Strachan, Hew, 'The Lost Meaning of Strategy', *Survival*, Vol. 47 No. 3, Autumn 2005, pp. 33–54.

Stuart, Reginald C., *War and American Thought: From the Revolution to the Monroe Doctrine,* Kent: Kent State University Press, 1982.

Summers, Harry G., *On Strategy: A Critical Analysis of the Vietnam War*, Novato: Presidio Press, 1982.

——*On Strategy II: A Critical Analysis of the Gulf War*, New York: Dell, 1992.

Toffler, Alvin, and Heidi Toffler, *War and Anti-war: Survival at the Dawn of the 21st Century*, Boston; London: Little, Brown, 1993.
Ullman, Harlan K., and James P. Wade, *Rapid Dominance, A Force for all Seasons: Technologies and Systems for Achieving Shock and Awe*, London: RUSI, 1998.
Van Creveld, Martin, *Fighting power: German and US Army Performance, 1939–1945*, Westport, Conn: Greenwood Press, 1982.
——*The Transformation of War*, New York: Free Press, 1991.
——*The Art of War: War and Military Thought*, London: Cassell, 2000.
Walzer, Michael, *Just and Unjust Wars*, New York: Basic Books, 2000.
Warden, John A., 'Air Theory for the Twenty-first Century', in Karl P. Magyar, ed., *Challenge and Response: Anticipating U.S. Military Security Concerns*, (Maxwell AFB: Air University Press, 1994).
Weigley, Russell F., *History of the United States Army*, New York: Macmillan, 1967.
——*The American Way of War: A History of United States Military Strategy and Policy*, Bloomington: Indiana University Press, 1977.
——'American Strategy from Its Beginnings through the First World War', in Peter Paret, ed., *Makers of Modern Strategy: From Machiavelli to the Nuclear Age*, Princeton: Princeton University Press, 1986, pp. 424–429.
——'The American Military and the Principle of Civilian Control from McClellan to Powell', *The Journal of Military History*, Vol. 57 No. 5, October 1993, pp. 27–59.
——'Response to Brian McAllister Linn', *The Journal of Military History*, Vol. 66 No. 2, April 2002, pp. 531–533.
Wheeler, Nicholas, 'Dying for "Enduring Freedom": Accepting Responsibility for Civilian Casualties in the War against Terrorism', *International Relations*, Vol. 16 No. 2, August 2002, pp. 105–125.
Williams, Phil, 'Thomas Schelling', in John Baylis and John Garnett, eds, *Makers of Nuclear Strategy*, London: Pinter Publishers, 1991.
Windsor, Philip, *Strategic Thinking: An Introduction and Farewell*, London: Lynne Rienner, 2002.
Wohlstetter, Albert, 'On Vietnam and Bureaucracy', July 1968, available online in *The Writings of Albert Wohlstetter* – www.rand.org/publications/classics/wohlstetter/D17276.1/D17276.1.html. Accessed 1 December 2005.
——'Between an Unfree World and None: Increasing Our Choices', *Foreign Affairs*, Vol. 63 No. 5, Summer 1985, pp. 962–994.
Woodward, Bob, *Bush at War*, London: Pocket Books, 2003.
——*Plan of Attack: The Road To War*, London: Simon & Schuster, 2004.
Woodward, C. Vann, 'The Age of Reinterpretation', *American Historical Review*, Vol. 66 No. 1, October 1960, pp. 2–8.
Wrage, Stephen D., 'Introduction: The Promise of Immaculate Warfare' and 'Conclusion: Prospects for Precision Air Power', in Wrage, ed., *Immaculate Warfare: Participants Reflect on the Air Campaigns over Kosovo, Afghanistan, and Iraq*, Westport: Praeger, 2003, pp. 1–20.
Zoellick, Robert B., 'Congress and the Making of US Foreign Policy', *Survival*, Vol. 41 No. 4, Winter 1999–2000, pp. 20–41.

Speeches, interviews, and government publications

Central Intelligence Agency, *Comprehensive Report of the Special Advisor to the DCI on Iraq's WMD*, 30 September 2004 – www.cia.gov/cia/reports/iraq_wmd_2004/index.html. Accessed 12 August 2005.

Defense Advanced Research Projects Agency, Statement by DARPA Director Dr Anthony Tether to the Subcommittee on Emerging Threats and Capabilities, Senate Armed Services Committee, 10 April 2002 – www.darpa.mil/body/news/2002/DARPAtestim.pdf Accessed 3 February 2006.

Department of Defense, *Quadrennial Defense Review Report*, Washington, DC, 2001 – www.defenselink.mil/pubs/qdr2001.pdf. Accessed 1 December 2005.

——'Secretary Rumsfeld Speaks on "21st Century Transformation" of U.S. Armed Forces', 31 January 2002 – www.defenselink.mil/speeches/2002/s20020131-secdef.html. Accessed 12 August 2005.

——'News Briefing with Secretary Rumsfeld and General Myers', 23 December 2002 – www.defenselink.mil/transcripts/2002/t12232002_t1223sd.html. Accessed 6 February 2006.

——'Beyond Nation-Building', Remarks as Delivered by Donald Rumsfeld, 11th Annual Salute to Freedom, Intrepid Sea-Air-Space Museum, New York City, Friday, 14 February 2003 – www.defenselink.mil/speeches/2003/sp20030214-secdef0024.html. Accessed 26 February 2004.

——'Deputy Secretary Wolfowitz Interview with Sam Tannenhaus', *Vanity Fair*, 9 May 2003 – www.defenselink.mil/transcripts/2003/tr20030509-depsecdef0223.html. Accessed 1 July 2005.

——'Strategy and the Idea of Freedom', Lecture by Douglas J. Feith at the Heritage Foundation, 24 November 2003 – www.defenselink.mil/speeches/2003/sp20031124-0703.html. Accessed 3 February 2005.

——'Richard B. Myers Testimony to the Senate Armed Services Committee on the Transition in Iraq', 25 June 2004 – www.defenselink.mil/speeches/2004/sp20040625-depsecdef0541.html. Accessed 3 February 2006.

——'Deputy Secretary Wolfowitz Remarks at the Aspen Institute', 16 July 2004 – www.defenselink.mil/transcripts/2004/tr20040716-secdef1041.html. Accessed 12 August 2005.

——'News Briefing with Deputy Secretary of Defense Paul Wolfowitz', 24 July 2004 – www.defenselink.mil/transcripts/2004/tr20040724-depsecdef1081.html. Accessed 5 December 2005.

——*FMI 3-07.22 Counterinsurgency Operations*, Washington, DC, October 2004, full text available online at www.fas.org/irp/doddir/Army/fmi3-07-22.pdf. Accessed 6 February 2006.

——*Directive No. 3000.05: Military Support for Stability, Security, Transition, and Reconstruction Operations*, 28 November 2005 – www.dtic.mil/whs/directives/corres/pdf/d300005_112805/d300005p.pdf. Accessed 19 January 2006.

——*Defense Science Board 2004 Summer Study on Transition to and from Hostilities*, Washington DC, December 2004 – www.acq.osd.mil/dsb/reports/2004-12-DSB_SS_Report_Final.pdf. Accessed 3 February 2006.

——*Quadrennial Defense Review Report*, Washington, DC, 2006 – www.defenselink.mil/qdr/report/Report20060203.pdf. Accessed 9 February 2006.

General Anthony Zinni, Address to the Marine Corps Association and US Naval Institute Forum, Arlington, Virginia, 4 September 2003 – www.mca-usniforum.org/forum03zinni.htm. Accessed 12 August 2005.

General William Westmoreland, 'The Battlefield of the Future', Speech to the Association of the United States Army, Washington, DC, 14 October 1969.

House Armed Services Committee, 'Statement of Arthur K. Cebrowski before the Subcommittee on Terrorism, Unconventional Threats and Capabilities',

26 February 2004 – www.house.gov/hasc/openingstatementsandpressreleases/108thcongress/04-02-26cebrowski.pdf. Accessed 12 August 2005.

Les Aspin, Address to the Jewish Institute for National Security Affairs, Washington, DC, 21 September 1992.

National Security Council, *NSC 68, United States Objectives and Programs for National Security*, 14 April 1950. Full text available online at www.fas.org/irp/offdocs/nsc-hst/nsc-68.htm. Accessed 19 January 2006.

PBS, 'The Immutable Nature of War': *NOVA* interview with Paul Van Riper, conducted 17 December 2003 – www.pbs.org/wgbh/nova/wartech/nature.html. Accessed 12 August 2005.

——'Transforming Warfare': *NOVA* interview with Admiral Arthur Cebrowski, conducted 15 January 2004 – www.pbs.org/wgbh/nova/wartech/transform.html. Accessed 12 August 2005.

——*Frontline* interview with Paul Van Riper for *Rumsfeld's War*, conducted 8 July 2004 – www.pbs.org/wgbh/pages/frontline/shows/pentagon/interviews/vanriper.html. Accessed 12 August 2005.

——*Frontline* interview with Colonel Douglas MacGregor for *Rumsfeld's War*, conducted 23 July 2004 – www.pbs.org/wgbh/pages/frontline/shows/pentagon/interviews/macgregor.html. Accessed 19 January 2006.

——*Frontline* interview with Former Secretary of the Army Thomas White for *Rumsfeld's War*, conducted 12 August 2004 – www.pbs.org/wgbh/pages/frontline/shows/pentagon/interviews/white.html. Accessed 19 January 2006.

State Department, 'President Bush Outlines Progress in Operation Iraqi Freedom', 16 April 2003 – www.state.gov/p/nea/rls/rm/19709.htm. Accessed 12 August 2005.

The White House, 'Radio Address of the President to the Nation', 15 September 2001 – www.whitehouse.gov/news/releases/2001/09/20010915.html. Accessed 1 December 2005.

——'Presidential Address to a Joint Session of Congress and the American People', 20 September 2001 – www.whitehouse.gov/news/releases/ 2001/09/20010920-8.html. Accessed 1 December 2005.

——'President Bush Delivers Graduation Speech at West Point Military Academy', 1 June 2002 – www.whitehouse.gov/news/releases/2002/06/print/20020601-3.html. Accessed 1 December 2005.

——*The National Security Strategy of the United States of America*, Washington, DC, September 2002 – www.whitehouse.gov/nsc/nss.html. Accessed 3 February 2006.

——*National Strategy for Victory in Iraq*, Washington, DC, 30 November 2005 – www.whitehouse.gov/infocus/iraq/iraq_strategy_nov2005.html. Accessed 6 December 2005.

Newspapers, magazines and web-only articles

Air Force Magazine (US)
Armed Forces Journal (US)
Army Times (US)
Boston Globe
Christian Science Monitor
Daily Telegraph (London)
Independent (London)

International Herald Tribune
Jerusalem Post
Los Angeles Times
New Left Review
New York Times
New York Times Magazine
Prospect (London)
The Atlantic Monthly
The Australian
Time
Vietnam Magazine
Wall Street Journal
Washington Post
Weekend Financial Times (London)
Weekly Standard

CBSNews.com, 'Kay: "We were almost all wrong"', 28 January 2004 – www.cbsnews.com/stories/2004/01/29/iraq/main596595.shtml. Accessed 19 January 2006.

Coalition Provisional Authority, letter purportedly from Abu Musab al Zarqawi to Ayman al Zawahiri, intercepted by the CPA in January 2004 – www.cpa-iraq.org/transcripts/20040212_zarqawi_full.html. Accessed 12 August 2005.

Codner, Michael, 'The Battle for Hearts and Minds', www.rusi.org/iraq. Accessed 28 April 2004.

DefenseTech.org, 'Army's insurgent manual author speaks', 17 November 2004 – www.defensetech.org/archives/2004_11.html. Accessed 6 February 2006.

GlobalSecurity.org, 'Memo by US Secretary of Defense Donald Rumsfeld on the Global War on Terrorism', 16 October 2003 – www.globalsecurity.org/military/library/policy/dod/rumsfeld-d20031016sdmemo.htm. Accessed 12 August 2005.

——'Global Strike Task Force', 26 April 2005 – www.globalsecurity.org/military/agency/usaf/gstf.htm. Accessed 12 August 2005.

Globeandmail.com, 'More cash flowing to robotics research', 11 May 2004 – www.globetechnology.com/servlet/story/RTGAM.20040412.gtrobotsapr12/BNStory/Technology. Accessed 19 January 2006.

Interview with Lt.-General Liu Yazhou of the Chinese Air Force by Dai Xu, for *Dongfang Wang* (Shanghai), 31 May 2004 – <online translation www.evening-post.org/blog/_archives/2005/1/8. Accessed 12 August 2005.

Kaplan, Fred, 'The Flaw in Shock and Awe', Slate Magazine, 26 March 2003 – http://slate.msn.com/id/2080745. Accessed 12 August 2005.

Kniazkov, Maxim, 'U.S. Army Reserve Becoming "Broken Force"', DefenseNews.com, 6 January 2005 – www.defensenews.com/story.php?F=586113&C=landwar. Accessed 1 December 2005.

Krepinevich, Andrew, 'Skipping "Skipping a Generation?"', CSBA Backgrounder, 5 January 2002 – www.csbaonline.org/4Publications/Archive/B.20020501.Skipping__Skipping/B.20020501.Skipping__Skipping.htm. Accessed 19 January 2006.

Libicki, Martin, 'www.U.S.DoD.com: Virtual Diplomacy Report 7', United States Institute of Peace, February 1999 – www.usip.org/virtualdiplomacy/publications/reports/libickiISA99.html. Accessed 3 February 2006.

Loughlin, Sean, 'Rumsfeld on looting in Iraq: "Stuff happens"', www.CNN.com, 12 April 2003. Accessed 12 June 2003.

Bibliography

Mazzetti, Mark, 'Good Marines Make Good Neighbours', Slate Magazine, 25 February 2004 – http://slate.msn.com/id/2096027. Accessed 12 August 2005.

Peterson, Steven W., 'Central but Inadequate: the Application of Theory in Operation Iraqi Freedom', National Defense University, 2004 – www.ndu.edu/library/n4/n045602I.pdf. Accessed 12 August 2005.

Rogers, Paul, 'Between Fallujah and Palestine', OpenDemocracy, 22 April 2004 – www.opendemocracy.net/themes/article-2-1858.jsp. Accessed 12 August 2005.

Rogers, Reginald P., 'Army changes from divisions to brigade units of action', TRADOC News Service, Department of Defense, 5 April 2004 – www.tradoc.Army.mil/pao/TNSarchives/April04/040604.htm. Accessed 19 January 2006.

Smith, Daniel, 'Iraq: Descending Into a Quagmire', Foreign Policy in Focus Policy Report, June 2003 – www.fpif.org/papers/quagmire2003-upd.html. Accessed 12 August 2005.

Sperry, Paul, 'No Shock, No Awe: It Never Happened', WorldNetDaily.com, 3 April 2003 – wnd.com/news/article.asp?ARTICLE_ID=31858. Accessed 5 February 2006.

Talbot, David, 'How Technology Failed in Iraq', TechnologyReview.com, November 2004 – www.techreview.com/articles/04/11/talbot1104.asp?p=1. Accessed 12 August 2005.

——'The Ascent of the Robotic Attack Jet', TechnologyReview.com, March 2005 – www.technologyreview.com/articles/05/03/issue/feature_jet.asp?p=0. Accessed 12 August 2005.

Transcript of the second US Presidential Candidates' Debate, 8 October 2004 – www.debates.org/pages/trans2004c.html. Accessed 19 January 2006.

Varhola, Christopher H., 'American Challenges in Postwar Iraq', Foreign Policy Research Institute E-Notes, 27 May 2004 – www.fpri.org/enotes/20040527.americawar.varhola.iraqchallenges.html. Accessed 12 August 2005.

Index

Abrams, C., General 70, 147
Abrams Doctrine 70–71, 103–106
Abu Ghraib 144
Acheson, D. 56
Adams, J. 25
Adams, J.Q. 24
Afghanistan 5, 139, 115, 143; civilian casualties 88; command-and-control system 118; counter-insurgency and post-conflict stabilization in 105, 130; minimalist approach in 116; planning for attack on 107; Provincial Reconstruction Teams 131; separation of politics and strategy 125; Special Forces in campaign 107; vision and reality in 112; war in 89, 101, 114, 135; *see also* Operation Enduring Freedom; Taliban
'Air Land Battle' doctrine 94
Albright, M. 80
Allied Force Operation 80
America/American: as lone superpower 7; casualty figures in World Wars 72; casualty tolerance 61, 72, 88, 89, 145; Civil War 19, 72; Cold War *see* Cold War; colonialism, experiment in 37; concept of free security 2, 23, 38–39, 138; 'crusading' tendency 18; cult of mechanization 46; entry into World War I 49; geopolitical context 17, 23, 24, 47, 138; ideal of war 67; participation in World War I 27; preference for unconditional surrender 31; public opinion in wartime *see* public opinion; search for science of war, cultural origins 45–56; stab-in-the-back thesis 68; super-power status 38; technological rationality 46; traditional 'republican' way of war 103; *see also* United States *entries*
American Exceptionalism 24, 138; cultural heritage of 2, 6, 30
American Expeditionary Forces 31
American military: automation of processes 109; autonomy from civilian interference 37; corporate influence on military culture 48, 95; culture 13, 128, 137–130; culture, future of 82, 144–148; education 31, 46; expectations and realities of war 120–127; experience, paradox of 140; funding 47, 110, 142; institutional hostility to counter-terrorism efforts 101; intervention from Vietnam to 9/11 75; and memory of Vietnam 61, 63; professionalism 27, 67; resources, profligacy in expenditure of 67; sensitivity towards American public opinion 29; separation of politics and strategy in 16, 32; 'small wars', experience of 34–38; sponsorship of new science of strategy 51; transformation, unconventional opponents 147; *see also* Army; civilians
American Revolution 23, 24, 25
The American Way of War 2, 18
Andreopoulos, G.J. 155n.106
anti-ballistic missile (ABM) systems 60
apoliticism 16, 26, 27, 30, 45
Arab-Israeli conflict 74
Arkin, W.A. 164n.20

Army: core mission as continental defence 28; officers, sensitivity towards congressional and public moods 29; preoccupation with conventional warfare 35; professionalization in state of isolation 28; *see also* civilians; military
Arnett, P. 78
Arnold, H., General 49, 50
Aron, R. 139, 174n.10
Aspin, L. 96, 166n.53
Atlanta, burning of 19, 20, 87
atomic age and Cold War 16, 25, 61
Avant, D.D. 153nn.56, 60, 155nn.97, 110
Axis of Evil 122

Ba'athist regime 4, 124
Bacevich, A.J. 125, 155n.114, 159n.4, 160n.24, 161n.47, 162n.65, 163n.84, 166n.70, 172n.69
Baghdad, fall of 3, 90, 125, 135
Balkans 141
Banks, W.C. 153nn.49, 50
Baram, A. 172n.74
Barnett, T.P.M. 149n.4, 168n.106
Barno, D.W., Lt.-General 131
Bassford, C. 150n.19, 152n.19
Bataan 72
Bathurst, R.B. 150n.29, 157n.50
Beach, I. 172n.92
Beard, C. 46
Betts, R.K. 33, 34, 65, 143, 152n.26, 154nn.84, 94, 155n.101, 159n.7, 175n.23
Beyerchen, A. 150n.24, 169nn.1, 5
'Black Hawk Down' incident 75
Blinken, A.J. 166n.63, 172n.78
'body-bags syndrome', Vietnam and 71–73; *see also* casualty tolerance
Bohlen, C. 56
Boot, M. 154nn.95, 96, 155nn.103, 107, 160n.10, 161nn.31, 46, 52, 162n.55, 175n.31
Booth, K. 152n.31, 158n.73
Bosnia 80, 96, 128, 143
Bradley, General 33
Bremer, L.P. 124, 171n.59
Brennan, D.G. 40
Brinegar, G.A. 161n.36
Brinkley, J. 172n.93
Brinsfield, J.W. 19, 151n.11

British: colonial experience 35; emphasis on 'pacification' 130; military, civilian interference in military affairs 28, 37; policing of insurgencies 124, 129
Brodie, B. 41, 51, 54, 154n.79, 157n.61
Brooks, V., Brigadier General 128
Brush, P. 165n.29
Brzezinski, Z. 57
Buncombe, A. 167n.89
Bundy, M. 58, 60
Burns, J.F. 172n.90
Bush, G.H.W. 63, 69, 85; stab-in-the-back thesis 69
Bush administration 1, 3, 4, 85; grand strategy 97, 101, 106, 145; post-9/11 period change in national security policy 84; precautionary principle 99, 137; radical optimism over political utility of force 89, 113, 136; *Regional Defense Strategy* 73
business and war, scientific management of 45
Byrnes, K., General 130
Byrness, J.F. 27

Calhoun, J.M. 19
Cambone, S. 97
Campbell, K.J. 160nn.21, 22, 162n.61
Card, A. 125
Cardwell, E. 105
Cardwell System 105
Carney, T. 128
Carter, P. 57
Casey, L.A. 151n.17
Cassidy, R.M. 162n.52
casualty-aversion 72; of American society 82; search for economies of force 49–52
casualty tolerance, American 61, 72, 88, 89, 145
Cebrowski, A.A., Admiral 87, 88, 101, 108, 124, 149n.4, 168n.106
CENTCOM 76, 136;
Chace, J. 153n.33
Cheney, Dick 79
China 29, 34
Churchill, W.S. 32
Chynoweth, B., Major 48
citizen-soldiers 29, 70–71
civilians: civil-military relations 27, 33, 69, 129, 139; emphasis on limiting and controlling force 40;

interference 28, 37, 75; neo-Clausewitzian 16, 31; strategists 6, 8, 12, 40, 52, 53, 55, 57, 61, 84, 90, 97, 139
Civil War 7, 21; expression of American Way of War in 18
Clancy, T. 175n.24
Clark, M., General 33
Clark, W., General 76, 80, 81
Clarke, J. 165n.40
Clausewitz, C. von 2, 5, 6, 7, 8, 9, 10, 11, 21, 44, 48, 66, 112, 139, 149n.12, 150nn.21, 22, 25, 28, 169n.1, 170n.26; characteristics of warfare 86; concept of force 8, 39; fog of war 85; 'friction' concept of 85, 113; grammar and logic of war 10; insight on war as continuation of politics 134, 146; and Powell and Weinberger doctrines 65, 67; war as instrument of policy 138; war as 'Remarkable Trinity' 142
Clinton, Bill 88; on air strikes in Kosovo 83; reliance on airpower 8
Clinton administration: and *al Qaeda* 84; *National Security Strategy* (2000) 83; Overwhelming Force, paradigm of 11; Pentagon's 'environment-shaping' 82; and risk-averse mindset of military 80; Somalia 75
Clodfelter, M. 155n.108, 162n.54
Codner, M. 129, 172n.89
coercive diplomacy 8, 33, 79, 81, 125; Albright's advocacy 80; Cohen, E. 32, 70, 82, 84, 152n.23, 153n.55, 154nn.77, 82, 157nn.38, 46, 51, 161n.35, 163nn.1, 92
Cohen, W. 86
Coker, C. 163n.94, 164n.14, 168n.118
Cold War 6, 13, 18, 43, 56; American strategy in 51; 'containment' strategy 11; crises, civilian and military approaches to 33; emphasis on scientific management 56; Limited War theorists 14; post-Cold War era and changing realities of war 79–82; strategic imperatives 16, 39, 94; structure of deterrence 99
collateral damage 20, 88, 89, 96, 111, 132; friendly fire 88, 132
Congress, US: Army officers' sensitivity towards 29, 76; fickleness of support for war 69, 73, 76; military funding shortages 47
containment strategy 11, 17, 56, 84
Cooper, M.H. 168n.95
Cooper, R. 96
Cordesman, A.H. 167n.87, 169n.21, 170nn.24, 37, 39, 172n.85
Correll, J.T. 155n.100
counter-insurgency 34, 36, 58; campaigns 73; counter-guerrilla tactics in Vietnam, failure of 91; defined 143; and evolution of American military culture 127–132; 'Social Systems Engineering' approach 58; Vietnam-era 'clear-and-hold' strategy 147, 173n.101
Cress, L.D. 153nn.48, 49
Creveld, M. van 48, 141, 142, 157n.37, 174nn.13, 14, 16, 175n.21
Crowder, G.L., Colonel 117, 118
Crowe, W., Admiral 64
cruise missiles 92
Crusader artillery system 97
Cuban Missile Crisis 39, 61
cultural conception and reality of war 31–38, 75–83
cultural sources of strategic absolutism 23–31
Currie, M.R. 92

Dao, J. 168nn.115, 117
Davidson, P. 73
Davis, A.C., Vice-Admiral 22
Decker, General 33
Defence Advanced Projects Research Agency (DARPA) 96, 109
Defence Science Board 133
DeLong, M., Lt.-General 109, 115, 118, 120, 124, 168n.113, 169n.15, 170n.30
Demchak, C.C. 168n.109
Der Derian, J. 162n.67, 164n.9, 168n.110
Diamond, L.J. 171n.63, 172nn.75, 82
Dickson, P. 165nn.30, 35, 166n.55
Dobbins, J. F. 124, 171n.64
Dominant Battlespace Awareness 87
dot.com boom 95
draft 105, 124; ending of 104; replaced by all-volunteer force 65, 70
Drew, D.M. 160n.12
Duelfer, C. 122
Dugan, General 69

Eccleston, R. 171n.57
Echevarria II, A. J., Lt.-Colonel 5, 149n.10, 174n.5
Edison, T. 49
Edwards, P.N. 91, 158nn.67, 68, 159nn.100, 105, 117, 165n.32
Eikenberry, K.W. 162n.48, 165n.43
Eisenhower, D. 32, 50, 52
Eisenhower–Dulles strategy of increased reliance on nuclear deterrence 43
electronic battlefield concept 91, 94, 96, 111, 128
11 September 2001 49, 63, 77, 78, 83, 84, 89; impact on Pentagon 97–110
Ellis, J. 46, 156n.25
Ellsberg, D. 42
Embick, S., Lt.-General 29
England, G. 107
Enthoven, A. 55
'environment-shaping', concept of 82, 83
'escalation', concept of 44, 57
Europe: attitudes towards war and peace 138; balance-of-power system, rejection by US 6, 24; power politics and imperialism 6, 21
European Union 138

F-22 Raptor 97
failed states 143
Fallows, J. 119, 167n.79, 169n.17, 170n.41,172nn.70, 81
Fallujah, siege of 124, 130
Feaver, P.D. 159n.8, 161n.46, 167n.84
Feith, D. J. 4, 136
Ferguson, N. 145, 155n.111, 175n.27
Finletter, T.K. 35
Fisher, R. 91
Fitzsimonds, J.R. 167n.74
Flexible Response 15, 36,57
'fog of war', concept of 10, 85
Ford, H. 47
Fordism 47
Franklin, H.B. 157n.43
Franks, T., General 89, 102, 103, 107, 115, 118, 120, 165n.24, 167n.86, 169n.14, 170nn.33, 36, 38, 44, 172n.68; war plan 116, 125
Freedman, L. 92, 146, 159n.99, 163n.89, 165n.36, 175n.29
Freedman, M. 53
'free security', concept of 2, 23, 38–39, 138

'friction' in war 66; in Afghanistan and Iraq 127, 134; warfare's unpredictability 85
Friedman, G. 118, 150n.18, 158nn.69, 71, 93, 166n.48, 170n.31
Friedman, M. 150n.18, 158nn.69, 71, 93, 170n.31
Friedman, N. 149n.4
Frye, A. 159n.109
Future of Iraq Project 126

Gacek, C.M. 152nn.25, 29, 154n.89, 159n.6
Gaddis, J.L. 61, 151n.15, 155n.104, 158nn.81, 84, 159nn.104, 106, 112
Gaither Committee, report of 56, 122
Garner, J., General 124, 126
Garnett, J.C. 155n.5, 156nn.14, 16, 159n.103
Gat, A. 48, 156n.32
Gelb, L.H. 3, 85
Gelpi, C. 159n.8, 161n.46, 167n.84
Gentry, J.A. 122, 171n.50
Germany 25, 50, 51
Ghamari-Tabrizi, S. 158n.77
Giap, General 61
Gibson, J.W. 57, 157n.40, 158nn.89, 91, 92, 95, 159n.108
globalization, impact of 143
'Global War on Terrorism' (GWOT) 100, 116, 123
Golden Handshake 71
Goldhamer, H. 60
Goldwater, B. 92, 96
Goodgame, D. 162n.75
Gordon, M.R. 162nn.60, 70, 73, 74, 76, 80, 164n.19, 169n.19, 171nn.49, 56, 60, 173n.97
Gordon, P.H. 166n.67
Grant, U.S., General 21, 29, 31
Gray, C.H. 150n.26, 157n.63
Gray, C.S. 9, 12, 45, 150nn.23, 30, 71, 156n.21, 169n.23, 174n.17
Green, P. 61
Grenada 88, 141; Operation Urgent Fury 77
Grotelueschen, M.E. 154n.75
Guantanamo Bay 144
guerrilla warfare 58, 62, 74
Gulf of Tonkin incident 57
Gulf War: 7, 77–79, 86, 93, 135, 140; air war, 'Instant Thunder' 79; see also Iraq; Saddam Hussein

Index 195

Haiti intervention 88
Halberstam, D. 76, 162nn.59, 63, 79, 82, 163nn.90, 91
Halper, S. 165n.40
Hancock, General W.S. 29
Handel, M. 65, 160n.11
Hanson, V.D. 150n.30
Harries, M. 161n.40
Harries, S. 161n.40
Harris Poll, 1973 68
Heideking, J. 152n.40
Helmly, J., Lt.-General 104, 145
Herken, G. 155nn.3, 6, 156nn.8, 11, 18, 157nn.58, 62, 158nn.72, 88, 90, 159nn.102, 113, 115
Herzog, A. 155nn.1, 2, 4, 156n.15, 158nn.76, 78
Heuser, B. 150nn.19, 20, 152n.20, 156nn.9, 12, 158n.97, 160n.13, 174n.12
Hilsman, R. 33
Hiroshima 51
Hirst, P. 175n.20
Hitch, C. 42, 45, 55, 61
Hoffman, B. 172n.86
Hoffman, F.G. 74, 154nn.80, 85, 155n.118, 160nn.23, 26, 162nn.49, 71, 164n.15
Holbrooke, R. 75
Holden Reid, B. 159nn.3, 5
Hollingworth, L. 128
Hopkins, G.E. 153nn.42, 44
Horner, C., Lt.-General 78
Horvath, J., Lt.-Colonel 132
Hounshell, D.A. 156n.31
Howard, M. 20, 151n.16, 157n.66, 170n.26
Hughes, T.P. 156n.22
Hull, I.V. 150n.30, 153n.60
humane warfare, concept of 87–90
Huntington, S.P. 2, 13, 17, 38, 149n.2, 151nn.5, 35, 155n.113, 156nn.23, 26
Hyde, C.K. 161n.46

Ignatieff, M. 100, 166n.71
Immaculate Destruction, concept of: cultural sources 90–97; discourse of 86; political utility of 89–90; strategy and tactics of 116–120; technical bias of 121–123; Vietnam Syndrome 115; vision 3, 5, 8, 83, 106, 113–116, 137
Individual Ready Reserve 104
Information dominance, concept of: 86, 122; imperfect environment 10;

incomplete, in war 85; *see also* fog of war
'Instant Thunder' air campaign 86, 117
Institute for Defense Analysis 91
Iran 100, 136, 141
Iraq 100, 139, 143; *al Qaeda* 145; 'catastrophic success' in 123–125; Civil Defence Corps 131; insurgency 120, 145; invasion of 4, 89; no-fly zone 96; politics, history and culture, complexities of 126–127; post-conflict stability operations, American failure in 5, 127–129; security organizations 121; separation of political and military considerations 125; and Vietnam, comparisons between 145; vision and reality in 112; 45
Iraqization 132
Iraq Survey Group 122; final report on Iraqi WMD 120
Iraq Syndrome 146
Iraq War 94; aftermath of 14, 135; casualty levels, low 88; and central paradox about American military culture 113; mutation in 143; planning process for 102; 'Shock and Awe' in 118; Special Forces in campaign 107; strategic concepts during 117–118
ISAF (The International Security Assistance Force) 114
isolationism 17, 23, 90, 139
Israel, Yom Kippur war 93; approach to counterinsurgency 130
Iwo Jima 72

Jaffe, G. 168n.99, 103
Janowitz, M. 34, 152n.27, 154nn.74, 93
Japan 25, 26, 51, 124
al Jazeera 144
Jefferson, T. 23
Jehl, D. 171n.48
Johnson, D.V., General 55
Johnson, L. 57, 104
Johnson, P. 152n.39
Johnson, R.H. 158n.87, 163n.93
Johnson, W.R. 155n.109, 159n.107
Johnston, A.I. 150n.30
Joint Unmanned Combat Aerial Systems or J-UCAS 109, 110
Jomini, A.H. de Baron 48
Jumper, J., General 87
Just War Theory: *jus ad bellum* 19, 25; *jus in bello* 19, 20, 21, 25

Kagan, F.W. 165n.25, 166n.49, 175n.31
Kagan, R. 138, 174n.9
Kahn, H. 41, 42, 44, 54, 55
Kaldor, M. 174n.13
Kaplan, F. 57, 60, 154n.91, 155n.119, 156n.7, 157nn.56, 64, 158nn.75, 79, 82, 83, 85, 86, 159nn.101, 114, 170n.35
Kaplan, R. 53
Kaufmann, W. 42, 55
Kay, D. 122
Kaysen, C. 42
Keegan, J. 11, 12, 150nn.27, 30
Keeny, S. 41
Keller, B. 165n.45
Kennan, G.F. 10, 17, 25, 52, 56, 151n.2
Kennedy, D.M. 51, 157nn.44, 47, 49, 53
Kennedy, J.F. 18, 34, 42, 45, 57; Cuban Missile Crisis 39; interest in limited war 36
Kennedy, P. 105, 135, 167n.92, 174n.3
Khafaji, Isam al 172n.73
Khe Sanh, siege of 91
Khong, Yuen Foong 163n.2
Kibbe, J.D. 167n.76
Killebrew, R.B., Colonel 134, 174n.107
Kissinger, H. A. 17, 34, 72, 138, 151n.6, 154n.92
Kitfield, J. 160n.16, 161n.37
Klare, M.T. 158nn.74, 96, 165n.31, 34
Kniazkov, M. 167n.90, 175n.25
Knickerbocker, B. 164n.16, 171n.54
Korb, L.J. 160n.17, 167n.91
Korea 33, 34, 37; ceasefire in 140; see also North Korea
Koreanization 52
Korean War 17, 33, 35, 69, 104
Kosovo 74, 76, 81, 83, 128
Krepinevich, A.J., Jr. 93, 154n.87, 155nn.102, 105, 162n.50, 165n.42, 166n.58, 172n.88
Kuang-Heng, Yee 163nn.94, 95, 97, 166n.66
Kutler, S.I. 160n.29
Kuwait 70, 75, 78, 79, 119

Lacquement, R.A. 161n.43
Laos 33
Larson, E.V. 145, 161n.45, 175n.28
Leahy, M., Colonel 110
Lebanon 75, 141, 146
Lemann, N. 163n.4
LeMay, C., General 20, 34, 41, 42, 45, 49, 53, 74

Lewis, J. 153n.46
Libicki, M. 164n.7
Libya 75
Lieber, F. 20
limited war 8, 15, 16, 17, 18, 43, 66, 67, 69, 137
Lincoln, P. 21, 23
Lind, M. 157n.60, 160n.27
Linn, B.M. 7, 150n.14, 153nn.62, 71, 155nn.99, 112, 157n.36
Lippmann, W. 17, 18, 25, 151nn.3, 8
Liu Yazhou, Lt.-General 86, 164n.8
Lockheed Martin 88
Lock-Pullan, R. 160n.18, 161n.38, 162n.53
Lodge, H.C. 27
Lord, C. 153n.71, 155n.117, 162nn.51, 69, 169n.23
low-intensity conflict 34, 36, 74, 75, 128, 133, 141, 142
Luce, S.B. 48
Lukeman, N. 168n.113, 169n.15
Luttwak, E.N. 72, 153n.71, 161n.44
Lynn, J.A. 12, 127, 150n.30, 172n.76

MacArthur, D., General 14, 16, 22, 33
McConnell, M. 165n.24, 169n.14
MacDonald, D. 51
McDougall, W.A. 152n.36, 158n.94
MacGregor, D., Colonel 103
machine gun, as expression of American military culture 46, 47
Mackenzie, D. 94,166n.47
McNamara, R. 39, 42, 54, 61, 91, 107, 136
McNaughton, J. 58, 91
McPeak, M., General 76, 80
al-Mahdi Army 130
Mahnken, T.G. 167n.74
Malaysia 124
Manhattan Project 51, 53
Mann, J. 160n.15, 161n.32, 162n.64, 168n.100, 170n.40
Marine corps 34, 35
Marshall, A.W. 60, 93, 94, 165n.38
Marshall, G., General 30, 32, 50, 72
Martin, J.J. 165n.38
Maslowski, P. 152nn.31, 32
Massive Retaliation 16, 34, 43, 53, 57
Mattis, J., Major-General 131
Mayers, D. 152nn.34, 37
Mazzetti, M. 173n.97
Mead, W.R. 151n.13, 153n.53

Index   197

military: Military Transformation 15, 84, 89, 113, 147; debate 97; reconceptualization 133
Millennium Challenge 2002 112
missile technology 53
Muller-Freienfels, R. 46
Munich 84
Münkler, H. 174n.13, 175n.18
Murphy, D. 171n.61
Murray, W. 157n.65, 164nn.5, 13, 170n.43
Murtha, J. 146
Mutual Assured Destruction (MAD), concept of 4, 53, 95
Myers, General 119, 123
My Lai massacre 89

Nagasaki 51
national interest, concept of 73–75
National Security Strategy 83, 89, 98, 99, 122, 136, 143
nation-building: American reluctance 58, 75, 116; in Bosnia and Kosovo 128; Rumsfeld on 114–115
Naylor, S.D. 169n.3
Nelson, J.D. 170n.28
Network-Centric Warfare 101, 108, 112, 134
New Alternatives Workshop 93
Newman, J. 41
'New Wars' theorists 141
9/11 see 11 September 2001
Nitze, P. 43, 51, 52, 56
Nixon, R. 30
Northern Ireland 124, 129
'No Substitute for Victory' philosophy 14, 16, 26, 33, 34, 37, 45, 69, 132; see also MacArthur
NSC-68 38, 51, 56
nuclear power 34, 42; 'counterforce' doctrine 94; bomb, justification for use of 25; deterrence 43, 56, 59, 84; US loss of monopoly 17

Office of Force Transformation 101
Office of Reconstruction and Humanitarian Assistance (ORHA) 126, 128
Offley, E. 164n.10, 171n.51
O'Hanlon, M. 165n.44, 170n.45
Operation Deliberate Force 80
Operation Desert Fox 80
Operation Enduring Freedom 88, 118, 120
Operation Infinite Reach 80
Operation Iraqi Freedom 1, 118, 120, 128, 135, 136; Phase III and Phase IV 128
Operation Just Cause 77, 141
Operation Scorpion 119
Operations Research 59; development of 53
Osama bin Laden, escape of 120
Osgood, R.E. 18, 43, 62, 151n.7
Overwhelming Force paradigm 8, 14, 63, 65, 66, 75, 77, 81; cultural sources of 67–75; excessive risk-aversion and inflexibility 64; and Immaculate Destruction, as rival paradigms 137; marginalization after 9/11 137
Owens, W.A., Admiral 86, 93, 164n.10, 165n.41, 171n.51

Pakistan 120
Panama 88; Paret, P. 170n.26
Patton, General 50
Pax Americana, concept of 7
Peacekeeping Institute at Army War College 128
Pearl Harbor 24, 84
Pearlman, M.D. 152n.18, 153nn.52, 58, 66, 69, 154nn.73, 81, 86, 157nn.41, 52, 59, 159n.1, 161n.41, 162n.72
Perito, R.M. 163n.88, 169nn.6, 8, 172n.87, 173n.95
Perle, R. 94, 116
Perry, W. 82, 86, 92
Pershing, General 31, 32
Peterson, S.W. 170n.25
Petraeus, D.H. 162nn.58, 62
Philippines 29, 35, 37
Podhoretz, N. 63
politics/political: dimension of war 31, 137; sovereignty in war 10, 137; utility of force 10, 14, 43, 139
population control 129, 130, 132
Porch, D. 163n.87
Powell, C., General 14, 64, 65, 69, 76, 77, 82, 88, 100, 108, 119
Powell Doctrine 64, 65, 66, 81, 82, 100–103, 106, 145; see also Weinberger doctrine
Power, T.S., General 20, 55
precision guidance 92, 94, 107
predictability, concept of in war 86, 87
preventive war: defined by 9/11 98; against Iraq 85, 137

Priest, D. 81, 108, 162n.81, 163nn.83, 96, 168n.108
Private Military Companies (PMCs) 105
public opinion: attitude to casualties 72, 87, 88; fragility of popular support 52, 72, 76, 78, 137, 146; support during wars 68, 69, 72, 73, 75, 76, 82, 137, 145
Pursell, C. 156nn.28, 29, 30, 157n.55

Qaddafi, Muammar 76
al Qaeda 77, 84, 88, 120, 145
Quadrennial Defense Review (QDR): of 2001 98, 122; of 2006 133, 147

RAND Corporation 41, 42, 51, 53, 54, 55, 60
Rapid Decisive Operations, concept of 118
Rapid Dominance, concept of *see* Shock and Awe
Rapoport, A. 24, 42, 59, 152n.38
Reagan, R. 69; stab-in-the-back thesis 69
Reardon, C. 153n.63, 157n.33
Record, J. 153n.68, 159nn.9, 11, 162n.77, 163n.2, 169n.18
Reid, B.H. 64
Remarkable Trinity, War as 66
republicanism/republican 23, 27, 104; influence on military, 29; US self-image 138
Reserves 104; call-up since 9/11 104; reducing dependence on 105
Reston, J., Jr. 149n.3, 151n.9, 11
Revkin, A.C. 168nn.115, 117
Revolution in Military Affairs (RMA) 8, 15, 88, 92–94, 97, 111, 122, 128, 134, 135
Revolution in Strategic Affairs 135
Rice, C. 99, 114, 116, 123
Rich, F. 175n.26
Rieff, D. 172nn.71, 77, 83
'Rio Declaration' (1992) 99
Riper, P. Van, Lt.-General 112, 113, 149n.11
risk-aversion in war 64, 66, 76, 84, 85, 100, 106, 137
Rivkin, D.B. 151n.17
Roche, J. 107, 110
Rochlin, G.I. 166n.56
Rogers, R.P. 167n.94, 172n.91

Rolling Thunder air campaign 58
Roosevelt, F. 25, 27, 50, 32, 38
Root, E. 23
Rose, M.F. 110
Rosen, S.P. 160n.21
Rostow, W. 42
Rowen, H.S. 42, 165n.38
Rumsfeld, D. 1, 5, 6, 15, 84, 97, 115, 116, 136, 145, 146, 169n.16; Afghan War 98; Doctrine 100, 106–108; on risk-aversion 85; 'unknown unknowns', concept of 98
Rusk, D. 68

Saddam Hussein 3, 75, 79, 111, 118, 120, 126
al-Sadr, Moqtada 130
Saigon, fall of 64
Saipan 72
Santoli, A. 160n.28, 161n.30
Sapolsky, H.M. 161n.34, 164n.17
Sarkesian, S.C. 153nn.54, 59
Scales, R..H., Jr., Major-General 107, 170n.43
Scarborough, R. 102, 166nn.57, 59, 73, 167nn.77, 80, 168nn.101, 105, 114, 169n.20, 172nn.72, 79
Schelling, T. 22, 43, 44, 54, 57, 98
Schmitt, E. 167n.89, 173n.96
Schofield, J.M., Major-General 48
Schoomaker, P., General 97
Schultz, G. 79
Schultz, R.H. 163n.3
Schwarzkopf, N., General 76, 78, 87
science of strategy 40; in Cold War 122; pioneered by civilians *see* civilians; war as 56–61
Scowcroft, B. 78
'search-and-destroy' operations 36, 74, 130, 132, 147; in Afghanistan 115; in Vietnam 74
Segal, H.P. 156n.27
Senate Armed Services Committee 80
Serbia 76
Shanker, T. 167nn.88, 89, 173n.98
Shapiro, J. 161n.34, 164n.17
Sheehan, M. 77
Shelton, H., General 103
Sherman, W.T., General 2, 4, 18, 19, 26, 28, 87
Sherry, M.S. 49, 59, 61, 151n.14, 153n.43, 155n.115, 156n.19, 157nn.39, 42, 45, 48, 54, 158n.98, 159n.111
Shinseki, E., General 102

Shock and Awe (Rapid Dominance) 85, 118; failure of 123–125
Short, M., Lt.-General 74
Shultz, R.H., Jr. 162n 68
Shy, J. 135, 150n.30, 152n.30, 154n.76, 174n.1
Sikorski, R. 169n.7
Single Integrated Operational Plan (SIOP-62) 34, 42, 57
small wars 34, 35
Smith, D. 171n.62
Smith, M.R. 156n.24
Snow, D.M. 160n.12
Snyder, J. 150n.30
Solana, J. 83
Somalia 75, 96, 141, 146
Sorley, L. 175n.32
Soviet Union 34
Spanish-American War 35
Special Forces 101, 107, 108, 130
Special Operations Command (SOCOM) 101, 102
Sperry, P. 170n.32
Spinner, J. 172n.94
stabilization: post-conflict 105, 114, 115, 124, 126, 127, 128; and reconstruction (S&R) missions 133
stab-in-the-back thesis 68–69
Stalin, J. 32, 52
Starry, D.A., General 71
states: European system 24; failed 143; inter-state industrial warfare 141; monopoly of violence, loss of 142; rogue 100, 122; and war as instrument of policy 4, 8, 18
Steele, B. 153n.45
Steenkamp, W. 167n.93
Stevens, R.J. 88
Stoler, M.A. 153nn.64, 67, 70, 154n.83
Strachan, H. 171n.66
Strategic Air Command (SAC) 16; nuclear targeting 42
strategy: abstraction and reality of war 59–61; culture as dynamic context 12; imperatives perceived in aftermath of 9/11 97; failures of America in Iraq 147; new studies 53; as technical process 44
Straussman, J.D. 153n.50
Stuart, R.C. 153n.41
Sullivan, G. 108
Sullivan, L. 91

Summers, H.G., Jr., Colonel 66, 68, 75, 160nn.20, 25, 161n.39, 162n.57
Sun Tzu 122
Swidey, N. 165n.37
systematization of war 46
systemic collapse in war, concept of 123; achieving 116–120
Systems Analysis 54, 59; role in Vietnam War 60

Talbot, D. 168n.116, 170n.46
Taliban 2, 88, 108, 114, 115; *see also* Afghanistan
Taylor, F.W. 47, 54
Taylor, M., General 36, 68
Taylorism 47
technology/technological: emphasis on 133, 134; force multipliers 102; and humane warfare 3, 87–89, 90, 113; ingenuity of American society 47; making war immaculate 15, 90; precision 86, 90, 94, 96, 111; revolution in warfare 90, 101
Terrill, W.A. 153n.68
terrorism/terrorist: failed states as havens for 143; 9/11 *see* 11 September 2001
Tetcher, T. 108, 109
Tet Offensive 64
Tikrit 130
Time-Phased Forces Deployment List 119
Toffler, A. 79, 150n.18, 162n.78
Toffler, H. 79, 150n.18, 162n.78
Tokyo, firebombing of 87
Toner, R. 160n.19
Tora Bora 120
'Total Force' policy 70, 71, 104
Trainor, B.E. 162nn.60, 73, 74, 76, 80, 171n.49
Transformation, concept of 112
'Transition to and from Hostilities', report on 133
Truman, H. 24, 25, 27, 33
Tyson, A.S. 173n.96

Ullman, H.K. 124, 164n.6, 170n.29
unconditional surrender 2, 16, 17, 27, 31, 32, 38
United States (US): Army reserve specializing in Civil Affairs 129; casualty-averse, more since Vietnam 71; counter-insurgency strategy, evolution of 130–132; dependence on

United States (US) (*Continued*)
Saudi Arabia, reducing 89; effectiveness against guerrillas 94; the Imperial Republic 139; intervention to reshape Middle East 89; interventions between Vietnam and 9/11 141; military culture, dialectical evolution of 38–39; military discourse on political dimension of war 39; military face in Afghanistan and Iraq 37; military professionalism 28; nuclear monopoly, loss of 17; security guarantee to Western Europe 138; standoff precision strike capabilities 81; and USSR, thermonuclear standoff between 14; *see also* America/American *entries*

United States strategy: in Afghan War 107; in Gulf War 79; thinking after 9/11 99; in Vietnam 58; in World War II, 'apoliticism' 30

unmanned aerial vehicles (UAV) 107, 109, 110

unpredictability of war 15, 85, 106, 137

Upton, E., General 27, 28

USSR (Soviet Union) 24, 34, 37, 51, 147; disintegration 96; nuclear war 38, 57

Varhola, C.H. 129, 172n.84
Vessey, J., General 71
Vietmalia Syndrome 75
Vietnamization 68
Vietnam Syndrome 63, 90, 135
Vietnam War 4, 7, 20, 30, 36, 37, 57, 68, 72, 84, 137, 146, 147; Advanced Research Projects Agency 37; body-bags syndrome 71; casualties 72; Combined Action Programme (CAP) 131; contribution of Systems Analysis 58; crisis of American military culture 61–62; decline of support in 89; defeat 60, 69; defeat as cultural source of vision of Immaculate Destruction 90; draft 104; effect on civil-military relations 70; electronic battlefield 91–92; failure of counter-guerrilla tactics in 91; fragging 67; Igloo White programme 91; lessons of 62, 64; *Linebacker* campaigns 92; military strategy in 18; political and cultural parochialism 60; 'Rolling Thunder' campaign in 79; traumatizing effect of 73

Wade, J.P., Jr. 164n.6, 170n.29
Wagner, A.L., Colonel 29
Wallace, W., General 131
Waller, Lt.-General C. 79
Walzer, M. 151n.10, 153n.45
war: changing reality of 140–144; conflicting visions, its relationship to politics 6; as continuation of politics 10, 11; as cruelty, discourse 87; as cultural phenomenon 11–14; as failure of politics 18–23; as form of 'bargaining' 44; 'grammar' of 9, 10, 21, 43, 66, 83, 85–90, 137; innate momentum 22; as instrument of state policy 8, 9; in Iraq, underlying political rationale 4; 'logic of' 21, 43, 66, 137; as political instrument 2, 6–11, 40; as 'Remarkable Trinity' of people, military and government 66; as science, conception and reality of 56–61; of social scientists 58; tendency to resist control 10; *see also* fog of war; 'friction' in war

Warden, III, J.A., Colonel 79, 86, 117, 118, 164n.11, 170nn.27, 34

'War is Hell' philosophy 18, 19, 20, 21, 42, 62, 87; *see also* Sherman

Warnke, P. 61
War of 1812 23, 49, 63
War on Terror 7, 14, 15, 97, 100, 104, 146; as 'the Long War' 147
Washington, G. 24; Farewell Address 24
Watson, M.S. 152n.28
Webb, J. 69
Wedermeyer, General 50
Weigley, R.F. 2, 7, 16, 18, 26, 28, 31, 53, 62, 70, 116, 136, 139, 147, 149n.1, 150n.13, 15–17, 151n.1, 152n.22, 24, 153nn.47, 57, 65, 71, 154n.72, 78, 88, 90, 155n.97, 156n.20, 157nn.33, 35, 158n.70, 159n.116, 160n.14, 161n.33, 169n.22, 174nn.6, 11, 175n.32
Weinberger Doctrine 65, 67, 79, 96, 100, 145; *see also* Powell Doctrine
Weiner, T. 164n.21
Westmoreland, W., General 30, 36, 69, 91, 92, 96, 147, 165n.33, 166n.54

West Point 46, 48
Weyand, F.C., General 71
Wheeler, E., General 36
Wheeler, N. 165n.18
White, T. 102, 107, 116, 128
White, T.D., General 55
Whiz Kids 54, 60, 136; *see also* McNamara
Williams, P. 156nn.10, 13
Williams, T.H. 152nn.21, 35
Wilson, W. 17, 31
Wilsonianism 24
Windsor, P. 63, 159n.1
Wiseman, W. 49
WMD 141; in Iraq, search for evidence of 89, 99, 120, 145; with rogue states or terrorists 89, 122, 143
Wohlstetter, A. 3, 53, 54, 56, 90, 92, 93, 94, 95, 165nn.28, 39, 166n.50
Wohlstetter, R. 98
Wolfowitz, P. 3, 78, 89, 93, 94, 95, 102, 114, 115, 116, 119, 126, 135, 136

Woodward, Bob 3, 103, 115, 125, 149n.5, 165nn.24, 26, 166nn.60, 61, 72, 167nn.78, 82, 83, 169nn.9, 13, 170n.40, 172n.67
Woodward, C.V. 151n.4
World War I 31, 27; chemists' war 58; slaughter, emotional scars 32
World War II 18, 25, 26, 27, 49, 59; dominance of absolutist mindset 33; new global responsibilities of US 51; as physicists' war 58
Wrage, S.D. 162n.56, 163nn.85, 86
Wylie, J.C., Rear-Admiral 22

al Zarqawi, Abu Musab 112, 121, 169n.2
Zawahiri, Ayman al 169n.2
Zhou Enlai 52
Zinni, A., General 103, 136, 137, 146, 147, 149n.11, 174n.8, 175nn.24, 30
Zoellick, R.B. 153n.51
Zuckerman, S., Sir 60

eBooks – at www.eBookstore.tandf.co.uk

A library at your fingertips!

eBooks are electronic versions of printed books. You can store them on your PC/laptop or browse them online.

They have advantages for anyone needing rapid access to a wide variety of published, copyright information.

eBooks can help your research by enabling you to bookmark chapters, annotate text and use instant searches to find specific words or phrases. Several eBook files would fit on even a small laptop or PDA.

NEW: Save money by eSubscribing: cheap, online access to any eBook for as long as you need it.

Annual subscription packages

We now offer special low-cost bulk subscriptions to packages of eBooks in certain subject areas. These are available to libraries or to individuals.

For more information please contact webmaster.ebooks@tandf.co.uk

We're continually developing the eBook concept, so keep up to date by visiting the website.

www.eBookstore.tandf.co.uk